The Rocky Road

a memoir

RICHARD OSWALD EAST

The Rocky Road

a memoir

RICHARD OSWALD EAST

Copyright © Richard East 2025.

All rights reserved.

The moral right of the author has been asserted.

No part of this book may be transmitted or reproduced in any form by means without permission in writing from the author.

This book is a work of non-fiction based on the life of the author. In some limited cases, the names of people or details of places or events have been changed to protect the privacy of others. Some language and terminology used is appropriate to the time and may be offensive to some readers. Contains adult content.

First published in Great Britain in 2025.

Developmental Editor: Hugh Barker
Copy Editor: Lynne Walker
Typeset and formatting: Laura Jones-Rivera
Proof Reader: Carol Charlton
Designer: Makenzie Oliver East
Cover Art: Ella Burke

Printed by Bookvault.

Rocky Road Publishing.
- First Edition -

Paperback ISBN 978-1-0685528-0-9
Hardback ISBN 978-1-0685528-2-3
Ebook ISBN 978-1-0685528-1-6

the-rocky-road.com

Big Dave
May your soul rest in peace

"Even if you fall on your face, you're still moving forward."
Victor Kiam

"Sometimes you just have to jump out of the window and grow wings on the way down."
Ray Bradbury

Contents

Introduction 1
Acknowledgements 3

Chapter 1: Falling Over 6
Chapter 2: The Great Betrayal 43
Chapter 3: The Long Way Home 72
Chapter 4: What's Normal? 104
Chapter 5: What a Surprise! 110
Chapter 6: Singapore Justice! 163
Chapter 7: Queenstown or Changi 176
Chapter 8: Did I Learn a Lesson? 197
Chapter 9: Back in the Game 208
Chapter 10: The Crazy Man Returns 258
Chapter 11: The Journey Home 260
Chapter 12: Life in a Loop 270
Chapter 13: South America 282
Chapter 14: Nearly Meeting My Maker 304

Introduction

This is a story of a life well-lived. While some may disagree, the title and first chapter suggest that it is indeed a life well-lived, albeit with some harsh lessons along the way. The question of whether I am proud of my misdeeds is not relevant in the context of this book. Instead, I have written an account of something—a time warp, a glimpse into a life that few would have lived and even fewer would choose to live.

With much encouragement from two people close to me, my friend Mick Hayes and my partner Gaynor, with whom I have shared more than half my life. It's not the whole story of my life; it's just a window, open wide enough to let people peer in.

When I told close friends, especially old friends, that I was writing about my life, they, more often than not, would say, "I would love to know what happened in your house when you were growing up."

I was brought up in a large, poor, working-class family with lots of brothers and two sisters, and I was the runt. There was plenty of fighting, plenty of law-breaking, and a whole ton of heartache, but I'm afraid that is for another

The Rocky Road

book. However, this book should go some way towards satisfying some of my friends' curiosity.

I haven't written this account looking for forgiveness, and I am not using it to somehow cleanse my soul. I have written it because two people thought it was worth writing.

The process has been a long learning curve; I mean, who writes a book, novel or biography for Christ's sake? I'm all but illiterate, but the words are mine and written by my fair hand. Don't expect a "masterpiece"; this is basic and raw, and, I hope, readable. If the literate snobs among you find it too simplistic, I suggest you put it back on the shelf and read something more challenging. This book is for the adventurer or the escapist; it is for someone who wants to read a ripping yarn, laugh and cry, and get a little concerned as they find the main character falling over and finding himself in yet another hole.

I hope you enjoy the ride!

Acknowledgements

There have been just a few people in my life who have influenced me in a positive way, though there have been plenty who have influenced me otherwise!

The first person I would like to acknowledge is Jerry Jarret, whom I spent a year of my life with. Jerry had a profound effect on me in that life-changing year. He was a surrogate older brother if you like. I learnt many things from this extraordinary man. Almost from the first day we met, he gave me confidence and a belief in myself. I acknowledge and thank him.

To Francis, who I mention in the book and who has sadly passed away. I wasn't crazy when I took on board her warnings, but she was correct in her predictions concerning all my friends. It didn't end well for any of us, as we all carried on doing what we were doing. She stayed in my life, and I bless the day I met her.

To all the lads from Asia—the ones who are still alive—including Brian Mounsey and Nawn, with whom I spent many special moments.

A special call out to my old friends Chris Giles and Mark Cunningham. Without them, this book could not have been written. We're still great friends.

The Rocky Road

And to Chris Matheson, who I convinced that going to Singapore with me "had no risks attached".

To Ella Burke, the most gifted artist, who painted the beautiful cover for this book and oversaw all of the design.

To Carol Charlton, who offered to proofread the book for me, but she got so lost in the story she forgot to proof it. Thanks for all the positive feedback, Carol; I couldn't have written it without you.

To Dave Eden, the author of Nut & Gut, who, after reading the first chapter, rang me and said, "What a load of rubbish! Start again, Richard. You can't begin a biography from the age of 20." I neglected to tell him it was a memoir. I love your honesty, Dave; it spurred me on more than you can imagine.

To Hugh Barker, who did an exceptional job of doing the developmental editing of this book. I had to admire his fortitude in correcting my appalling English.

Also, to Lynne Walker, who did the copy editing. Lynne put the final touches to an OK book and turned it into something that far exceeded my expectations.

To both of my sons, Makenzie and Cameron, who, when they came into this world, gave me focus and taught me to be a father, along with everything that came with.

Lastly, I thank my dear partner Gaynor, who changed my life completely; she has been one of the most positive influences in my life.

Chapter 1

Falling Over

Life had always been a rocky road for me, but it was about to get rockier. I was on my way to India, the "Jewel of Asia", to pick up drugs and smuggle them back to the UK. My name is Richard (Dicky) East. I was a wayward character with not a lot of sense and a crackpot idea to smuggle drugs into the UK. It was 1982; I was 19 years old and on the run from the cops, and I had nothing to lose, or so I thought.

The inspiration for this drug-smuggling caper was my brother, Big Dave. He lived for the most part in India. He was ten years older than me, a bodybuilder, a biker, covered in tattoos, with long hair and a huge beard. He rode with a biker gang who called him Dirty Dave on account of the fact he never washed or bathed. As legend had it, he kept one pair of socks on for over a year for a bet, and he won! He had a strong personality with real self-confidence: a leader, one of those personality types that you could rely on to take control in a bad situation. Sometimes, he could be self-absorbed,

Falling Over

but generally, he was good fun to be around, especially if you were in awe of him.

I was honoured to have him as my big brother, but he had some control issues. I remember him one year, returning from one of his trips to India, just turning up at our house uninvited and making himself at home.

One morning he took over the front room, which was the TV room. He pulled up a chair in front of the television, and no one could watch it from that point on. He just sat there, blocking out the TV like he owned the place.

Growing up in a house with lots of brothers and sisters, control of the TV was sacrosanct. Remote control TVs were new, and if you wanted to watch something on the TV, you had to be first in the front room and have your hands on the controls. Ultimately, this gave one person power over the front room; that person had the right to change the channel, annoying everyone in the process. This would lead to calls of "MUM, he keeps turning the telly over; it's not fair." My mum would shout from the kitchen to leave the telly alone; this would be ignored, and then a fight would break out. There would be fists flying, and language you wouldn't hear from a gutter rat bellowing out at full volume. This, all over which station was on the telly! This was my prep for life. If you didn't get what you wanted, shout louder than the other person; if that didn't work, punch them in the face.

When Dave abused this protocol, no one would dare say a word. So there he sat, in control. To rub salt into the wound, he then got out a yoghurt pot full of cannabis resin, rolled himself a joint and puffed away to his heart's content.

The Rocky Road

A remarkable scene at the time, as there weren't a lot of drugs about in those days. I didn't know anyone who took drugs, and there, right in my front room, was this big hairy guy with muscles, tattooed up to the eyeballs and smoking joint after joint. He loved the cricket, and the Ashes were on the TV. He sat there for days watching the cricket until the last drop of oil in his pot was gone. He dominated the front room, dominated the TV and consequently pissed up everyone's legs and dominated the house. My sisters were unimpressed. Big Dave was home, and didn't we know it, whether we were impressed or not!

His life was a dream: he would spend all winter in India and the summer in the UK. Sometimes he would spend a couple of years in India, but mostly, we would see him in the summer—and more often than not, he would have a new girl in tow. Right now, that was Veronica. Veronica was tall, slim and very middle class. Like most of Dave's girlfriends, she was a gentle, kind soul, and very bright. On his return, he would share stories of his travels: the Himalayan Mountains, Delhi, the Ganges, Amritsar and the Golden Temple, long adventures on motorbikes, and the vast beaches of Goa. It all sounded very exotic and stirred up a bit of wanderlust in me, along with the idea of travelling to somewhere like India.

He would often lecture my brothers and sisters and me on the virtues of life, talking about different religions, explaining the difference between Pakistani and Indian culture, discussing racism, politics, vegetarianism, animal welfare and on and on. He was a very intelligent guy; he had no formal education as such but was well-read. He could quote Huxley, Gurdjieff,

Falling Over

Lao Tzu, and even Geoffrey Boycott! But he also had his faults and contradictions, and, at times, he was a little careless. He would invariably return with a few ounces of brown sugar, or heroin. He sold it for a profit, which would fund his lifestyle back in India, and his "habit". This lifestyle pretty much went on for a good ten years; from the age of 20 to the age of 30, he lived this life, not doing a lot, taking drugs and living in paradise.

On his last visit home, I was astounded by how much money he was making. He would share the details of his little drug smuggling operation with me: he would buy brown (heroin) for £3 per gram, bring back 4 to 5 ounces (112 to 140 grams), and cut it with vitamin C powder or the like. Depending on how cheeky he felt, this could increase the total amount to anywhere between 150 to 225 grams. The numbers were ridiculous; with a £336 outlay, he could make between £12,000 and £18,000. You don't need to be Einstein to work out that it was good business. Needless to say, it piqued my interest, and without much cajoling, I was on a plane to India to meet him.

The flight to India was just like any other: cramped and uncomfortable with plastic food. It was a nine-hour overnight flight but trying to sleep was impossible. There was no position that was comfortable; your neck would get crooked, your hips sore, and you would get a dead shoulder from leaning on the window for too long.

This route was notorious for turbulence. On our descent towards Bombay Airport, the turbulence began. It was extreme and quite frightening. It felt like the plane was going

The Rocky Road

to fall from the sky at any moment. There was a rattle and a shake, accompanied by that noise that only a plane in a turbulent atmosphere makes, a creaking sound as if the wings were about to be torn off. My heart would be in my mouth as the bloody plane dropped like a lead weight, then she would catch herself, level out and then fly along gracefully only to drop out of the sky again. But we finally landed, and I was in one piece. The bumpy ride should have been an ominous sign! The gods were screaming, "Don't do it, Dicky, don't do it!"

Nothing can prepare you for the heat and the smell of Bombay. It was baking hot, and the smell was rank. Once I made it through the airport and stepped outside, the smell was even more overwhelming—a mix of aviation fuel and something dying. The noise of a thousand conversations filled the air. In the background, planes were landing and taking off, while taxi cab drivers shouted to attract passengers. Bus conductors were calling out their destinations, and some people seemed to be shouting just for the sake of it. It was my first experience of organised chaos!

Somehow, this mad, frantic mess of noise and people functioned, and things got done. I wasn't overwhelmed by the madness of the noise and the incredible smell. I was here, and I was in one piece.

Dave gave me a detailed set of instructions: how to get from the airport to the hotel, where to buy a ticket for the ferry from Bombay to Panjim in Goa, and then the final leg, the taxi ride from Panjim to Colva, my final destination.

The taxi journey to the hotel was extraordinary. Carts rattled by, towed by these majestic-looking cows. One cart, loaded to the brim with boxes, pots, clothes, and who knows what else, was as tall as a mountain and pulled along by a massive beast with horns! Nothing fell off, nothing got spilt, but the guy in control would give the beast a jolly good whack across the backside. The beast wouldn't react; it just plodded along and did its job. The madness surrounding this beast was breathtaking; it shared the road with untold motor vehicles, including a million black and yellow cabs, tuk-tuks galore, lorries, cars of every shape and size, and other beasts pulling carts. The scene was surreal, amplified by the heat, the hustle and bustle, and crowds of people in an array of different, foreign-looking clothes: kaftans, turbans and badly made suits. The colours were vibrant; the women wore beautiful sarees and often adorned their foreheads with a bindi: a red dot or a jewel.

Numerous open-fronted shops sold everything from beautiful silks and cloths to car engines. Street vendors were knocking up chapattis, and Indian guys on corners brewed tea for passers-by: only in India! All they needed was enough rupees for a kettle and a cup, and they had a ready-made business.

And you couldn't help but notice the poverty; there were beggars hobbling about with their hands out for some change and boys with twisted bodies, maybe a limb missing. It was ugly and beautiful at the same time; almost from day one, I was to recognise the extremes of beauty and ugliness, vast riches and obscene poverty. All that on my short journey to the hotel, my first experience of this exotic, beautiful country, where I was on a mission to smuggle drugs, part of

The Rocky Road

the ugly side of India. Exhausted from the long flight, I ate at the hotel before crashing for the night.

The next day, I made my way down to the ferry wharf and purchased a ticket for the overnight ferry to Panjim in Goa. I had a ticket that allowed me to sleep on the top deck; you could get a cabin, but for some reason, Dave had said to get a top deck birth, better described as a "sleep on the deck" ticket. Afterwards, I went back to my hotel, grabbed something to eat, and had a long, relaxing shower to cool myself down. I then packed all my gear and headed back down to the ferry wharf.

Once again, the ordered chaos was everywhere; there were more people than available spaces. I'm not sure how I achieved it, but I found a space on the deck, put my bag down, and took out my sleeping bag, laying it down to create my own little sacred area. To my surprise, my fellow travellers seemed to honour this space. I was set for the night. I left my belongings where they were, without fear of anything being stolen. Then, I looked around the boat, familiarising myself with the toilets and where food could be bought. The boat was a steamer, a big old jalopy with a wooden hull and four decks. She was called the *Konkan Shakti* and had been in service for 30 years or more.

The toot toot of the ship's horn sounded, the lines were untied, and we left Bombay. The cool, fresh sea air on my face was a welcome relief after the hot, humid climate of the city. Immediately, the smell of Bombay disappeared, and the salty sea air washed over me and cleansed me. I had no thoughts of smuggling drugs; I was just loving this sense of freedom;

Falling Over

watching the chaos around me was somehow cathartic. I felt free and happy.

The scene before me was mesmerising, with people of all shapes and sizes, including the odd Westerner, but mostly Indians. They talked and chatted or played cards while the kids ran amok. The Indians had an innate ability to share space, with ten people in a four-foot square area, everyone on top of each other, absolutely encroaching on each other, touching, feeling, and sitting one on top of one another. They found comfort in being so close, valuing the importance of human contact. In contrast, an Englishman demands his auric space, and we are agitated when people invade that space. Some have been known to knock another man out for being too close. "Get out of my space, you moron," then whack, and it's all over. But the Indians live and breathe each other; it's a very refreshing thing to observe, and I watched and admired it. However, I was English, so I still wanted my space.

We sailed up the east coast, with land always in sight on one side and the open sea on the other. At one point, we spotted a whale, which caused quite a furore with hooting and hollering and screams of delight. The boat trip was calming and easy as we chugged along till dark when everyone settled in for the night amid lots of chatter and laughter. The sea air and the steady hum of the ship's engines made me heady and tired. Observing people somehow soothed my soul, so I watched and listened as I slid into my sleeping bag. I eventually drifted off to sleep and woke to the ship's horn signalling our arrival into port. After disembarking in Panjim, I headed straight over to a tuk-tuk driver.

The Rocky Road

Anyone who has made this trip knows Colva Beach is some 32 km away, so it makes sense to grab a taxi or a bus.

A tuk-tuk is a small, three-wheeled vehicle with open sides, typically used for short distances around town. It has an engine that sounds like a two-stroke motorbike—high-pitched and whiny—and is completely open to the elements. When I approached the tuk-tuk driver, he wasn't too sure. I don't think he'd ever had this request: Panjim to Colva in his tuk-tuk! Anyway, we struck up a bit of bartering—Indians love this; it's their food of life. Then, a price was struck, and off we went. Raj and I talked a great deal on the journey, about family, village life, beautiful women, Indian politics, and Kathmandu. We were chatting away with this stunning scenery passing us by. The roads were OK: some tarmac, some dirt, and lots of potholes. We would sweep along these quiet, empty roads, where the verges were sandy and more often than not, the road would be lined with palm trees. As we motored along, dogs would chase us, especially when we were passing through tiny villages.

There always seemed to be a couple of mangy-looking dogs mooching about, looking for a truck or a tuk-tuk to chase up the road. Great white-headed eagles and buzzards would climb the thermals way up above us. We meandered along the road with the warm air on our faces, the clear blue sky above, and the sun beating down on our bodies.

I was still feeling quite content; it's such a beautiful country! We carried on, and the landscape changed. The tree-lined road opened out onto this vast open landscape of lush green paddy fields. The view was spectacular.

Falling Over

I got Raj to pull over for a minute. He shut off the engine, and the silence was deafening. The beautiful landscape took my breath away.

Raj said, "Beautiful?"

"Yes, Raj, beautiful." We sat in silence for a few moments before I said, "Shall we carry on?"

"Not far now, Mr Dicky," said Raj as he fired up the tuk-tuk, and off we went. The beauty of India! Finally, we reached our destination, Colva, a quaint little fishing village with a couple of restaurants, a small hotel, a few beach bars and pancake stalls, and a beach that went on for ever. Old fishing boats were pulled up on the beach, and the fishermen's nets lay strewn all around, drying in the sun.

I paid Raj and bid him farewell. As I watched him disappear around the corner, I felt quite alone. I had enjoyed his company, and my new friend was now gone in a puff of smoke.

I took out my trusty list from my backpack to see if I could find Dave. Following the instructions he had given me, I wandered up the road to find him. To my surprise, there he was, sitting in a restaurant. There's something warm and comforting about a familiar face in a far-off land.

Dave introduced me to his friends, and I told them about my journey. I mentioned taking the tuk-tuk from Panjim to Colva, but no one could believe it. They were laughing their heads off at the idea of a fucking tuk-tuk ride from Panjim! At 19 years old and struggling with some anger issues, I didn't appreciate them digging me out; it made me feel inadequate and silly, so I was embarrassed. If I had been back home, I would no doubt have knocked one of these long-haired hippies, but I wasn't back home; I was here, in a strange place, surrounded by these odd-looking blokes who were laughing at me. They had long beards, long hair, round John Lennon glasses, and long flowing shirts with funky trousers and Jesus kickers! Odd was the word; I couldn't calculate the threat even though I knew it was there. The moment soon passed, though, and my brother handed me a cold beer as I sat down with him and this motley crew.

I was outside my comfort zone here; these guys were articulate, well-travelled, posh, and well-educated. They talked music—Led Zeppelin, Bob Dylan (whoever that was), and Pink Floyd. I sat and listened; this was not a conversation I could or wanted to participate in. Back home, I went to the gym and boxed. At the weekends, I went to the pub, got drunk and had a punch-up. The conversations I had with my friends were more mundane, revolving around gossip, cars and girls, while these guys delved into discussions about the meaning of life, for fuck's sake!

I was uncomfortable in this situation, but it wasn't the first time; earlier in the year, I had got together with a friend, Cody, who had suggested we go to Israel together to work on a kibbutz. At the time, the cops had been hot on my tail, and I jumped at the chance. Israel sounded good to me, and off we went. I had known Cody for a long time. We had been good friends for most of our lives; he was one of the nicest and funniest guys, so I knew this would be fun.

We left from Heathrow. On the plane, Cody took out a map of Israel, and I couldn't believe what I was looking at;

Falling Over

we were going to the Bible! In my tiny brain, I had always thought of the Holy Land as some mythical, imaginary place, and now here we were, flying straight into it. It felt surreal. Jerusalem, the Dead Sea, Galilee, and—excuse me cursing—Jesus fucking Christ, Bethlehem.

When we got to Israel and to the kibbutz, we settled ourselves in. Cody immediately slipped into the "travellers" culture; he had a healthy knowledge of music, which everyone wanted to talk about. He had followed the punk scene, went to live shows, and could talk the talk. By contrast, I was inadequate and intimidated in this situation. Cody developed a good rapport with the guys from back home and soon decided to tag along with them when they decided to leave Israel. He left me there—but more on that later.

So here I was in India with the same feelings, not knowing quite what to say and how to say it. After an hour, Dave and I finished our drinks and headed off to where we were staying.

Colva was a lovely fishing village with houses dotted among the palm and coconut trees and little sandy footpaths leading off in all directions. We followed one of these, arriving at a double-fronted shed, but a shed, nonetheless. It had a little veranda at the front, which connected the two doorways, allowing a reasonable area for six or more people to sit.

A couple of hippies were sitting and smoking some kind of pipe with a cloth around it, which I later discovered was called a chillum. One of these guys took a huge toke on this thing and blew out an impossibly humongous plume of smoke. He then turned to us and greeted Dave. Dave introduced me, saying, "This is my little brother Dicky.

The Rocky Road

Dicky, this is Andreas and his brother Helios. They're our neighbours." As it turned out, we were actually staying in one of these little sheds! And our neighbours were these full-on, kaftan-wearing, garbed-in-beads Greek hippies. They looked like ZZ Top, with long dresses on.

Andreas was shit-faced; he wore a big smile and stared off into space. However, they were kind, gentle human beings, and I grew to love them. They were great neighbours and kind to me, even, if one night, they got me so stoned that I was comatose and couldn't walk.

Dave opened the shed door to reveal… another shed! It was like a shed in someone's back garden, but a beautiful garden, I might add. It was lush, green and full of coconut trees. I had a straw mat to sleep on, and with my sleeping bag, it was comfortable enough. At this point, I needed to go to the toilet. Dave pointed me to another shed and said, "It's over there. There's no paper here, so you have to wash yourself afterwards. Use the pot of water next to the toilet."

You know when you don't really take in what someone has said? I opened the toilet door to be met by a concrete platform with a three-to-four-inch slit in the floor, and you could see the outside world through it. It was all enclosed apart from this hole. It was an odd-looking setup, but obviously, you got down on your haunches over the hole and did your business. So I positioned myself over this hole and started to relieve myself when, all of a sudden, a giant pig thrust his snout up through the hole in the floor and practically took his dinner straight out of my bum. How I didn't scream like a girl, I don't know. It was so shocking it took my breath away.

Falling Over

Every home in the village had a domestic pig for human waste disposal—recycling at its best. I had to laugh to myself. When I made myself decent and walked back, there was more laughter at my expense; my brother was rolling about laughing: "Did he get you?"

"Ha ha, very funny, you bastard." It took quite some time for them to calm down. Andreas was stoned and had the giggles, so there was no stopping him.

It had been a long day, so I went for a snooze after this little episode. My brother gave me a nudge in the early evening, and we went off to find something to eat. Dave led me along one of the little sandy tracks and we ended up at this Indian lady's house in the middle of nowhere, again surrounded by a beautiful garden; you could hear the sea, the waves crashing down onto the beach. We climbed up onto the veranda where a table was set for dinner; a couple of English girls who Dave knew were already sitting down, and a little while later, we were joined by Derek and Clive (honestly, that was their names). These two likely characters smuggled grass and resin back to the UK. They had some factory set up somewhere nearby where they processed their products. Apparently, they had blown up their last factory and were lucky to be alive.

So we were sitting down to eat together, two wayward grass smugglers, two smack smugglers and a couple of nice girls from leafy Hertfordshire. The lady of the house was a typical sweet Indian woman, with a long saree, a bindi, and a wobbly head. She made some polite conversation when we were all seated, then disappeared and came back with some poppadums with different dips. The industriousness of the Indians never ceased to amaze me; this was her home, but in the evening, she turned her veranda into a mini restaurant for travellers. We had a lovely meal of poppadums, a veggie curry with rice, a potato and spinach dish, some okra and, for dessert, a sponge pudding with lime green custard. We pretty much ate here every evening; the food was lovely, and it cost very little, which my brother liked.

After dinner we made our way down to the beach, grabbed a couple of beers in a bar and talked for a while. I had never really spent much time with Dave; he was ten years older and left home when he was 16, only returning to borrow money from our mum or to get some free lodgings when he had nowhere to live. He was an intriguing fellow with all his muscles and hair, a sort of toned-looking Giant Haystacks. He could handle himself as well; he was an intimidating man, there was no doubt about it. I heard many years later that, back home, he would go round the local council estate beating up the drug dealers and stealing their drugs. I don't know how true that was, but he looked like the type of guy who could get away with that sort of behaviour. He was the big brother hero for myself and my twin brother, a hard man with a serious reputation. He was also bright and intelligent, and he spoke like the rest of this crowd about music, religion, politics, with an opinion on anything and everything. He was right at home here.

We spent the evening talking about nothing much, while he smoked a couple of spliffs with different people; to smoke was to share, so it was a real social event, a great icebreaker, and a great way to meet new friends. I liked it, even if I didn't say much or smoke the forbidden weed.

It was dark on the way back to the shed; you could see no more than three feet in front of you. I had never been in the true darkness of night before—no streetlights, few houses, and the moon was new. Dave got out a torch, something I realised I needed to buy.

When we got back, the Greeks had a few friends gathered on the little veranda; the chillum was being passed around, and music filled the air. As we sat down for a moment, I was offered a toke, but I declined; it really wasn't my thing. I left Dave with the Greeks and went to bed, falling asleep listening to the chatter, laughter and the music coming from just outside the door. For all my woes, this place felt special. It was a natural paradise, and still, in this moment of solitude and calm, I couldn't hear the warning calls.

The next day, I was woken by the birds singing just outside the door. The shed had no windows, so it was pitch black inside. I got up and opened the door; the light was blinding. I stepped outside, rubbing my eyes, and as they cleared, the cool, fresh air swept over me, and I sat down. The peace and tranquillity! As well as the birds singing in the trees, I could hear the insects with their own morning chorus, crickety-crackety sounds as loud as the birds. I sat there for some time, taking it all in; what a way to start your day. No wonder Dave stayed here for most of the year; you felt at one with God.

After a while, I decided to take a shower, which consisted of a bucket of water and half a coconut shell. The shell was used to scoop up the water from the bucket and launch it over your head. Each scoop of cold, refreshing water took your breath away. The clarity of mind and the sizzling sensation over your entire body as the cold water washed over you made you feel alive. This was my ritual every morning while I was in Goa, 9,000 miles from home, without a care in the world!

As I sat on the veranda, I could hear Dave rousing himself. After some time, he appeared through the door, all sleepy and rubbing his eyes. He headed over to the water urn and threw water over his head, waking him up. He wished me good morning and asked if I fancied some breakfast.

Pretty much all the cafés and restaurants were open affairs with those canopy-type sun shades made of thin sticks layered thick, like some scaled-down thatched roof, with plastic tables and an odd assortment of plastic or wood chairs. We found somewhere to eat and had a long, drawn-out breakfast; everything you did there took time as you were rich with it; everything was deliberately slow. It was a lovely pace of life. Most days, we would spend our time just doodling about, wandering off to Dave's friends' places or sitting on the beach and eating the best banana pancakes in the world.

The beaches were pristine, the water was turquoise blue, and the sand was golden. Indian men wearing two-piece suits would roll up their trousers to paddle in the sea and ogle the half-naked white girls. The Indian women, by contrast, were dignified and wore long sarees and headwear with no skin showing. The beach was quite the sight with its mix of half-naked and fully-dressed people.

Falling Over

On the way back from a trip one day, Dave took me to a local weightlifting gym, which he told me he'd used. It was in the next village, maybe two miles away. It was like any typical weight gym with lots of grunting and lots of sweat, rusty old bars and cracked mirrors. I signed up, and then Dave took me on the most direct route back to Colva, trying to give me a sense of direction so that if I wanted to go to the gym on my own, I would know my way.

When we got back to Colva, he took me to a push bike hire place, which was basically a front garden with some old bikes in it. I struck up a deal for a bike, and the very next morning, bright and early, I was up and off to the gym. I jumped on this rickety old black push bike I had hired, no gears, a classic-looking relic from a bygone age.

There was one road to the next village, slightly elevated and passing through some paddy fields. There was the odd farmer out in the fields, who would wave, but apart from that, it was quiet. The early mornings here were so fresh. The sun would come up over the horizon and I would pedal along wishing this would never end. That feeling of contentment washed over me once more; I loved this journey, which I made many times, feeling the same contentment and joy in my heart.

The days were long and balmy; we didn't do much over the coming weeks before Veronica arrived, so we just hung out, getting a tan and eating nice food. I did witness Dave injecting most days, which was surreal. I didn't get the attraction and thought it was a waste of money. I had to watch this person I had just started to get to know, who was above average intelligence, start gouching or nodding out—take your pick, they mean the same thing. This grown man standing bolt upright one minute would be bent over double the next, with his face nearly touching the ground. I saw this on more than one occasion, though generally, he would be sitting with his chin on his chest and looking like some sort of retard. It could be embarrassing, but I went along with it, as he never seemed to be bothered by how stupid he looked.

One of the most mortifying times was during a dinner at the Indian lady's house with Derek and Clive. We had just finished our main course, and they were talking about the oil they had sent around the world and how it was a shame that the pot they had sent to Dave never made it to England. Red flag! The dishonesty. I had watched him smoke the whole lot while watching the Ashes.

While I was taking this little nugget in, all three of them decided to smoke a joint of smack. Now they were all nodding at the table; I was lost. Was this really happening? Then the desserts arrived, and they all suddenly sat bolt upright as if nothing had happened and carried on the conversation exactly where they had left off. It was funny, but embarrassing.

The Greeks were great company. When I caught them in the morning, they were different people, chatting about home and life, really engaging and funny. However, in the evening, they were more often than not stoned.

One evening, we came back early, and Andreas and Helios were just getting started. A couple of friends were over, so we all sat around together, and Andreas cajoled me into having a smoke on the chillum. I had never smoked hash before. Smokers have a wicked sense of humour if they suss out a newbie; for some reason, they just want to get them smashed out of their heads, and this was no different. They got me to smoke this pipe, which spun me out to the point that I couldn't move, I couldn't feel my legs, and I couldn't feel my brain. I sat in that seat for what must have been hours with these people around me laughing at my expense. In the end, I mustered up enough energy, strength and courage to launch myself out of my seat and fall into my room. The laughter was raucous as they watched me trying to walk. I slept like a baby though.

***

I was enjoying my time in Colva, even with these weird episodes, but time was moving on and talk came round to the mission at hand, which Dave assured me would be absolutely fine. He said he had done it many times, and it was a breeze. On reflection, I realise now he should have acted like my big brother and forbidden me from getting involved in any shape or form with heroin; heroin comes with a universal karmic payload, as I would find out, and so would he.

We decided to take a trip to Bombay to meet his man and pick up four to five ounces of brown. The bus station at Margao, where we were due to take the overnight bus, was busy; it was a ramshackle affair, and it was hard to tell one bus from another. Dave seemed to know where he was going, and I followed along. The heat and the dust didn't make it any easier. Again, men were shouting—it only ever seemed

The Rocky Road

to be men—and one guy shouted, "MAPUSA MAPUSA." The Mapusa bus was leaving shortly, and he had to fill the seats. The dust was swirling up in the wind, stinging our faces and getting stuck in our throats. Finally, Dave found our bus and we climbed aboard. Dave's experience showed as we sat at the front of the bus, which he said was the most comfortable place; the rear was hot and bumpy, no place to be on a long journey.

It turned into a terrifying experience! We pulled out of the bus station and off we went. The engine roared loudly, and pink dust filled the air from the road. The wheels churned it up, blowing it through the windows like a hairdryer blasting warm, gritty air into your face. I was choking and trying to get into a comfortable position. It was a bit crazy in the daylight hours, but night-time was when it got really hairy.

We got away from the town and made steady progress on the flat roads. Then we started to climb up through the hills, which were truly precarious, with sharp turn after sharp turn, hairpin bends like the ones you see in Switzerland, with deep ravines tumbling down and disappearing into the forests below. There were no crash barriers protecting you from the roll of death down the bank, and as I looked out of the window, peering down to the forest below, I could see the odd truck or bus burnt out and smashed to pieces. I couldn't imagine anyone surviving that. And here I sat, a willing participant on the great Indian rollercoaster ride of death.

These roads were so close to the edge, and the driver pushed the bus to the limit. Every now and then, we would stop; the driver would jump out, disappear for a few moments,

Falling Over

then jump back on, and off we would go again. After a few of these unscheduled stops, I asked Dave what was going on. It turned out that the driver was stopping to pay homage to Pushan, the god of journeys. Along the road, there were these little temples—worship sites—and the driver would stop, jump out, prostrate himself in front of Pushan, ask for a safe journey and leave a token or gift. He was buying luck! That seemed fair enough to me. I was really accepting of different cultures, whatever floats your boat, or whatever drove your bus.

Night driving and day driving required different skills. What I witnessed left me scarred for life. It was a game of chicken. As an oncoming bus approached, the drivers would wait and wait until they could each see the white of each other's eyes, and then they would grab their steering wheels and turn as fast as possible, swerving to miss each other. It was a risky game, and if it went wrong, the evidence was strewn all over the mountainside! Right now, I wished we were in the rear of the bus. As the driver kept praying to the temples, I kept thinking to myself, "Stop praying and drive properly!"

A few miles out from Bombay, there was a godawful smell. I said to my brother, "What's that smell?"

He said, "Oh, that's Bombay; we're nearly there."

Bombay in the 1980s had the smell of 8 million people, there was pollution on top of pollution, gas-guzzling lorries and cars, and god knows what, but it was bad. It was a smell you couldn't quite describe, but it wasn't pleasant, and we were heading straight into it.

The bus finally dropped us off in what seemed like the

middle of nowhere, so we made our way by foot towards the docks. We came across a pack of dogs in the distance barking and howling. My brother told me to get a pace on as they would take you down given half a chance.

We sped up and found a cab which dropped us off near the waterfront. We found a cheap hotel and chucked our gear in the room. I had a shower to wash off the bus journey while Dave kept his reputation by not showering at all, then we headed off to find his connection. We ended up in a small café and waited. After some time, a dodgy-looking Australian guy called Gregory turned up. It was all quite straightforward: he slipped my brother a package and my brother gave him an envelope. We left, and that was that. It was no biggie, really uneventful.

We dropped the gear off at the hotel and spent the day wandering around. We went to Dypsies ice cream parlour, grabbed an ice cream and picked up a couple of ferry tickets to Goa. Bombay was hot and humid, and rushing around wasn't an option, so we took our time. My brother showed me a couple of the sights in Bombay: the magnificent Taj Mahal Palace Hotel; the Gateway of India, a huge arched building commemorating King George V, and the Victoria railway station, another impressive structure.

At one point, a man started to follow us, calling out and asking questions like "Where are you from?" "Are you British?" "What language do you speak?" And on and on it went. I can't say it bothered me; it was just someone who wanted to talk to an English person. However, it rankled my brother, who told him to "fuck off".

Falling Over

The man didn't, so my brother said, "Fuck off, you bastard. We don't want to talk to you." This did the trick, and he fucked off. Bastard is a very offensive word in Indian culture, and you should never say it. Dave's behaviour surprised me; after all his lectures on racism and tolerance, that didn't seem to be tolerant at all. I wasn't sure what to make of it all; could this be the same guy with all the good advice? Anyway, we had some food and disappeared back to the hotel for the night. We got up the next day, eventually made our way back down to the wharf and jumped aboard the ferry.

We were camping out on the top deck again; the feeling of the fresh air on your face was a welcome relief from the heat and smell of Bombay. We found a corner on the deck and made ourselves at home. Dave got talking to some Americans, one of whom was a big guy dressed like a South African hunter with a bushwhacker hat, a beige hunting jacket and a pointy beard. His name was Bob, and he had a friend with him called Roscoe. It soon became apparent that Bob and Roscoe were also smuggling heroin. Bob was the brains of the outfit and Roscoe was the donkey. They were on a kamikaze run! Bob was calculating and manipulative; how he had talked Roscoe into this scam, I shall never know. He was loading Roscoe up with heroin, like a donkey, suitcases packed full of the stuff, and was sending him back to the States to his doom. Ruthless!

It seemed Dave had found a fellow junky in Bob, and in their wisdom, they had decided to cook up some smack in a couple of spoons and shoot it up on the deck. The audacity of these two; the deck was rammed with people, kids, families. I couldn't believe what they were attempting. Bob gave Roscoe orders to be the lookout; it was obvious that Roscoe was not the full ticket, as he sat bolt upright like a meerkat looking out for a bloody eagle. He spoke with this southern drawl which did him no favours; he looked and spoke like a simpleton, drawing the attention of the passengers. I had to tell this guy, who was maybe fifteen years my senior, to relax; he was eyeballing everyone and making people nervous, especially me. He was slow and simple, and the more he tried to look inconspicuous, the more ridiculous and obvious he looked.

Bob and Dave, on the other hand, were not being cool either; oblivious to the fact that they were carrying a large quantity of smack between them, they carried on with their junky business on the boat, cooking up a couple of hits in spoons, tying off their arms and injecting themselves, in broad daylight on a passenger boat. I was too young and did not have the confidence to tell these two to pack it in. I was messing about in a dangerous game with some dangerous guys, but I didn't recognise the signs.

When we got to Panjim, Bob and Roscoe went their own separate way, and Dave and I headed back to Colva. Thank God for that.

Now we had the goods, the idea was to make these little bullet-shaped packages, put 2 to 3 grams in a condom, tie it off, then repeat the process, adding six more layers. This would allow for any breakdown of the layers you were relying on to protect you from dying. This was a dangerous game, a life-or-death game for someone too stupid to realise the potential consequences—me!

Falling Over

The closer the time came to leave, the more nervous I got. The time in Colva now became blurred, with the joy of the scenery, the lovely cool mornings, showering in the open, riding to the gym all gone.

We returned to Bombay a couple of days before departure. We were holed up in a nice hotel on the day of the flight, and I was supposed to swallow these things before I got on the plane. This was not happening. I couldn't swallow them; they were too big and too uncomfortable to swallow. Dave was trying to encourage me, but I couldn't do it. Time was running out and I needed to be at the airport, so Dave had the great idea for me to just put the drugs in my carry-on bag and eat them on the plane. I argued about this, but somehow, he persuaded me to do exactly that. The insanity of it. This was the junky side of him. He didn't give a shit; get on that plane and to hell with the consequences.

We got a taxi to the airport with Dave encouraging me, trying to give me confidence not to worry and saying it would all be fine. At the airport, he was full of encouragement, still trying to pump me up. He saw me to the departure gate; then I waved goodbye to him... and my life!

I went through departures, passport control, and nothing else, just straight to the departure lounge. This was in the heady days of peace before the Americans blew up the Twin Towers, blamed it on some Arabs and made everyone's life a misery thereafter. So, I was through at the Bombay end, in the departure lounge, and ready to board. But I wasn't sure what I was going to do with these drugs in my bag. I felt exposed; this wasn't good, and it certainly wasn't safe. The thought crossed my mind to flush them down the loo on the flight.

Just then, we were called to our aircraft, and I duly boarded. Economy class was packed, so I sat at the back of the plane in the smoking seats. (Yes, folks, we used to smoke on flights, then they relegated us to the back of the plane, but we could still smoke.) I was crushed into my economy seat with another passenger sitting right on top of me. That's something that hasn't changed: the size of the economy seats.

How I was supposed to swallow these goddam things, I really had no idea. When the plane took off, I made my way to the toilet, where I decided to have another go at swallowing them; to my surprise, they weren't so bad and I could manage them. I spent the whole flight up and down to the toilet; I got some odd looks from the flight crew, but nothing alarming. By the time we got the sign that we were approaching Heathrow, I had swallowed them all.

I felt a great sense of relief now and a confidence. I had nothing in my bag, and nothing on me, as it were. I felt a calm come over me; I was relaxed and pleased to be home. I grabbed my bag, departed from the plane, and went through passport control. There were no issues, just a straightforward check of the passport and through to the baggage lounge. I picked up my backpack and went through the nothing to declare channel, but for some reason, the customs officer stopped me.

Again, I wasn't nervous or agitated; I was full of confidence. There was snow on the ground and Christmas was just around the corner, so everyone was in a holiday mood.

Falling Over

The customs officer asked me where I'd been and asked for my passport. I said, "Goa in India, and now I'm back here in the freezing cold, I'm not sure I'm happy with that." We both chuckled, and he gave me my passport back and wished me well. It had worked, and now that I was through to the arrivals, the relief and the rush were overwhelming.

***

I wanted to get back to my sister's place where I was staying and get this shit out of me. I passed all the drugs, then weighed it all up—four and a bit ounces.

I headed off the next day to my mum's house to pick up my prearranged phone call from Dave in India at noon. He had to go down to the post office to make international calls. When he called in, we were both relieved that I had made it, me more than him. He had given me some instructions on distribution; he had a close circle of friends, drug friends, heroin users who he used to supply. I had the prices and the quantities, as well as information on who to trust and who not to trust. I went to town, chopping up, cutting, bagging quarters, eighths, half a gram, and even a gram; it was unusual to sell in grams, as mostly it was eighths. It's amazing how quickly the money rolled in; I bought a motorbike and zoomed around all day, dropping off gear.

Dave wanted me to give Veronica some cash so she could join him in India. She was sweet and kind, and I really liked her. She didn't have a habit, but she had had to watch this spoon-cooking and jacking-up process over and over again. I gave her money, and she left for India. In the meantime, Dave and I would speak regularly. We worked out a plan to smuggle two kilos of brown into the country. He had made some good contacts in India, and he could get candlestick holders made up, packed with heroin and sent in the post. The pound signs were adding up. I thought I could make a million pounds before my 22nd birthday easily; greed was kicking in.

To fund our little project, I had to send Dave a lot of money; the best way to do this at the time was through Standard Chartered Bank. Give them your passport details, the passport details of the recipient, hand over the money, get your receipt, and hey presto, it was done. The money would be there in a couple of days. All Dave had to do was take his passport and pick it up. No worries about tracking and no questions about sending large quantities of money; it was safe and secure.

I offloaded the rest of the drugs. I had a lot of money kicking about. The problem when you're making easy money is that you lose a lot of respect for it. I didn't know how much I had, but I had a lot of it tucked in all sorts of places; I had a big stash at one of my sisters' houses just stuffed in a cupboard, and I told her to help herself, which she did.

I bought this lovely Honda Super Dream motorbike inspired by an old friend who used to own one when we were younger. Honestly, I felt like Superman. I paid cash for the bike. I would just buzz around all day on it without a care in the world: no licence, no insurance and no MOT.

Dave would be returning to England soon, and he was bringing more drugs back with him, which meant more

Falling Over

money. I was wrapped up in the greed, the danger, and the adrenaline, pushing the boundaries as if I was still at school.

* * *

My school days were dominated by a lot of misbehaving and fighting. I remember the first day at senior school, when my twin brother Paul and I were quite innocent. We were looking forward to getting to big school, following in the footsteps of my sisters and brothers who had gone before us. On the very first day, one of the teachers, a supposedly learned person, commented on "THE TWINS": "Here comes trouble. The East boys. Hope you're not like the rest of the family."

Our brothers and sisters had led the way, and we didn't really stand a chance as a welcoming committee awaited us. Adult teacher after adult teacher, making comments about "THE TWINS" like we were the Krays or something.

After the first year and a half, we started to play up to our unearned reputation. At this point I don't think we were particularly bad, but when you're being dug out on a daily basis and told you are bad at that age, you don't have the wherewithal to bat it off for the nonsense it was. We became disruptive; daily fights would break out, we would start turning up late for registration in the morning, disrupting any and every class without a care for authority. We were not scared of the teachers at all, and they knew it.

Smoking cigarettes was the grown-up thing to do, so plenty of that happened at school. By the time we reached the last year of senior school, we ran the school or felt like we ran it. When I found out from a friend that I had been expelled, I marched straight into the head of year's class while he was teaching and demanded to know what he thought he was doing. He apologised and said I wasn't expelled. One teacher insulted my girlfriend, so I dragged him out of his classroom, pinned him up against the corridor wall and threatened to give him a beating. Still, I never got expelled. Both my brother and I were creations of our teachers; neither of us really wanted it, but we definitely knew how to play the role when it was offered. So we left school with very little education and carried on behaving badly, with lots of fighting and stealing.

My family had gathered a reputation as one of those rough families, a big family you didn't want to mess with, living in the "roughest road" just causing mayhem, and the cops would pay a visit to our house on a regular basis. I was still a person of interest; the cops wanted to talk to me about a case of mistaken identity, well that's the way I saw it. A violent incident had happened in the village and my name had been put forward, giving me good reason to keep clear of the family home, only paying the occasional visit. Why I happened to be round the house on this particular morning, I don't know; I don't think there was any good reason for me to be there. I had my bike parked out front and I was just leaving; I put my crash helmet on and bid everyone farewell, then opened the front door. There, across the road in an unmarked car, were two CID officers. So, quite casually, I turned around, walked back into the house and shut the door. I said, "Fucking hell, the cops are outside. I'm out the back door. See ya later." I left my elder brother Toby and my sister Mary in the house and went out the back door and over the neighbours' gardens. I made it over the fences, through the shrubbery and out onto the main road, running as fast as my legs could carry me. Little did I know, but one of the neighbours had seen a strange man running through her back garden and phoned 999. This brought a lot of police very quickly. It was a small village, and I had to think fast about where I could hide out. I stopped running, knowing it might be attracting too much attention, so I decided to visit an old girlfriend's house, which was really close by. I went straight round the back.

Jason, her little brother, was playing in the garden. "Hello, Jason. Is your mum in?" I said. He was a funny little kid; whenever I was round the house, he would play me tape recordings of his farts, and then he would burst into laughter and run upstairs. He was also destined for trouble; you could see it all over him. Anyway, he went and got his mum, and she invited me in for a cup of tea. Laura's mum was cool; she had a soft spot for scallywags; her son Jason was one! We got on like a house on fire. I went in and sat down while she put the kettle on in the kitchen, and she called out, "What have you been up to then? You look like you're running away from the police." Jesus, was she psychic or something? She sat down with me and gave me a right grilling: "Go on then, who's chasing you? Why are they chasing you? What have you done? Come on, you're up to no good, it's written all over your face."

She was relentless, but I assured her in my best bullshitting way that everything was fine, then I made my excuses and left. There was more pressure being interrogated by Laura's mum than by the police; also, I didn't like lying to her. She had always been good to me, a real alternative mum. So I was back out on the street, which was not good, as the cops could come past at any moment. I was mulling over my next move when a friend from way back drove past in his car. I shouted, "Oi Peter! Where are you going?"

He pulled over, wound down his window and shook my hand. "Long time no see, Dicky. What are you up to?"

"Not a lot. What you doing?"

He said he was on his break and was going home for his lunch. Without even an invitation, I walked around the car, jumped in the passenger seat, and said, "I'll come with you, its ages since I've seen you. Let's have a catch-up over lunch."

You could see he was taken aback, but he said, "OK, let's go." And off we went.

On the drive to his place, he said, "There's definitely something going on in the village. There are police everywhere, bikes at the top of the hill, vans at the station, it's like they've locked down the whole village." That seemed like a bit of an overreaction by the cops. Now the problem I had was that Peter lived in the village, so I was still trapped, if you like. When we got to his house, I asked if I could use his phone, and I rang my house.

My sister answered. "Hello, Janice, how are you?" she said.

I said, "Are they in the house?"

"Yeah!"

Shit! I spent about 45 minutes round Peters chewing the cud and trying not to look agitated; finally, he said, "Do you want a lift somewhere? I've got to go back to work." I asked where he worked, and he said in the next town, so I

Falling Over

said I would come with him so he could drop me down the road from where he works. As we drove out of the village, there were police everywhere: bikes, vans, marked cars, and unmarked cars. Jesus, they seemed to be keen to talk to me. I couldn't work it out; I wasn't that interesting.

I was living in digs by now, so I headed off to my place. The next day, I called the house, and my sister answered the phone. "Fucking hell, what was all that about?" I said. It turned out that they had arrested my sister and brother and had taken them to the police station because, get this, they weren't being very cooperative! The police had a search warrant, so they came into the house and turned it upside down. They wanted to know who the male with the blue crash helmet was. My brother and sister, God bless them, swore they hadn't seen anyone with a crash helmet, as they had been the only people in the house. The police officer got angry, but they both stuck to their guns and said they hadn't seen anyone, so they cuffed them and took them to the police station. My sister said the police told her that a bank robbery had taken place in the next town, and they suspected it was the man with the crash helmet. Now I was a bank robber!

I asked my sister what they did in the house; she said that they went through the place with a fine-tooth comb, taking the records from the shelf and looking in the sleeves, looking between the pages of books, generally turning the place upside down. I was more interested in the record and book search; what were they looking for, bank notes? I suspected they were on to me over the drug dealing. Even with this suspicion, I persevered, like I had a death wish.

The Rocky Road

The cops took the motorbike and told my brother that if I wanted my bike, I could come and get it from the police station. I just went out and bought another bike; as I said, I had too much money and I didn't care.

The whole thing blew over and no one went to court; more importantly, no charges were brought against my sister and brother.

Dave was on his way home at this point. In India, he had introduced me to one of his close friends, Johnny—an intense guy who was the same age as my brother; they trained in the gym together and now they took smack together. I spent a little time with Johnny; he was smart and articulate, an academic sort of guy. He had his own gig going with another friend of his, and they had recently returned back home. I felt pretty uncomfortable in his company; he was one of those intellectual types, and I struggled to keep up as I was young, with no life experience and a limited vocabulary. This guy used big words, and he was confident and intimidating, so he freaked me out.

Dave turned up the following week. I met him at the airport and dropped him off at his friend's. We arranged to get together the next day for a chat. When he turned up at my place, I made him a cup of tea and we discussed what was happening; he had the candlesticks made, and they were going to be delivered to my address, which was in bedsit land. I had given my landlord a false name, and Dave had put the same name on the parcel. The parcel was arriving any time in the following two weeks, so I had to keep my eyes open for it. In the meantime, Dave had brought some smack back with

Falling Over

him, and he was busy selling that. I didn't get involved, but I spent the next two weeks looking for the parcel.

Dave rented a house not far away, and I would pop up to see him every now and the, just to touch base. He'd got enough money together to buy a trike, which I didn't think was a good idea! He had two kilos of smack coming in and he was on this really loud machine; it was not cool. The gods were definitely calling out my name, but it was too late!

Then it happened; the postman was at the door with a parcel. I took it from him and put it on the floor near the front door. I went outside to my car to check no one was watching and came back in. I grabbed the parcel, chucked it in a bag and went out in the car. I drove to a secluded spot and undid the parcel; the candlesticks had broken in places and smack was leaking everywhere. I couldn't believe this had got through in the post. Were there no checks in the postal service? I got the package and, in my wisdom, decided to drop it off at a close friend's house. I told him it was nothing and asked if he could do me a favour and look after it for a few days.

So I had the merchandise, and it was safe and secure. I decided to go up to Dave's house; I hadn't seen him for a couple of days. When I got there, no one was around, and it was deathly silent. I couldn't find him anywhere; it was a bit suspicious, and I didn't like it. I dropped in on a couple of his friends, but no one had seen him. No one knew where I lived apart from Dave, so I knew my place was safe. I decided to go and pick up a couple of bits and head off somewhere.

When I pulled up at mine and walked across the road, I noticed the front door was wide open. I was in bedsit land;

there was nothing too much to worry about, so I wandered through the front door, only to be met by armed police and the customs squad. They had kicked my door in and were coming out of my room.

"Hello, son, what's your name, then?" I had been nicked many times, so I knew the drill. Moreover, I was clean, as I had nothing incriminating on me. So I said, "Richard East. Who are you?"

"We're customs, son, and you are nicked."

Then I was arrested, handcuffed and manhandled into the back of a police car and driven to the local police station.

Chapter 2

The Great Betrayal

The truth is, underneath the bravado, I was a flawed character with the same issues as anyone growing up; maybe my issues were more than other people's, or maybe they were less; who knows? I was painfully shy, but my lack of confidence looked like overconfidence, and an ability to cover things up with a punch in the face. I make no bones about it, I liked a fight, and if I felt under threat, I could deal with it. However, it was a coping mechanism for inadequacy, not for being confident. My twin brother had the same character; he loved a good fight, and we both played up to the reputation of Big Dave, the big brother with the big rep.

Both Paul and I hero-worshipped this guy; he had been in trouble with the law, and he would fuck the cops off and didn't give a shit. As it turned out, I was better equipped to deal with them than him, but that realisation came too late!

At the police station it was the same old same old, nothing new for me. I was processed by the station sergeant: name, date of birth, empty your pockets, sign here, and off to the interview room. They had nothing on me; I knew it and they knew it. They left me in the interview room on my own for a while, just so I could stew in my own thoughts; it was a softening-up process. Eventually, the door burst open and two plain-clothes cops came in. They played out this big drama scene; one of them slammed down a big bundle of papers on the desk, the other one pulled off his jacket in an exaggerated fashion, then hung it on the back of a chair, all with a flair and aplomb fit for the West End. They both sat down with a *crash bang wallop*, and now we were into *The Sweeney* with Regan and Carter. I could see I was in for a long day.

The short one, who was all hunched over, reminded me of Quasimodo; he looked angry and pissed off. He introduced himself as Jonas Buckwheat, a senior officer with customs. The other one was tall, clean-shaven, with a much more relaxed attitude. He was with the drugs squad, and his name was Sergeant Bob Tucker. I hadn't been questioned before by the drug squad, or customs, but I was guessing they would use the same interrogation tools as any other copper.

As Tucker was talking, it was obvious that this was going to be the good cop, bad cop act. Tucker started by being overly friendly, saying, "It's Richard, is it?" I nodded. "So you're Dave's little brother, are you?" I nodded. "You like your brother?" I nodded. "He sent you a parcel, did he?"

I just looked at him. "Cat got your tongue?" he said. "We know he sent you a parcel." I shrugged and pulled a nonplussed face. Someone had been blabbing, but how they knew this, God only knew. "Look, we know he sent it to you, he's already told us," Tucker said.

The Great Betrayal

Now I knew these two were talking absolute bullshit because there was no way Dave would have told them anything. While I was digesting this little bit of information, Quasimodo jumped up: "You're nicked, son. You are in big trouble, do you understand? This is Class A drugs, so you're going down for a long time, make it easy on yourself and hand over the parcel. DO YOU UNDERSTAND?"

I sat there.

"Well, what have you got to say?" he added.

"No comment."

Then Buckwheat started becoming even more aggressive, repeating that I was in trouble: "Dave's told us all about it. Give us the parcel."

Sergeant Tucker decided to step in at this point with the softly-softly approach: "How do you get on with your brother, Dave?"

"No comment."

"He's told us all about it, the parcel, the candlestick holders, and the two kilos of heroin."

"What do you say? We know everything, Richard, so come on, tell us where the parcel is and it will go a lot better for you." Buckwheat was sitting there all smug and holier than thou. I didn't know why he was so smug. Dickhead, I thought. They seemed to have a lot of info, but I couldn't work it out. My brain was on fire. I knew this tactic well: your co-defendant has grassed you up, and we know everything. The cops would throw in a couple of curveballs, some tiny fact they suspected, and say, "Your mate has told us everything."

The Rocky Road

The way to deal with this was to make no comment and demand they get your solicitor. There was, however, one problem; they knew things that they really shouldn't have known, like the candlesticks, for fuck's sake! That was a biggie. And my address? No one knew where I lived apart from Dave... nah, he couldn't have, could he? My mind was working overtime, but I kept to the script. I just said, "No comment; get my solicitor," every time.

This irritated both of these officers; they questioned me for a couple of hours, going over and over the same questions to no avail. I knew this questioning would go on for the next two to three days, but I had the drugs stashed and they had nothing on me. It didn't matter about the candlestick story —I could find out later how they knew about that—all I had to do was sit this out, and I could.

After a good two hours of questions, they'd had enough, and the customs officer blew his top again, saying, "Take him away and throw him in the cells." I was taken away and put in a cell.

Once in the cell, my mind started replaying the last few hours. The police cells are cold and lifeless; it's just you and your thoughts in there. Over and over again, the scene plays out: "the heroin, the parcel, the candlesticks" over and over and over. I had doubts; maybe someone else had been nicked and talked, but that didn't make sense. Only Dave knew about the candlesticks. It was a conundrum. I was lying on the bed in the cell half dozing, when the door opened and in came my brother. This was odd; what was he doing in my cell? The cops would never allow this; once they have been arrested, all suspects are kept apart. The cops would go from one suspect to the other, trying to piece together a good case for conviction; separation was imperative. I had been arrested many times, and this was not something I had allowed for. This was not good. The sirens were blasting my ears off—red alert, red alert, the ship's sinking, Captain. Then the betrayal?

My brother, the idol of my childhood, was about to say something to me that I couldn't comprehend: "Now listen, I have this all under control. I want you to give them the parcel; give them the parcel; it's fine. I have this sorted… don't worry."

"What?"

"Give them the parcel. I have this all under control, do you understand? It's not a problem; just give it to them and let me deal with it," he repeated to me until they took him away. So it was Dave who had given them the information. I didn't know what to think at this stage.

No sooner had he left than they were back in my cell questioning me. "Now give us the parcel; you heard Dave. He wants you to give us the parcel." Ultimately, I had the utmost confidence in my brother. I thought he knew what he was doing; this was his area of expertise. He knew how to deal with the drugs squad; he'd dealt with them many times. By contrast, I was a bit of a scallywag, fighting and thieving and getting nicked, but somehow, this was different; this was playing off-script. But I assumed that Dave had his own way of dealing with the Old Bill, so I went along with it, much to my detriment and everyone else's. I decided to give them the parcel, despite my conscience telling me not to.

The Rocky Road

The drugs were at my mate's house, so I negotiated with the cops to pick the parcel up with some discretion, as the person who had the candles wasn't aware of what he was holding for me. They assured me it would be done with care. No drama. I told them where it was, and they sent half a dozen cars round to my close friend's house and made a right scene—sirens blaring and blue lights flashing. The honesty of the police!

I didn't know what to do now. I was stuck in a cell, thinking about my situation. What had just happened? Had he really come into my cell and talked me into giving them the drugs? They had so much information. The fuckers knew about my address, the parcel, the candlesticks, and even the fact that there were two kilos of smack. Dave had told them everything!

The cops had got me on the hook, and they were reeling me in. The next interview was difficult; I had never cooperated with the police. I had been nicked so often that I took it as an occupational hazard. I knew you should bat them off and laugh at them but not talk to them. When the cops say, "Anything you say will be used against you," they mean it.

In my time I would often get nicked through carelessness. There was one occasion when I was with Cody, and we were on our way to drop off some stolen filters. I had been working for a local motor factor, and during my last week working there, I had decided to help myself to half the store as a going away present. I had oil filters, air filters, brake pads, brake shoes, you name it, I had it. Cody had a contact who could take all the oil and air filters. He worked for this guy, Tommy, a garage owner, and he would take the lot. So off we went.

The Great Betrayal

The car was rammed with filters of every shape and size. On the way we got held up at some traffic lights, and, as luck would have it, the Old Bill were also stuck at the lights. They were looking at us with a keen interest, and it made us laugh. Clearly, this was not the right attitude to take when carrying stolen goods. When the lights changed to green and we drove off, I saw the cop car in the rear-view mirror looming down on us with their lights flashing and their siren blasting out. We turned into the garage, so they followed us in. Bugger, we were in trouble now! The cops got out of their car and came over as we got out. I said, "Are you all right, officers? What can we do for you today?"

"East and Giles!" one of them said. "Now what would you two be up to?"

"Nothing," I said, "just delivering some filters to this garage. Why? What are you two up to?"

"Hmm," the officer said, "filters, eh? Where are they from, then?"

I gave him the name of the motor factor I used to work for.

The WPC said, "Delivering filters in your own car? Where's the van, and why are you using a private vehicle?"

"Oh, the van broke down," I said. At this point I made an excuse and said I needed to use the toilet, leaving Cody to talk to the cops while I went into the garage kiosk. I asked the girl in the kiosk if I could use the landline. She handed me the phone.

I rang the motor factor and got reception. "Hi," I said, "Is that you, Jenny?"

"Yeah," she said. "Is that you, Richard?"

"Yeah, it's me. Listen, can you do me a favour? The police are going to call you in a minute. Please, please tell them that I still work there; have you got that?"

"OK," she said and put the phone down.

"That should do the trick," I thought. I went outside to the waiting police officers. "Are you still here? WHAT. DO. YOU. WANT?" I said, emphasising the words.

"These filters…" one of them said.

"Look, I haven't got all day. What exactly do you want? We're trying to deliver filters and you're harassing us," I said.

"We suspect they are stolen."

"Oh, you do, do you?" I said, still with oodles of confidence. "Look, just ring the motor factor and check it for yourself." The two cops walked away so they could talk in private. I took this opportunity to tell Cody what I had done. "Let's hope it works," I said.

One of the cops went off to ring the motor factor, and when he came back, he said, "You two are nicked," and proceeded to handcuff the pair of us and shoved us in the back of their police car. I looked at Cody and he looked at me. We both started laughing until we couldn't stop. The male officer put his head through the open window into the rear of the vehicle and said, "It's not funny, you two. We're taking you to the police station," which made the laughing even worse.

The two PCs got in the front of the car and told us to pack it in, but we had got caught up in one of those giggling fits, the type that only you and a close friend can get into. We laughed all the way to the police station, where we finally calmed down. They put us in separate cells and locked the doors. We were

The Great Betrayal

left to fester for hours. When my cell door was finally opened, in came the two constables: "Come on, East, come with us". They took me to an interview room and sat me down.

At this point, the uniformed boys and girls generally hand you over to the CID, as they have the interrogation skills, but, for some reason, these two thought they would question me.

"Right, where are the filters from?"

I thought they were kidding. What did they think they were doing? This was way above their pay grade. I was very uncooperative and just looked at them, and in the end, they took me back to the cells for the night.

In the morning, the CID opened the door and took me to be interviewed. This was more like it, back to normality. These guys knew what they were doing but they didn't mention the filters; instead, they wanted to know about a car I had previously owned, a yellow Mark 3 Cortina. "What about it?" I asked. It transpired that my old car had been involved in an accident in Leighton Buzzard, and it was still registered to me. "Well," I said, "I reported that car stolen way back when." They informed me that the car was in a hit-and-run accident; they said it had turned up, burnt out on "East Lane". (They couldn't see the irony in that.)

"Well, officers, I can't help you there; someone stole it and I reported it. Check your records." One officer then informed me that the driver in the alleged hit-and-run fitted my friend Cody's description.

I said, "If that bastard nicked my car, I'm going kill him, the fucking bastard." They didn't get much else out of me after that.

Two days later, my solicitor turned up and they had to let me out. They let Cody out too. Outside the police station, dishevelled and in need of a bath and a change of clothes, Cody said, "You wouldn't believe what happened in there!"

"Go on. What happened?"

"Do you remember that old Cortina you had, that yellow one?"

"Yeah."

"They only accused me of nicking it, crashing it in Leighton Buzzard, and then torching it."

I began to laugh.

He said, "What's so funny?"

"I know," I said through tears of laughter. "They came into my cell and said you fitted the description of a hit-and-run driver in Leighton Buzzard. So I said I was going to kill you and called you all manner of names."

"I didn't nick your car, Dick," said Cody.

I said, "I know, that was me in Leighton Buzzard. I thought it would be funny to see what they would do, so I made out I was really angry and I wanted to kill you. Anyway, it wasn't exactly a hit-and-run; I bumped another car and drove off. They gave you a good grilling though?"

"Yeah," Cody said. "They cracked on with it for three days. They wouldn't let it go, they just kept saying you stole East's car. We know you did it."

"What did you say?" I asked.

"Nothing. It wasn't me."

We laughed.

"Did those two uniformed cops try and question you as well?"

"Yeah, the WPC was trying to be clever, so I said, 'You're not too good at this, are you, darling? I suggest you go and get one of your male colleagues to help you.'"

"Jesus! What did she say?"

"She nearly cried, then got up and left. After that, the CID questioned me."

And that was the never-ending battle; the cops would be forever nicking us, and we would battle them with confident words as they came at us with their well-trained psychobabble and intimidation.

We were out of their grasp now, breathing in the fresh early morning air, free as birds, with no damage done. Ready to fight another day. We walked all the way home, sharing each other's version of the previous three days. Upwards and onwards, as they say!

This time, though, I was stuck with the drug squad and the customs. I'd given them the 2 kilos of smack. This had somehow turned into one kilo, though I'm not suggesting any corruption. I had obviously admitted to the 2 kilos since I'd given it to them. Then they asked about Dave. It transpired that they had nicked six people: four guys and two girls. They were trying to lever the guys using their women. Dave had been nicked with Veronica and Johnny with Jocelyn. They also had Johnny's mate, Matt.

So I made a statement and was placed back in the holding cells. They questioned me some more, then remanded me to Brixton. It turned out that we were sent to Brixton, while the girls were sent to HM Prison Holloway. A week later, we would be taken back to the police station.

The Rocky Road

I finally got to see everyone as they were loading us onto the sweat box, a purpose-built van with tiny little cells on board, with room to sit and stand, and that was it. The cells also had a tiny wee little window. Watching the world go by from my claustrophobic, cramped cell, feeling every bump in the road, observing people going about their daily business, all free without a care in the world, brought everything into perspective. I was in the shit.

When we arrived at Brixton, we were taken to a holding room; this was the first time we had all been together and were able to speak. Dave's friend Johnny asked me what had happened. In my mind, I still believed that somehow Dave had it all worked out, and even though I had given the cops the drugs, Dave was there to rescue the day. There was tension in the air as I explained myself.

Johnny asked if the cops had mentioned him and what they knew about the drugs. I told him what happened. He held his head in his hands; he couldn't believe it.

Dave butted in and said, "It's fine, I've got it all under control."

"We're fucked," Johnny said. "You gave them the drugs? Why?"

"Because he told me too," I replied. Johnny looked at Dave, who gave a shrug. Just at that moment, he was called through to be processed. After he had gone, Johnny gave me a stern warning not to trust Dave and told me that I should be very careful.

The processing was mundane with a certain degree of humiliation: name, date of birth, empty pockets, strip naked, what size clothes, grab your clothes, get dressed and go through into the wing. Here, a screw (prison officer) was waiting to allocate you to a cell. I went through the process and into the wing. "Come with me, B76181 and B76167," said the officer. From now on, I was a number, B76181, or 181 for short. They took us up to Landing 3 and put us in a cell. Each floor was numbered from 1 to 4. I was banged up with Dave.

When we entered the cell, I said, "Johnny doesn't look too pleased."

"He'll be all right."

"Why did you make me give them the parcel?" I said.

Dave said, "It's fine. Don't worry about it. It's all under control; I'll tell them you had nothing to do with it."

He talked and talked, and I stopped listening; the shiny edges were burnished now. I didn't see the hero anymore; I could only hear Johnny's words, "Do not trust him".

I was knackered, so I got on my bunk and fell fast asleep, only to be woken by the jangle of the keys and the door opening for the evening slop out. Slop out; it was an endearing term for not such an endearing process.

There are no cleaning facilities in the cell, no basin, and no running water, just a bed. And, of course, your trusty bucket with a tight-fitting lid. The bucket is for toileting purposes. It was Neanderthal, to say the least, as anyone who has experienced this will attest to the smell once the lid was removed. It is unique and forever etched on your brain, forever. And this wouldn't be the first or the last time I smelt this lasting aroma!

Slop-out procedure: the door is opened, one takes a toothbrush and the bucket ("the piss bucket" as it's fondly named), and half the prisoners on the landing go down to the recess where there is a toilet and a huge basin. You empty the piss bucket and, if possible, brush your teeth, and you may be able to sneak in a quick dump, depending on which screw is on duty. The smell from all the buckets being emptied is something to behold; it's slightly heady, and a little nauseating. Brushing one's teeth while on the verge of passing out is an experience not to be forgotten.

This procedure takes place like clockwork. Five minutes, and then you're ordered straight back to your cell, where the door is unceremoniously slammed behind you. The echo of the keys as the screw locks the door, the footsteps as he walks along the landing, then silence!

The prison system is full of life's more interesting characters, so the silence doesn't last long before there is some hollering and banging. This can go on for some time, sometimes all night, but generally, it's short-lived and the night is silent again.

We were opened up at 7 am the next morning to slop out again and for a quick wash. Then you got your trusty blue plastic cup filled with hot steaming tea, a good dollop of porridge in your trusty blue bowl and back to your cell with your bountiful breakfast—prison wasn't called porridge for nothing! At around 10 am, the cell doors would be opened for a couple of hours, where you were free to wander around the landing and go to other cells. At 11 am you could go to the yard to walk round and round it like a robot; it was like a scene from *Midnight Express*.

I wasn't happy with Dave, but I still had this big brother thing going on inside my head. A lifetime of adoration can't be expunged in a day. He had me half-convinced that he had it under control, even though I knew he hadn't. At exercise, I walked with Johnny. He was not pleased; he wasn't happy with Dave, and he wasn't happy with me either. I had handed over something I shouldn't have. He couldn't work out why I had given them the parcel, despite my best efforts to explain. He said Dave had fucked us all up and dropped me and him right in it. We were in a lot of trouble, and it was down to Dave. He again advised me not to trust my brother at all.

It was at this point I realised what an idiot I had been; they had no evidence, and I had handed it to them on a plate. It was a crushing thought. If he had left me alone with the drug squad and customs, I would have seen them off, and we would have been in a much better position. I was more cautious around Dave now, even though I was in a cell with him. I began to spend most of my time with Johnny and his co-defendant, Matt. I was already crushed, but there was a lot more crushing to come.

Brixton is an old Victorian prison, very much like Slade prison in the TV series *Porridge* with Ronnie Barker. It had metal landings on each floor with rickety old steps and walkways, each cell with a big heavy door and an eyehole in the middle. The screws liked to have a quick look in the cell before they opened the door; it was best to be safe, just in case the con was ready to pounce or, worse still, preparing to throw his piss bucket over them. The prison was old, it was gloomy, and it was fucking sad, with a lot of sad fucking people in it!

We decided to get our bail terms renewed weekly. That meant they had to take us to court every week on a Friday. The magistrate had to reinstate the bail terms and send us back to Brixton, week after week after week. Prison is a cat-and-mouse game: them, the screws, versus you, the inmate. Any points you scored were a bonus. Going to court on a weekly basis was our way of being inconvenient. It was a pain in the arse going through all the processes, booking out of Brixton, being loaded into the sweat box, sitting in a tiny little cell, then being unloaded at the courts. The magistrate would then remand us back to Brixton. Back in the box, name, date of birth, number, strip, prison clothes and back on the landing—some goal-scoring.

It was a pain in the arse, but we did it all the same. After a few weeks of this, the girls got bail, and so did Matt, leaving me, Johnny and Dave. Johnny was pleading not guilty and would spend many hours trying to find some holes in the prosecution's case. His main objective? He wanted to extract himself from the two kilos, or now the one kilo, which had nothing to do with him.

Customs and the drug squad were trying to make out we were some sort of international drug-smuggling operation, and Johnny was up to his teeth in it. But Johnny was determined. He was bright, a really clever guy, so he thought he could win. If not, he would go down fighting.

Personally, I was up to my teeth in shit. I was now carrying a dead weight—my brother! He was still the big brother, but without the shine, that light was getting dimmer and dimmer by the week. I spent more and more time with Johnny. We

The Great Betrayal

ended up in a cell together, and so began a baptism of fire. Apart from discussing the case against us, Johnny would talk about Buddhism, Daoism, Christianity, the Sufis of Islam, and all the great religions of the world. He did most of the talking—Freud, Jung, politics, and he was also a great music fan. These were the subjects I had felt so uncomfortable with while travelling, but now I found myself stuck in a cell with a guy who made me listen and learn. In many respects, this is what my big brother should have done. Johnny taught me about life and its many treasures.

We still went up and down to the court every Friday, but bail was always refused, and we were sent back to Brixton. On returning from one of these bail hearings, Dave and I got put in a cell together. Johnny was horrified and called out to me, "Will you be all right?" I waved a hand and said, "No problem, it's fine." I wasn't intimidated by my brother anymore, and I didn't listen to the bullshit. The door closed behind us, and there I was, stuck in a cell with him again.

Johnny was concerned about Dave, and he had reason to be. Dave had picked up some dope from the visit to the courts. I don't know how, but he had it. He said, "Shall we have a joint?"

"Yeah, sure," I said.

So Dave rolled up a little one skinner, popped in a roach and lit it. After taking a good few lugs, he handed it to me. I stood by the open window, blowing the smoke out. When the joint was down to the roach, and I was taking the last toke, the door suddenly burst open and in rushed two screws.

The Rocky Road

"Sit down," they shouted. I flicked the joint out of the window and sat down. "No worries, son. One of our colleagues is waiting at the bottom of the building. We're not stupid, son. You'll be up in front of the governor after the weekend." They searched us, and I watched them walk out and slam the door, the sound of the keys louder than ever and the silence that followed even louder.

Finally, my brother said, "Now, we've had it".

I said, "It was finished; I can't believe there was any hash left in it." So there we sat, stoned and paranoid, until the next morning when they opened the door and allowed us to move around the wing.

I went over to Johnny's cell and told him what had happened. "Let's go and talk to Peter Savage. He knows the score, let's see what he has to say." Peter was a Scouser; he was in the music business, a coke dealer. He had that Scouse attitude, slightly aggressive, and he spoke through gritted teeth. He could be blunt and always said it how it was. I explained the predicament we were in. His advice was to deny the whole thing. It was a bank holiday weekend, so the governor wouldn't do anything until the following Tuesday.

He said, "They will come and get you on Tuesday and take you down to the block where the governor will hold a kangaroo court. Just deny it was a joint. Tell her it was only a roll-up and there wasn't any hash in it. They will try and push it, so tell them you would like it sent for analysis. The results take months and months, and sometimes they don't even bother sending it off. It's an expense they can do without."

The Great Betrayal

Dave and I had all weekend to go over the plan; all he had to do was deny it had anything to do with him. He had the easy bit. I had to stick to my guns. It was a long weekend, but finally, Tuesday arrived, and they duly turned up to take us to the kangaroo court. They put us in a holding cell together with other accused felons who had been misbehaving in the prison. A screw opened the door, called out 167 and took Dave away. I sat and waited and waited. The door opened, and the screw said, "181?"

"Yeah," I said, and he took me to a cell that looked like a little court. The female governor was sitting behind this big old desk with her Senior Officer beside her. I was told to stand and face the two big, burly officers in front of her desk. There was just enough space between them for the governor and I to see each other and communicate. It was an intimidating situation. The governor asked for my name and number. She said, "So what have you got to say for yourself 181?"

"About what, Governor?"

"About these drugs?" she said, holding up a clear bag with a roach in it, and a rather large piece of hash.

"I don't know anything about any drugs."

"So you're denying these drugs are yours?" she said.

"I've never seen those before," I said.

"The officers came into your cell, and you were smoking cannabis; as the officer approached you, you threw the offending item out of the window where an officer was waiting below to pick it up. What do you have to say, East?"

I said, "I was smoking a roll-up, not cannabis."

The Rocky Road

"Look," she said, holding up the clear plastic bag again. "You are saying this is not yours?"

"Yes, that's right. If you send it away for analysis, it will come back negative. I don't smoke cannabis."

"Well, you're saying this is not cannabis, are you?"

"Yes, Ma'am. If you send it off for analysis, you will see it is just tobacco," I said.

She looked smugly at her senior officer and said, "That's not what your brother has told us." She let the silence engulf the room as she continued, "He said it is cannabis and has admitted his guilt to the offence." More silence. The bitch was enjoying this. I stood there with the walls of the cell closing in on me.

The silence was louder than ever. I stared at the governor for what seemed an eternity and then muttered, "My brother?" I frowned as I spoke.

"Yes, your brother," she said. Her smugness was pouring out of every cell of her body by now. There was more silence in the room, and I just stared at her, not knowing what to say. "Would you like some time to think about it, East?" One of the big officers guided me out of the kangaroo court and put me into a cell on my own. I sat there going over what had just happened. I kept thinking, "*He didn't admit to it, did he?*" Nah, that was impossible. Over and over and over again, the thoughts went through my overwhelmed mind; I was going into meltdown mode. She had to be bullshitting me. Suddenly, the door to the cell opened and in walked my brother! I had definitely been here before; talk about déjà vu.

He said, "The screws have said you haven't admitted to it; it's fine. Just go back in there and admit it. There's no punishment, all she does is knock a week off your EDR (Estimated Date of Release)."

In the stunned echo as his words bounced off the walls around me, I said, "You told them?"

"It's OK," he said, "they just add a week to your EDR."

"You told them?" It sounded like someone else's voice, not mine. Then I snapped out of it. It was my voice, and he really was standing in front of me, we really were in a cell, and yes, he had just fucked me again. I told him to get the hell out of the cell. The screws led him out and shut the door. I could have cried. Betrayal number two!

The screws came back to collect me, looking as disappointed as I felt; it was a copycat version of the police station. They put me back before the governor, who now looked positively radiant, all sparkly-eyed, sitting proudly, like the cat that got the cream. She looked at me, then looked at her senior officer, and said, "Well, have you had time to reconsider your position, 181?"

With a deep sigh, I said, "Yeah."

"So you admit it's cannabis, then?"

"Yes," I said.

"Yes what?" she said with her head tilted and a look of satisfaction on her face.

"Yes, it's cannabis, Ma'am," I said through gritted teeth.

"OK, that's a loss of all privileges for seven days, and seven days added to your sentence when received. Now get him out of my sight."

As one of the officers led me out of the sham court, I asked him, "What just happened in there? What did that mean?"

The Rocky Road

He said, "You're down the block, son, for seven days."

"What? Down the block? Where's my brother?"

"Oh, he's gone back up to the wing," he said.

That didn't make sense, so I said, "So what did he get?"

"They took seven days off his EDR. He's back on the wing, son." The screw looked at me and apologised, for what I don't know, but you could see he felt for me. He took me to the block. The block is even colder than the rest of the prison, and the doors look like something from another era—dungeon doors: big, old, black monstrosities. As the screw opened one for me, it creaked on its hinges. Inside was a cardboard chair and table, the bed bolted to the floor. I took off my shoes, and the screw searched me, and as I walked into the cell, a chill went down my spine as the door slowly shut behind me. I was stuck down here for a week, with one hour of exercise a day and no natural light.

A while later, a screw opened the door, handed me some books, and said, "Are you OK, East?" I said I was fine. God, even the screws were sympathetic to me. More time passed, and then the door opened again. The screw said, "You have a visitor, grab your shoes, son."

They led me to the visiting room, a long Perspex screen with chairs on one side for the cons and chairs on the other side for the visitors. Dave was waiting for me; we had a double visit together. I sat down on my haunches not far away from him. He tried to speak to me, but I told him to be quiet; I was so angry. The screws called us into the visitors' area and sat us down. My sister had turned up with an old friend, Paul MacBride. My sister said, "You look really upset."

The Great Betrayal

I said, "This cunt has just got me put in the fucking block." Dave tried to defend himself, but I just said, "Shut the fuck up, you are a cunt." I was past any warning signs; he had shown his colours, but where Dave was concerned, it wasn't over for me yet.

I spent the next three days in the block, and then they came to take me to the courts for the bail hearing. I got to see Johnny and Dave. I explained to Johnny what happened and that Dave was a liability! We had our hearing at the court and returned to Brixton. I was thrown back down the block to finish my solitary confinement while Dave and Johnny went up to the wing.

The weeks rolled into one endless, monotonous slog. We returned from court one Friday, and I was thrown into a cell. The door was slammed shut behind me, and I was stuck in this cell for the night with this middle-aged guy, but he seemed harmless enough. Prisons are full of lawbreakers, but some break bigger laws. This guy seemed normal, but the more he paced up and down the cell, the more concerned I got. It was starting to get a little creepy, so I sat with my back against the wall—if this kicked off, I wanted to be prepared. He started to talk about his case and why he was on remand. His boyfriend had been brutally murdered. He then went into fine detail about the event, how the body was dismembered, how someone had ripped the guy's rectum out with a sharp instrument, and how it wasn't him but his boyfriend. He had been caught up in a love triangle, and this lover had brutalised the other boyfriend. There was far too much detail! For fuck's sake, not a murderer, not gay, but fucking both wrapped into one: a homosexual murdering lunatic. It was the longest night of my life! In the morning, I got the screws to move me.

We were held in Brixton until our committal to Crown Court. Three months passed us by, then we had our hearing. After the court case, they transferred us to Pentonville, another old Victorian London prison. This wasn't much different to Brixton, old and dilapidated; the screws were the same, semi-literate and brutish. The cells were exactly the same, cold and heartless, a place where the personality and the soul go to die! I now shared a cell with Johnny 24/7: twenty-three hour bang-up, one hour of exercise a day, bland food but plenty of tea and duff—sponge pudding for the masses. We whiled away our time playing chess, backgammon and draughts. We trained every day in the cell, and Johnny was still educating me on philosophy and psychology. We were there for four months, and I learnt a great deal about myself. Johnny was good at getting inside your head, he could get you to open up. It was a truly enlightening time for me. I took an interest in Jung and Freud, tried to read Dickens, which was impossible, and loved reading Dick Francis, Neville Shute, Wilbur Smith, and *Jupiter's Travels*, Ted Simon's book on his four-year motorbike ride around the world. Escapism! We did *The Times* cryptic crosswords together every day, while Johnny gave me his advice on prison life: be thoughtful, make good choices, use your time well, and don't let the bastards get you down.

Dave, by now, had put himself under Prison Rule 43. For some reason, he felt under threat and requested to be placed under the protection of the rule, a system where a prisoner can ask to be segregated for his own safety. There are two categories: black Rule 43 for the vulnerable under protection and red Rule 43 for sex offenders. Sex offenders are automatically put on a red rule for their own protection. They are the most despised and hated people in prison. Other convicts attack them whenever given the chance. Dave had put himself under the black Rule 43 for self-protection; from that point on, we had to request the governor to see him.

* * *

Johnny and I had wangled ourselves jobs as pot washers, which meant our cell door was left open most of the day. It was easy work. After each meal, all we had to do was wash up the food trays, and that was it. We got on with the screws and tried not to offend them in any way; it was easy for a while.

There were a lot of drugs in the prison, and we were stoned pretty much all of the time. The screws loved it; if everyone was stoned, the wing was mellow, no trouble, and peace was to be had at Pentonville. When the drugs dried up, however, it could get tense. The atmosphere would be charged, and scuffles would break out. We all suspected the screws brought it into the prison when it was dry. Once the hash was back on the wing, it was back to peace and love, no more fighting, and everything was chilled.

Other drugs had started to make their way into the prison system, such as pills and heroin, so something had to be done. The screws started spinning the cells, searching for the harder drugs. Remand prisons have a high turnover, so this doesn't allow the prisoners to collude or create any useful bonds or unions; however, a lot of us had been in Pentonville for many months, so we were able to collude! Everyone liked to take drugs, so everyone was pissed off with the screws turning over our cells and strip-searching us. We, the prisoners, decided we weren't going to be humiliated by these strip searches anymore, and we were going to refuse them. Prisoners had rights!

A few days later, Johnny and I got the spin; we got turfed out of our cell. Once out, we saw that half the landing was getting the same treatment at the same time. We all made eye contact, then a casual nod, and we were all going refuse to be strip searched—prisoner power! It was a done deal—no strip searches. The screws came out after searching our cell and asked one of us to go back inside for the strip search, so I put myself forward and went into the cell first. Two screws came in behind me. I knew one of them; the other was young, and I'd never seen him before. The screw I was familiar with said to me, "Right, East, we need you to strip."

I said, "No, I'm not stripping."

"Come on, East, just take off your top, put it back on, then take off your bottoms and put them back on."

"No, I'm not doing it." The young officer got agitated and tried to push past his colleague to get at me, but the officer held fast and told the guy to back off.

"Right, get out, East," he said. As I stepped outside, I looked at Johnny, shook my head slightly, then moved out of the way. Johnny went in and gave them the same treatment and came out. We were standing on the landing now with screws and cons all milling about; it all looked rather chaotic. Then the S.O. turned up. He had heard about the two cons refusing to be searched, so he came over to us and said, "Get those two fuckers down the block," and then stormed off. Oh dear, that hadn't gone down so well!

I was now down the block in Pentonville Prison! The screws took my shoes and marched me to the cell. This wasn't the same as Brixton; the structure was more robust, with heavier doors and four-foot-thick walls. It had an ominous stench about it.

The regular cells in the Victorian prisons of London—Brixton, Pentonville, the Scrubs and Wandsworth—are all the same; they are cold, dead spaces. Many people commit suicide in London prisons, and it's not hard to see why. On entering a cell in the block, you feel hopeless, lonely and, above all, vulnerable. You can feel the past; it's oozing through the walls—the beatings, the torture, and the screams that no one heard!

I was taking in my surroundings, the cardboard chair, cardboard table, and the bed bolted to the floor, just like Brixton, when I heard the keys in the door, and three screws came in.

The S.O. was a small ginger-haired Jock with a deep Glaswegian accent and a severe case of "small man syndrome". I couldn't understand a word he was saying, so when he mumbled something, I said, "Sorry, sir, what did you say?"

He took a provocative step forward and repeated himself.

"Eh, East, you nay take a strip search, eh?" he said in this thick accent. I explained that I was an innocent man, I was only on remand, and I didn't think it was necessary or appropriate to be strip-searched, so he said, "Right, East, strip," which I started to do.

He said, "What are you doing, son?"

I said, "I'm stripping, sir."

"Why?"

"Because in the present situation, it's necessary. I'm in the block, and you need to check that I haven't concealed anything with which I may injure myself." He took a moment to digest this. I had been deliberately calm, articulate and quietly spoken. These goons were expecting and looking for some resistance. I had taken the wind out of their sails immediately, so they had nothing to bite on. I was neither aggressive nor provocative. Violence begets violence. I was in the shit, and these three wanted to give me a kicking.

I stripped and put my clothes back on, and then the S.O. said, "So your brother has put himself on a Rule 43? Why's that, son?"

I said, "I don't know, you'll have to ask him."

"Well," he said, "your brother has stated that you and your co-defendant are going to get him and kill him, and he needs to be protected from you. What do you say to that?"

"Have you seen the size of him? I hardly think I'm going kill him." But it was the final stab in the heart, the final betrayal. My brother had inadvertently compromised me to such a degree that I was now having to fend off three uptight prison guards who wanted nothing less than to give me a jolly good beating. The S.O. was deliberately trying to provoke me so all three of them could vent their childish anger on me and give me a good kicking. He looked at me in a befuddled sort of way, and without another word, he about turned and took his thugs with him.

Fuck me, that was close. They went next door, where Johnny gave them the same treatment and sent them on their way with their tails between their legs.

We spent a week in the block, and then they let us out. We received a small round of applause from the other cons, but we also noted a lot of embarrassed faces. No one else had taken part in the protest, even though we had all agreed that none of us would accept a strip search. So much for solidarity!

We carried on with our remand time and got the sack from our pot-washing post. We were back training, playing long games of chess and devouring books. Johnny was good company, like an older brother, pointing me in new directions, challenging my views and generally giving me shit.

The court hearing was fast approaching; Johnny was pleading not guilty, and Dave and I were pleading guilty.

The court case arrived. Dave and I gave our pleas, and they took us back to prison, now as convicted prisoners awaiting sentence. Johnny was found guilty and received his sentence of nine years; Dave also received nine, and I got four and a half years. Four and a half years at 21 was like a life sentence. I struggled to see the end of that tunnel. But, in comparison, it was light; Dave and Johnny received nine. We were all taken to our respective prisons, and I didn't see either of them again for a long time.

Chapter 3

The Long Way Home

I learnt many things from being banged up with Johnny, and his friendship was dear to me. I was now in a much better space to deal with my sentence, much more thoughtful. I knew I could make this easy or difficult for myself; that was up to me. I was determined not to let the system get to me, get me down or, quite frankly, beat me.

I was from a poor working-class background, a council house, food tokens at school, second-hand clothes, a big family, stealing and fighting: a no-hoper. If it wasn't for Johnny, I would have had a completely different mindset in dealing with prison. I would no doubt have tried to fight my way through it, with the outcome of being crushed by the system. As it was, I was in an institution surrounded by inmates who could neither read nor write. Mostly, they were repeat offenders, in and out of prison with no help at the end of their sentence, something I would experience myself. Now, though, I was convict B76181, a number!

After the sentencing, I was bundled back into the sweat

box and whisked off to Wandsworth Prison, another Victorian pile of rubble. It was the same induction process as any other prison: name, date of birth, religion! That was a far more interesting question now I had spent so much time with Johnny discussing religion and philosophy, but I wasn't sure what to put down. In the end, I put down C of E, even though it didn't mean anything to me.

They allocated me to the hospital wing, E-wing. There wasn't anything wrong with me, so I wasn't sure why they put me there. I was banged up on my own now, a single cell, cold and lifeless, the same sort of cell as the ones in Brixton and Pentonville, "a place where the personality and soul go to die". The difference was I now had a window, a large window, barred, of course, but it looked out over a small park.

Wandsworth has an illustrious history. Notably, it was the execution prison; the last hanging was in 1961, one Henryk Niemasz, who shot his lover and received the death sentence. The gallows were still there, and it was on my wing. They kept it in full working order, testing it every six months; maybe they were expecting hanging to make a comeback! The cat o' nine tails had also been used there; it had still been dished out in the 1950s! It was used as a form of discipline, lashing the prisoner half to death—great discipline! The Great Train Robbers were held here, and Ronnie Biggs made his escape over the wall. They never caught him, and he lived out his days in Brazil.

This was a 23-hour bang-up prison: up in the morning, slop out and grab some porridge and then exercise at 10 am for an hour. The highlight of the day was watching Concorde bank round in the sky above the exercise yard. Then back inside at 11 am and lunch at 1 pm. A long afternoon, slop out at 5 pm and grab some tea and cake (duff) back in the cell. All meals were dished up on metal trays and eaten inside the cell. Once every two weeks, you had a library visit. The library had a limited number of books, but it was the highlight of a mundane fortnightly cycle. The days slowly but surely melted into one, and weekends held little importance; it was just slop out bang-up, slop out bang-up.

Being creatures of habit, humans adapt to their environment very quickly; the cyclical pattern of the prison's false reality is so easy to fall into. The prison system is a well-oiled machine, and the sooner they have you programmed, the better. This applied to the screws, also programmed robots following orders; they were just as institutionalised as the prisoners themselves.

Every morning, you could hear the rattle of the keys hanging from the belt of the screw as he made his way along the walkway doing his morning headcount, stopping at every cell and peering through the eyehole at the captive animals. I soon developed a morning ritual of yoga. Each morning as I heard the footsteps of the screw, with his keys jangling from his belt, I would go into a full lotus position and stand on my head; I would hear the eyepiece in the door move, and then it moved again as the screw did a double take. The same screw would open the door half an hour later to let me out; he would look quizzical, as if he wanted to ask a question. Then, ever so slightly, he would shake his head and move to the next cell. It was a tiny point scored, the point being a baffled screw; in an otherwise pointless day, it was childish entertainment.

One day I got called out to go to an appointment with the psychiatrist. I was confused. I thought they had the wrong East. I wasn't the one in need of his services; Dave was. Johnny had warned me about psychiatrists being "mad as a box of frogs". I had my interview with him; he was crackers, mad as a March hare, not making eye contact, looking absent-mindedly around the room, asking me questions about how I felt about prison. It was pointless, but again, one of the small moments of entertainment in a world of mundane repetition.

I would read in the morning, have a snooze after lunch, then dismantle my cell and turn it into a mini gym. The bed was a heavy old metal affair; I would strip it down and stand it on its end, so I had the legs sticking out and used them as a pull-up bar. The small table doubled up as a makeshift barbell; it was cumbersome and difficult to curl, but it worked. I would run on the spot, do burpees, star jumps, squat thrusts, sit-ups, all manner of different exercises, all based on my boxing training. I would carry on until I was exhausted, heaving for breath with sweat dripping off me; then I would put my cell back together. The buzz of training, the elevation of the heartbeat, my lungs burning with exertion, the sweat dripping off me: this combination had a remarkable cleansing effect; my system was oxygenated, and my mind was clear. My body would normalise quickly. My heartbeat would go back to an even rhythm, my breathing would calm, and my mind would be crystal clear. I found this a perfect time to meditate, so I would sit for an hour and get lost in my mind.

In the evenings, after slop out, they would bring round tea. The door was opened, and a con would be there with a great big urn. He would fill your plastic mug with sweet tea and, if you were lucky, a slice of duff, and then that was the end of the day.

I would while away my time in the evenings writing letters. I wrote every day—my therapy for staying sane. The window was quite high in the cell, so after writing, I would take the chair and place it on top of the bed; this gave me the perfect height to allow me a view of the road and out across the park. The rainy evenings were mesmerising. It's easy to forget the beauty of the world around you until it is taken away, then it all seems more stunning and beautiful than ever.

The days rolled into weeks, and the weeks into months. Wandsworth was an allocation prison, the processing hub before moving on to a permanent long-term prison. As the months drifted by, nothing much really happened. Though I bumped into Kenny Noye; he was infamous for killing a police officer and getting away with it, and the Brink's-Mat robbery. He was on the landing with half a dozen screws round him. He gave off a menacing aura, and the screws were obviously paranoid around him.

Six months passed by, and then they moved me to High Point Prison in Newmarket. It was a category C prison, mid- to low-security; it looked pretty new and was surrounded by fields with two large fences around it. High Point is split into two sections: the South side and the North side. On arrival, you are taken to the North side of the prison. As we pulled up in the transport we noticed a huge crowd, a welcoming committee. It looked like the whole prison had come out to welcome us.

I got out of the bus and started to wander up to the office with the other cons. This felt like the walk of shame, as every con in the prison watched you walk by. I clocked an old friend, Colin, who came over. Colin and I lived in the same avenue. He was Dave's age, and he had spent a lot of time in prison. He was an old-school hardman and a thief, a proper fighter. He greeted me warmly and wanted to know if I had brought any dope with me. I hadn't, which he was disappointed with.

The walk of shame was really a vetting process; the other cons wanted to see who was carrying and who wasn't. It was important, as this prison ran on dope. Colin gave me the rundown of the North side of the prison. It was a dead-end prison with nothing going on and a bit of a free-for-all as the cons were out in the grounds all day with nothing to do. If there was plenty of hash about, the prison was cool, but when the dope ran out, the tension grew, and scuffles would break out, just like Pentonville.

Colin said I was best off on the South side and the way to get there was to sign up for the plumbing course. I did exactly that, so they allocated me the South side. While I was waiting to be moved, I spent a short time with Colin. When I explained what had happened with my brother, he said, "Don't judge your brother; we all make mistakes." Very philosophical!

Just before my move, Colin got called to action; one of his pals came over complaining about his cellmates. He shared a cell with three others. Because Colin's mate snored, they wanted him out of the cell, so they trashed his gear. Colin said, "I'll be back in a minute, Dick," and went off with his friend. Some moments later, they returned, and they were laughing. They had gone round and given all three of them a beating. Colin didn't have a hair out of place; he was a scary dude.

I got my move to the South side, and they put me in with an odd-looking guy called Jimmy. He seemed harmless; he kept himself to himself, and we got on fine. It was odd for me to share a room with another person, after spending such a long time on my own. I had become phobic about other people, so it took a little bit of time to get used to another person in my cell, but I did get used to it.

The South side of High Point had three units, with something like forty prisoners in each; the door on the unit was locked at 7 pm each evening, then opened at 8 am for breakfast. Instead of cells, you were housed in these units with rooms. The rooms were never locked, but you had to be back in your room by 9 pm for a roll call. The day was a long, mind-numbing procession of roll calls. In the morning, a screw came round, opened your door and checked you off. Breakfast was in the canteen across the way, another check-off. If you were in education, you wandered down to the education facility at the other end of the prison, so another roll call. At lunchtime, it was back to the unit for another roll call, and after lunch, it was back to the unit for another roll call. Then you were called to afternoon education and another roll call, and then back to the unit, another roll call. Before you went to have your evening meal, there was another roll call, then back to the unit for 7 pm and another roll call. Then there was another, the last one at 9 pm!

I soon gathered a close group of friends around me, all either drug dealers or drug smugglers. This was an age when drug smugglers and drug dealers weren't violent; these people took drugs, and while they were at it, they supplied the stuff. The cons who were in for drugs weren't violent; most of them were intelligent and thoughtful, not your typical criminal and definitely not at all criminally minded. They were good company, especially if you were banged up with them. This was a group of smokers, and we got stoned every day. Ian Scott-Stewart was a well-spoken, well-educated Oxford boy, who was in for dealing coke. There was Dutch, six or seven years older than me, and he was in for smuggling grass, as were the Irish boys. Stuart Spicer was my age, an ex-junky, a dealer, a wide boy, a real Arthur Daley type who could get anything, any time. He was full of funny stories, and he could charm you as well as the guards.

The weeks passed by, and the guys in the room opposite me wanted a word; they told me the bloke I was sharing with was a known paedo (a nonce), and they were going to give him a beating. They proposed to do it that evening before my cellmate got wind of it. All I had to do was pretend I was asleep while they set about him. "Don't worry, Dicky, you're not going to get hurt," they said. Cheers!

So that evening when it was dark, they crept into my room and beat this guy with these rocks in socks, and God knows what; the screams were blood-curdling as they dragged him into the hall, beating him as they went, then as quickly as they had come, they disappeared back into their rooms. The screws found him on the floor in the hallway, half-conscious, bleeding all over the place, whimpering like a baby. One of the screws came into my room: "East, East, wake up," they shouted. The light was on, and there was blood everywhere—up the walls, all over the floor and out into the hallway. "What happened, East, what happened?" the screw yelled.

"I don't know. I was asleep," I said.

"What do you mean you were asleep? Didn't you hear the screams?"

In my most innocent tone, I said, "No, I'm stone deaf in one ear; if I lie on my good side, I can't hear a thing. Sorry, I heard nothing. Why, what happened?" The screws stood there looking at me like I was talking out of my arse. Then they moved me to another room, a single room! The next day, I had to go in front of the governor and tell him the same story. He also looked at me like I was talking out of my arse. They never found out who did it.

The guys opposite who had given the paedo a beating laughed when I told them what my excuse was. One of them said, "You told them you were deaf, and they believed you?"

"Yeah," I said, "but I really am half deaf," which for some reason they thought was even funnier.

When I was growing up, I was one of those poorly kids, always ill, mostly with tonsillitis and earache. I was up and down to the doctor's every week. My mother knew there was something wrong with me other than the tonsillitis; she suspected there was a problem with my ears. So, when I was around five or six, Mum took me to an ear, nose and throat specialist, Dr Silverman. We went up to see him a couple of times. He couldn't find much wrong with me, so he decided to book me in for some hearing tests. My mother and I duly turned up for the appointment, which Dr Silverman was overseeing himself. He was an elderly gentleman, tall with grey hair and round glasses. He spoke with a slight accent, and he had this gentle, caring way about him. My mum admired him greatly, and she spoke of him fondly for many years.

When we arrived at the hospital, I was taken to a sound room. It was dark and dingy with a table and chair. On the table was a board with some coloured lights and a series of buttons. There was also a pair of giant earphones. The doctor explained that they were going to create noises within the earphones, and I was to press the red button when I heard the sounds come through. That was simple enough, so we began the experiment. I sat and pushed the buttons to the sounds they fed me, beeps and high-pitched sounds of every kind. For some time, I sat in total silence as I didn't hear a thing.

After a while, Dr Silverman came and got me and took me back to my mother. She asked if everything was OK, and Dr Silverman said he knew what the problem was and could demonstrate his findings to my mother. He got me to stand up, placed my chair in the middle of the room right opposite my mother, sat me down facing her and then disappeared to retrieve a pair of earphones with only one earpiece. He asked me to put the earpiece on my left ear, then stood in front of me and asked an array of questions: two plus two, what colour is the sky and that type of thing. He then got me to change the earpiece to my right ear and again asked me some simple questions, which I answered correctly. My mother was observing this while sitting directly in front of me. It all looked perfectly normal, and the doctor walked over to my mum while I sat looking at her. He said, "Your son is completely deaf on his left side."

This confused my mum, who asked, "How do you know that?"

Dr Silverman stood behind me as I sat with the earpiece covering my right ear and shouted at the top of his voice, "RICHARD!" I sat there motionless, so he shouted again, and I still just sat there. My mother wept as I sat in front of her motionless, making no reaction to the shouting going on behind me. Dr Silverman then walked to the front of me and asked the same questions, which I duly answered. He explained that I was deaf on the left side and had developed the necessary skills to adapt to my surroundings. I was an accomplished lip reader to the extent that sound and lips moving were one; I could hear through my eyes.

* * *

There was a routine at High Point. Like all prisons, it's run by the clock, and you soon find your rhythm. In among the roll calls, you ate, got educated, went to the gym, smoked dope and slept, in that order.

The Long Way Home

Pretty much everyone in the prison was stoned. There were plenty of drugs at High Point. Everyone was aware of Alan and Jim; between them, they pretty much supplied the whole prison. There were a few cons that could get small quantities in, but Alan and Jim ruled supreme. These guys could get large amounts in past the guards, and it all came through the visits!

The visitors' room was large, with just tables and chairs and no glass screens to separate visitors from cons; touching was allowed, and this was the route into High Point. On ending a visit, the prisoner was beckoned through a door leading to a long corridor. The corridor was the transit lounge between the visitors' area and the prison. Once in this transit lounge, you sat and waited to be called through another door, with not a single screw in sight. The fault in the system! Not only a fault, but a fault with a toilet. For some reason, the prison authorities thought having a toilet in this area was a good idea.

On one occasion, Jim and I had visits on the same day. We took our visits, waved goodbye and entered the transit lounge. Jim immediately dived into the toilet, calling out as he disappeared behind the door, "Watch out for those bastards. I'm off to the toilet."

He had been in the toilet for a few seconds when the S.O. whose surname was Clarke appeared. "White? Where are you, White? Get in here," he shouted at the top of his voice.

"Coming, sir," Jim shouted from inside the toilet.

Clarke ran over to the toilet and pulled on the door, shouting, "Get out here now, White."

Slowly but surely, Jim unlocked the door and opened it, asking, "Are you OK, sir?"

"Get in here, you little toe rag." Jim gave me a knowing wink as they both went through the door to the prison.

I followed shortly after. "Come on, East. Get in here," the screw demanded. As I went through, the door slammed behind me.

"Strip," he said, so I stripped naked as a jaybird. "Down on your haunches," he ordered. I did as I was told and got down on my haunches. Then I stood up, put on my clothes and went through into the prison. Sometime later, I bumped into Jim and asked him what had happened.

"Fucking hell," he said. "The fuckers nearly got me. That fucking idiot was banging on the door while I was trying to push three fifties up my arse, plus a lump of hash. I could hardly walk." He was laughing. "Fuck me," he said, "that was close. Do you want a smoke, Dicky?" he said. "Come on, I'm frazzled."

I scored some shit off Jim and invited Ian round for a smoke. Ian was an interesting guy, much older than me. When he wasn't selling coke, he sold rare Middle Eastern rugs. He had been to Oxford University with the infamous dope smuggler Howard Marks. We had all read *High Time: Life and Times of Howard Marks*. Ian knew him, and he told us of a time when he and Howard had put together a smuggling operation and had procured the services of a Captain Jo and his boat.

They were bringing Lebanese hash to Europe using Jo's boat, which they loaded up, and he set sail for the port of Piraeus in Greece. He was heading down the Med with a ton of hash, but as he neared the port, he got spooked, so he decided to unload the hash on a small, deserted island whose only residents were goats. He dropped it all off and headed into port to check everything was safe. He waited around for a few days, and it all looked clear, so he returned to the island to retrieve his booty. All he found was a herd of stoned goats, and the Greek authorities. He was nicked, put on an island and locked up in the local police station. They left him there to rot. Ian and Howard hired some mercenaries who went to the island, broke Jo out and set him free. It was one of Ian's proudest moments!

Piraeus was not unfamiliar to me; when I had left Israel, I took a ferry there from the port of Haifa. Haifa was Israel's main port, and in 1982, it was like a military base, with soldiers and armoured vehicles everywhere and lots and lots of checks. At the time, it wasn't a good idea to have an Israeli stamp on your passport. Many countries in the surrounding area wouldn't allow you to enter their country with such a stamp. Israel understood this, so you received a separate entry and exit form with the relevant stamps.

It was tense in the Middle East. As I wandered through the port, I got stopped by a uniformed girl who asked for my documents. As she held onto my passport, she asked me where I was born. I was born in Bedford, but for some reason, I said Hertford. This set off alarm bells, and she called her colleagues over, and they grilled me about my place of birth. I finally convinced them I had made a genuine mistake, and they let me board the boat.

I had teamed up with a couple of guys who were heading for Nafplion on the Peloponnese peninsula. We boarded the

The Rocky Road

ship together and made ourselves at home on the deck. We had deck tickets, and this would be our home for two days and two nights. We had sleeping bags, which we laid out to create some space for ourselves. Looking around, I saw a small number of backpackers and an array of different colours and creeds sharing the deck with us, all travelling on the cheap.

The ship left port, and we chugged along heading for Cyprus. It was a gloriously sunny day with a lovely cool breeze; it was perfect. Little did I know that I would be in a very similar situation, but halfway around the world, in the not-too-distant future!

We ate together, chit-chatted about nothing in particular, and I asked the guys why they were heading to Nafplion. They said it was for work. They were going to pick oranges for a month and then move on to Spain for the grape season. It sounded like a good idea, and I asked if I could tag along, which they were cool with.

We pulled into the port of Limassol for a quick stopover, then headed back out into the Med and down to Greece. The sky was still clear, and the sun was warm on our faces. As the ship sailed towards Greece, the sun began to drop over the horizon and the night slowly but surely drew in its curtains. We were in the inky black darkness of the night. With no light pollution and the new moon in full swing, the night sky began to reveal its treasures. The heavens filled with a million twinkling lights. The Milky Way sliced through the middle like God had drawn his sword and slashed through the night sky, leaving this glorious spectacle for all humanity to witness. I climbed into my sleeping

The Long Way Home

bag and rested my head on my makeshift pillow. Lying there watching the night sky, looking up to the heavens, I could feel the ship's motion, ever so slightly swaying and rocking with the gently undulating waves. The sensation was surreal. I felt like I was floating through space, which I indubitably was, on this giant spaceship we call Earth.

The second night was overcast, and we didn't get our kaleidoscopic vision of colours and light to entertain us. The next morning, we arrived in Piraeus. We disembarked, found the bus station and got ourselves to Nafplion. This was a sleepy little town with tumbleweeds blowing down the dusty old main road. We headed over to a bar where some travellers sat drinking. They told us that, every morning, the local farmers came to the bar, selected the workers they needed, took them off to labour on the farm and then dropped them back at the bar in the evening. We asked about accommodation. One of the drinkers directed us to a nearby building site where all the backpackers were sleeping. We headed off and found the site; it looked like a multi-story car park with concrete floors and no walls. It was a half-finished building project. Sixteen guys were pitched up here. We all introduced ourselves and settled in.

We spent the night there, and the next morning, we headed off to the bar. Not one farmer turned up, so we stayed all day in the bar and got drunk. The next day was the same, and several more days after that. One morning, a couple of blokes turned up from Brighton, talking the talk and walking the walk. They reckoned they had been there, done that, and they were the boys about town. They stayed in the bar with us and got drunk. In the evening, we took them back with us to the car park hotel. As we were walking back, some Greek moped riders came up on the path and nearly ran us off it, tooting as they went flying along, laughing and cheering. The two wise guys from Brighton took offence and said if it happened one more time, they were going to "fuck those Greeks up". Another bike came tearing along the path; this one had a passenger on the back, so Tweedle Dee and Tweedle Dum of Brighton set about them, and a big fight ensued. In the end, the two guys jumped back on their bike and sped off into the night. As we made our way back to the building site, these two were slapping each other on the back for a job well done, saying they were tasty geezers! When we met up with the other residents of our makeshift hotel, they said there would be big trouble now. The locals tolerated us but wouldn't tolerate us fighting them. No sooner had they said that than the police turned up with their guns out and arrested us all. We got carted off to the local police station and locked up: sixteen guys in one cell!

We had been locked up for two or three days when up popped this head in among the many bodies strewn all over the floor. The head demanded to know where he was. Nobody had noticed this guy, who had been sleeping off some heavy drinking. He reeked of drink and vomit, and, by the looks of him, he hadn't had a bath for some time. He got up and started lurching around the cell. It was tight for space, and he was falling all over people. Someone shouted, "Sit down, you fucking arsehole. What's the matter with you?" Then he got aggressive, raising his voice and shouting obscenities. This

The Long Way Home

attracted the attention of the cops. They came to the cell and told him to sit down. He tried to communicate with them, but they weren't having any of it. Eventually, it all calmed down, and one of the guys explained to him that we had all been arrested and that we didn't know what was going on or what was going to happen. The cops would ignore us whenever we tried to speak to them. Another four or five days passed. We were all rancid; it looked like a jail full of drunks off the street—we stank and looked like shit.

Finally, about fifteen heavily armed coppers turned up and escorted us out of the jail and over to the court. When we got inside, it was full of police; I counted one for each of us. This did not look good. We were sat in two rows in front of the judge, surrounded by the police. One of the police officers could speak Pidgin English and was the court interpreter (and, I think, our defence lawyer!).

The drunk decided he didn't like what he was seeing and stood up, trying to make his way along the seats. As he did so, we all began to stand. Every police officer in the building pulled out their weapon and pointed them at us. We sat down and dragged the drunk onto his seat. There was a hushed silence in the court, and then it began, all in Greek. The judge ordered the first defendant to stand. There was then some dialogue between the judge and the interpreter/lawyer. The interpreter said, "The judge wants to know what you were doing in the building."

The defendant said, "I was sleeping there." The interpreter translated, and the judge said something and slammed down his gavel. The interpreter said he had just been sentenced to twenty days in jail for "tramping" (meaning vagrancy). Then the next one stood, and exactly the same process took place. Bang went the gavel, and he was given twenty days. This happened a few more times until we got to Tweedle Dee from Brighton. He stood up and told the judge that he had just arrived that day and was looking for a hotel. The judge asked for his passport, and someone passed it over to him. He checked the stamps and immediately released him. Tweedle Dum then stood up and said he was with Tweedle Dee and had also only just arrived. Again, the judge checked his passport and let him go. All we saw was the two instigators of the violence waving goodbye and shouting out that they would let the Consulate know we had been arrested. What a pair of cunts. We all got twenty days, apart from the drunk, who had been spotted in the town defecating in one of the local's gardens; the judge gave him an extra twenty days for being such a filthy mongrel.

Nafplion Agriculture Prison! This prison was straight out of a Spaghetti Western. It had a big courtyard, all dusty, with not a single living thing growing in it. Each cell housed thirty prisoners, so we all got thrown in together. All food was cooked in lashings of olive oil; there was nothing to do all day but smoke cigarettes and chat with other backpackers. We were a diverse bunch, mainly English, though the drunkard was Dutch. He was having a hard time of it. He was obviously detoxing from the alcohol, and he paced around cursing—in English!

They gave him a bed with bed bugs, and in the morning, he was covered from head to toe in bites, red raw and in absolute agony. It wasn't a pleasant sight. That day, the guards called all the English prisoners to the office. The Consulate had rung to talk to us. I waited my turn and got to speak to a rather posh individual who sounded like Bertie Wooster: "Afraid there's not a lot one can do, old chap. Are the locals treating you well?"

We exchanged words, and then he asked if I needed anything. I said, "You couldn't send me up a newspaper, could you?"

By all means, old chap. *The Times* OK?"

"Yeah, that'll do. Cheers."

"Tally ho, old boy. Hope they don't treat you too badly. They're quite civilised, don't you know." And he put the phone down.

The sentence was short and uneventful. Once our time was up, they took us to Athens to some holding cells at immigration, where we had to wait for empty seats on an Olympic Airways flight. We were to be deported back to the UK, free of charge. One of the guys complained and said he had the right to be flown wherever he wanted. We took him aside and told him to be quiet. He was annoying the officers, who had the authority to hold us for as long as they wanted. We had already been in the tank for four days, and his behaviour could extend that for however long these officers wanted.

The next day, we were escorted through Athens International Airport. The officers exposed their guns as they marched us through the terminal building. We had been handcuffed together, so as we made our way through the throngs of holidaymakers, we could feel the eyes of all

The Rocky Road

the people on us, almost bringing the place to a standstill. Finally, they bundled us onto our flight, and the officers left the plane.

Free at last, we got smashed on the flight, and by the time we got to Heathrow, one of the guys could hardly walk. We informed the aircrew that our friend was disabled and asked for a wheelchair on arrival. They obliged, and we carried him off the plane, down the steps and into a waiting wheelchair, where another guy helped him through the airport with me. It was a blast; we were all steaming drunk, but we made it all the way to arrivals, which was where we left him!

* * *

Anyhow, Ian and I were having a joint in my room when Dutch, the Irish boys and Stuart turned up. Everyone was flush, so we had an indulgent evening with two spliffs on the go. When things got slim, with no dope, we would resort to spotting. Spotting is a term used to describe taking a tiny piece of hash and popping it onto the head of a needle, lighting a flame under the hash and inhaling the fumes: pure hash, no waste! The joints were a welcome change to spotting.

The music was playing, the backgammon was out, Ian and I were enjoying a game, and the room was thick with the sweet smell of hash. We were relaxed and enjoying the evening when the door opened, and there stood the senior officer of the unit, S.O. Hewitt. Fucking hell!

"Mr Hewitt," I said.

"East," he said, putting his head into the room, sniffing the air as he looked round.

"Spicer."

"Mr Hewitt."

"Scott-Stewart."

"Mr Hewitt."

"The Irish boys."

"Mr Hewitt."

"Dutch," he said at last.

"Mr Hewitt," said Dutch.

We all sat staring at the S.O. I had a spliff in my hand, just under the table, and Spicer was in the corner with another one just out of sight. The tension in the room was tangible; we were bang to rights, but then he just bowed out, shut the door and went away. There was a serious panic. Everyone had to get back to their rooms and stash their gear.

"Jesus, can you believe it? What's he doing creeping around the unit at this time of night?"

"Calm down, everyone," I said. "The only person in trouble here is me. Just relax and finish the joint. He's gone and he's not coming back." I explained that Hewitt had pulled me to one side earlier that day and asked me some questions. I proceeded to fill them in.

"'East,'" he had said, "'how's everything in the unit?'" I told him everything was fine, so he asked if there was anything I could tell him to help with the smooth running of the unit. I said, "'I don't have anything to do with the people in this prison. In the evening, I shut my door and that's it. I'm not interested in these people, sir. I just want to get on with my bird and get out of here.' So he obviously thought this over and decided to pay me a visit to see if I was bullshitting him or not. Honestly, he won't do anything; he's going to give me some grief, but you lot are safe."

They didn't believe me, but it panned out exactly as I had predicted. The next day at roll call, he just glared at me, and that's how it went for three or four months. I think he was disappointed by his own lack of judgement; he had thought I was being honest! However, he never searched my room, and he was not vindictive, so nothing ever came of it. Once the smoke had settled, we returned to our old pattern, getting stoned and enjoying each other's company. They were good friends.

* * *

I learnt all about plumbing and got a City and Guilds qualification. I was denied my parole because the suspected paedophile Leon Brittan was the Home Secretary, and he had it in for convicted drug smugglers. Kids were fair game, but not drugs! I had about six months to go, so they re-categorised me to a low-risk inmate and moved me to Springhill Open Prison near Aylesbury.

Springhill is a category D prison, meaning it is completely open; the attitude was different: no more yes sir, no sir, three bags full, sir. I didn't even get searched when I arrived. There was a con working in reception, and he did most of the processing. I got shown to my bed in a billet divided into cubicles; the plasterboard partitions didn't block out the noise or give you much privacy, as all there was for a door was a curtain. It was a shock to the system moving from a solitary cell to a billet with twenty others, separated only by those curtains. The noise was disturbing, to say the least, and there was no privacy; I did not like this prison at all.

I was nearing the end of three years behind bars, and freedom was beckoning. Prisoners got a third off for remission, meaning I would be out within six months. First, though, I was going to be tortured in this hellhole. Open prison is a farce: no fences, no cells, no locks on doors, wandering around like you were free, even though you weren't. Prison in itself is about locking you away from your loved ones and not being free. Being locked up is the punishment. Here, you were keeping yourself prisoner, the keeper and the prisoner. It was fucking mad. Most people were serving short sentences for non-crimes, and whinging. I hadn't been around this wallowing in self-pity before: "Oh, poor me, my wife and my kids." This type of behaviour usually came from the repeat offender. My assessment: if you love your wife and kids so much, stop committing crimes! It took its toll on me; it was soul-destroying, and I wanted to go back to a London nick where there was some semblance of sanity. As luck would have it, Peter Savage, who I had known in Brixton, was there.

Peter was a Scouser, with ginger hair and a goatee; he had these big, rimmed glasses and a thick Scouse accent. He was short, five-foot-seven, but with a sting in his tail. He had secured a red-band job, working in the officer's mess. The red band secured a state of privilege, a trusted convict within the prison system. Peter had nurtured an aura about himself in the prison; he didn't have much to do with the other prisoners but let it be known that he had the ear of the screws, and he could get you in big trouble whenever he wanted to. Basically, "Fuck with me and I will fuck with you." The truth was he hated the screws, but he also hated most of the cons. He just wanted to get on with his bird with the least amount of aggravation and go home.

We talked, and he won me over. He said I would get used to it; it would take a little time, but I would be fine. His advice was to relax and take it easy. He gave me some hash. "Go for a walk around the grounds," he said, "and smoke in peace." I went for a smoke and chilled out for a while. This was going to be a chore, but at least I knew one person, and now I had access to hash, so maybe I could smoke my way through these last few months.

A couple of weeks in, and some guy started really pissing me off. I had spent the best part of two years on my own in peace and quiet, apart from the paedo incident. I had enjoyed my own company. Pretty much all the people I associated with were drug smugglers, intelligent and well-travelled, but not what would be considered standard prison fodder. I had minded my own business, not fighting the system, just getting on with my bird, and then I ended up here in this self-imposed prison with whingers, like this great big guy bounding about early in the morning waking everyone up. He was so ignorant. One morning, I heard him come in, and he was talking really loudly, so I shouted out, "Shut the fuck up, people are asleep, you ignorant bastard."

The Long Way Home

I heard him say to his friend, "Who said that?"

The friend said, "The new guy in there."

"Yeah," I said, "it was me. Now shut up and fuck off."

The curtain was pulled back, and there stood this lump of a guy. I'm five-foot-eight, I was ten and a half stone; this guy was six-foot-two, maybe six-foot-three, and a good seventeen stone. Men are no different from their primate cousins; we face off, puff out our chests and glare at each other, mentally weighing up our chances. If we both think we can win after weighing up the other, then we go for it. The chances of me winning here were zero, but I thought I'd at least give this lump a run for his money.

He said, "Who are you talking to, son?"

He was also older than me by ten years, so I said, "I'm fucking talking to you, cunt. Now, fuck off with your banging about in the morning. No one appreciates it, so fuck off."

"You cheeky little bastard. Come up the recess." Up the recess meant let's go fight.

I said, "Come on, then."

"I'll see you in there," he said and left. I should have been a lot wiser, but I was pissed off, so I went to the recess. I stood there waiting and waiting, and he didn't turn up. Just as I thought to myself, "*What a fucking jerk, he's not coming,*" the door opened and in he came.

He said to me, "You're a cheeky little fucker, so I'm going to beat the shit out of you."

"Go on, then," I said, so he produced a cosh and started to attack me. I thought he was having a laugh. A small bloke like me, and he needed a cosh. I was giving him as good as I got, and he had the weapon. At one point, I had him on the ground, all locked in so he couldn't move.

He said, "I'm going to fuck you up."

"Really? You're not doing a very good job of it." I let him up, and we went at it again, and I got him all tied up again. The problem was, I didn't have the weight or the strength to knock him out, he was a big motherfucker, and he could take it. I was super fit, and he was panting away like a beached whale. I think he was embarrassed as well as confused. He had obviously assessed the situation and thought I was going to be a walkover, and I wasn't. In fact, I had the better of him. We stopped, and he carried on with the threats, and then I stepped in close and said, "Put the cosh down, and I'll give you a beating, you prat." On hearing that, he whacked me right round the head with the cosh and caught me a beauty.

I didn't flinch. I turned to him square in the face and said, "Put that down and let's go for it." He called me some more names, but I could see in his eyes that he had had enough. That was the end, and we left the recess. He was still mumbling some nonsense, but I said I couldn't be bothered; I was also knackered. I thought, "That'll do."

I went back to my cubicle, and he followed me in, saying, "You think I'm one of these idiots in here, don't you? I'm not. I'm doing sixteen years for kidnap, and I'm going to get my blade, and I'm going to slice you up." He disappeared off to get his weapon. Oh dear, I really had fucked up, this guy was obviously a face. Nonetheless, I waited in my cubicle for him. I thought I was going to have to fight for my life now; this had got rather heavy. He returned and said he couldn't find

The Long Way Home

his blade, so he was going to sort it out later. He called me some more names and left.

I was up Shit Creek with no paddle, so I wandered off to find Pete to get his thoughts on the matter. When I got there, Pete said, "I've already heard, Dicky. What happened?"

I told him. Then I said, "He's talking about blades now. I think it's going to get messy, he's not happy. He can't beat me in a bare-knuckle fight, and he knows it, so he's going to resort to weapons. It's not really my gig, but I suppose, when in Rome." Peter said he had previous; he had already lost sixteen months for slashing someone at Albany Prison. Great! Peter said to leave it with him.

I got a message that Peter wanted to meet in the laundry room. This did not sound good at all, and it looked like I was going to have to fight my way out of this situation. The laundry room was a quiet place where two cons could have a tear-up without attracting attention, so maybe Peter had arranged for a bare-knuckle fight, winner takes all. I turned up to find Peter alone. We chatted, and he said he'd smoothed everything over with the big guy.

Then the big guy turned up. I thought, "Fucking hell, here we go. But we just exchanged glances and that was it: no fight, no drama, no shake of the hand, just a knowing that it was over. Because Peter had this authority about the place, he wielded power, and in this case, he was the broker and the deal was done.

Life at Springhill Prison was torture, but in the end, they gave me a cell to myself, and because I had completed the City and Guilds plumbing course, I was put with a maintenance

The Rocky Road

crew. I worked with a civvie (a civilian worker), doing the maintenance for Grendon Underwood Prison, which was right next door to Spring Hill. Grendon Underwood was a secure facility for serious sex offenders. The maintenance man advised me never to talk to the inmates; they were unpleasant, even if they looked normal. It was an odd experience working in this facility. A lot of the cons wanted to talk to me, and I would tell them to go away.

Every day we had two tea breaks, and on these tea breaks, we would be joined by two screws that were also maintenance. They were two of the most obnoxious, racist and bigoted people I had ever come across. On one occasion, I was assigned to one of these morons, so I had to spend all day with him. He said to me that these cons were the worst type of people on the planet. All day long, cons would come up to us and he would tell them to "fuck off". He would then proceed to tell me the con's name, his crime and his history. He knew about all of them. It made for an unpleasant day. I got chapter and verse on every con that we passed, and Grendon Underwood housed some of the most dangerous people in the country, who had committed some of the most heinous crimes imaginable. The days here went slowly. The civvie was an amiable sort of chap, so I had no complaints about him. It was the thought of wandering around in this hellhole every day that made it slow and arduous.

I got a couple of months off for parole, so they allowed me some home leave; they gave me three days out, then I had to return to do another four weeks, and then I was free. Shane, a long-time friend, picked me up from the prison for my three days of release. We had a history of stealing, fraud and some violence. He was a staunch friend who would always be there for me. We exchanged a few words, and I sat in silence as we sped along, leaving the prison behind. The ride home was like being in a fish tank, except I was the person on the inside of the tank watching all the little fishes swimming about on the outside. I was stuck in my mind, looking at the world as it was. I was trying to evaluate the situation; the open countryside was beautiful, and the sense of the car's motion was strange. My adrenal glands were obviously in overdrive, and I couldn't quite grasp the enormity of the moment.

We arrived at my home with lots of family and friends to welcome me back. The day moved along at a dreamy pace, and in the evening, my brothers and sisters had organised a small party.

I slept, or didn't sleep, and got up in the morning. My sister had made big fried egg baguette sandwiches for breakfast, which was heaven, and then I went for a walk round the village, simply because I could. I bumped into old friends and chatted about nothing. Walking free was a wonderful feeling. I didn't do much with the freedom, just strolling around aimlessly, and that was enough.

The next evening, I popped into London to see Ian Scott-Stewart, who had finished his sentence and was back selling rare antique rugs in Kensington. I needed to score some hash, and Ian was the man. I spent the evening with Ian and his lovely ex-wife, an artist. I had lost the feeling of inadequacy that had beseeched me in India. These two were bright and academic; she was from the artsy-fartsy world and spoke with a very upper-class accent. She had this artistic, flamboyant way about her; she was beautiful and carefree, and I thought she was lovely. I had the most wonderful evening with them in their Bohemian house with half-finished portraits stacked up against the walls and a general feel of ordered chaos. Ian slipped me some dope when his ex wasn't looking, and I discreetly popped it into my pocket. The evening came to an end, and I bid them farewell and wandered off into the night. Home leave, and here I was, wandering around the streets of London with a couple of ounces of hash in my pocket!

The weekend soon passed, and I was back off to the prison with my two ounces of hash up my backside; in prison terminology, this is bottling, so I had the hash bottled. Two ounces was a struggle, but generally speaking, I had spent the last three years with hash bottled and secured, it was the only safe place!

When I returned to the prison, I was given a cursory search and changed into prison clothes, and then I was back into the system, two ounces the richer and refreshed from my stint of freedom. I still tended to keep my friend group to drug smugglers and dope dealers. I went round and gave most of the smuggled hash to all the friends I had got to know; obviously, I was more popular than ever during the last four weeks of my sentence. But the four weeks were slow; I was stoned most of the time, which kept my gate fever under control.

The day of my release arrived, and I had to go through the process of signing pieces of paper and picking up my

The Long Way Home

belongings. The big guy I had had a fight with was now in charge of processing inmates for release. We hadn't had any interaction since that time; now, we met each other's eyes, gave each other a nod of respect, and he went through the processing. At the end, he held out his hand. I took it, and we shook hands, then looked each other directly in the eye and smiled. "Good luck," he said. I was taken aback by the gesture but didn't miss a beat and wished him all the best, which I meant. He was doing a long sentence, and he was working the system to get out of there as soon as he could. If I had gone to the screws, I could have jeopardised it for him. He was just paying me a little respect for being a staunch guy and keeping my mouth shut. It's not an easy thing for someone of his character to do. So I was humbled by the gesture; he was much more of a man than I gave him credit for.

And then I left the prison!

Chapter 4

What's Normal?

In many respects, prison was useless. If I hadn't spent time with Johnny, my brother's close friend, things could and would have been very different. Ultimately, I discovered a love of reading, the wonder of meditation, and the ability to self-reflect. Above all, I was more comfortable with myself. It has to be said that the long periods of isolation, the 23-hour bang-ups, and the periods in the different punishment blocks, all created within me not only the want but the need to be on my own, to find spaces within my life to isolate myself. I enjoyed my own company now, probably a bit too much at times. But to sit and reflect on oneself is an art, and incredibly important for the soul. Would I break the law again? We are curious creatures, full of complexities and contradictions, and, at that moment, there was not a chance, but in the future, who could know? But I didn't want to be banged up again. I would say it was a definite maybe.

The drive home was very similar to the home leave journey, only now I wasn't going back. Shane picked me up again.

What's Normal?

I was free of the confines of the prison, its rules, the guards with their never-ending rattling keys, doors being slammed, the yes sir no sir—all gone in a whisper! The feeling of alienation and somehow being separate from my surroundings was intense. My senses were hyper as we passed the open fields, all green and lush, and the bright blue sky. I was hyped up, and, at the same time, I had a sense of melancholy. On this drive to freedom, I was battling the aftermath of gate fever and the realisation of being free.

* * *

So what is normal?

I stayed with one of my sisters back in the village. I was over-excited; my body was producing chemicals on a grand scale, especially dopamine. I felt like I had taken a line of speed, and it was never going to stop. I was going at one hundred miles an hour and somehow pacing myself at the same time. This went on for days, if not weeks. I got stoned every day. I could drink a bottle of spirits without a thought and feel nothing. I wandered around aimlessly, bumping into old friends and generally being lost.

I met up with one old friend, Mark, who gave me a huge bear hug; he was overjoyed to see me. His unashamed self-expression and his open joy was very refreshing. Most Brits are an inverted lot who can't express themselves properly, so Mark's gregarious and open character was a breath of fresh air. Mark invited me up to his flat that evening. He said a few friends were coming over, and I was welcome to pop in

The Rocky Road

for a smoke. When I turned up, Ian Brock was there. He was the cousin of a girlfriend I dated at school and was two or three years younger than me. I had always had a lot of time for Ian. I remembered him from school days. I would look out for him, and if anyone bothered him, I would sort it out; he was my girlfriend's cousin after all.

I would spend as much time as I could with these guys, generally getting stoned. I didn't know many people who smoked dope, so their company was a welcome distraction: stoners! Up in the flat, we would watch programmes as we got smashed and listen to music and talk, which was not so different from High Point—good weed, good music, and most importantly, good friends.

I was still struggling, lost in my thoughts, and being over-analytical. I could ramble on about the universe, God, the sky falling—the ramblings of a madman. I was not happy. This was it, this was freedom, and this was normal.

One evening, Mark put on the TV, and Dame Edna Everage was being interviewed by Parky. I had a meltdown. I got up, shouting, "Do you fucking guys realise what you're fucking watching? It's a bloke dressed as a woman. Come on, this is ridiculous. This is not funny, and it certainly isn't entertaining. I can't believe you watch this fucking shit."

In unison, they all said, "Woah, woah, calm down, Dicky; it's just entertainment, take it easy."

I was surprised by my own lack of self-control. I was also surprised that they allowed me back after that.

* * *

What's Normal?

While I was in prison, five of my friends, Mack, Sebastian, Keith, Monty, and Cody, with whom I had travelled to Israel, all upped sticks and moved to Hong Kong. Cody and I were exchanging letters, and he offered to put me up if I came out as he had just got a new place with Mack, and they had space. They were teaching English, working on films and travelling the world. But my parole officer wouldn't allow me to leave the country until my parole was up. The officer was well-meaning but useless. She was an academic with no common sense at all. There was no good reason not to let me go; I suspected she had control issues.

The weekly meetings took place in her office, a square white room with a desk and two chairs. It was cold, with no life, and the conversation was the same. The idea was for me to talk, but I would sit and look at this person and wonder why I was sitting there. It was pointless, but ultimately, she had control of my life, and I resented it. She was neither helpful nor constructive; a dead space as far as I was concerned. I was trying to readjust, and this woman was supposed to be helping, but I couldn't see how. She prevented me from leaving the country, and that was all I could see. She was no help in finding me work or somewhere to live; no wonder criminals kept reoffending and going back to prison if this was all the help they got. I finally found a job under my own steam, driving for a local firm, which made my parole officer very happy!

I was truly lost at this point. I was drinking copious amounts of alcohol, yet I never felt drunk. I drank and drank, but nothing; I would feel as sober as a judge. In my state of

The Rocky Road

heightened gate fever, with my adrenal glands working overtime and my dopamine levels off the scale, I took a shine to my friend's sister, who was much younger than me. She had flair and personality; she was very funny and a pleasure to be around. She was far too young (not law-breaking young, but young all the same). She had this carefree attitude that was refreshing and a zest for life that I didn't see in other people. She was kind and generous and somehow fell in love with me. The romance was short. I didn't see it, or I couldn't see it, but she loved me dearly and would have given her life for me. By contrast, I was lost in the disappointment of freedom and the oppression I felt at being stuck on this island. I was longing to get away and break the chains that held me prisoner here. She was the victim of my ignorance, and I broke her heart. She was young, and I crushed her hopes and dreams—an unforgivable act. Shortly after we broke up, she went to live in Australia, where I was destined to see her again.

I was still at my sister's but wasn't welcome, so my other sister stepped in to put me up. I went from a house to a home; I took my sister's dog out for long walks and enjoyed the company of her children. Children are honest, the honesty that only children have without the baggage of life. They didn't challenge you like an adult. The questions were real and not twisted. It was amazing to watch them play and interact with each other. My sister was generous and never made me feel unwelcome; she's very honest and an upfront person.

The weeks were slipping by, and I was gathering stuff to travel: a new backpack and sleeping bag, maps, and odds and

What's Normal?

sods for a backpacker's life. I was excited. All the time I had spent in prison was accompanied by the desire to travel the globe. I had a map of the world on the wall of my cell with crosses all over it on all the places I wanted to visit, and here I was, realising my dream.

The months had flown by, and I had pretty much acclimatised myself back into society. I still smoked dope every day, but I didn't really drink anymore. I was a lot less analytical but wasn't completely grounded. Freedom still felt like prison because I didn't have the freedom to make the choices I wanted, and it was frustrating.

My last parole appointment came and went, and I thought the whole process had been a waste of time. My parole officer hadn't helped me in any shape or form; the only thing I felt was disappointment, and sadness for all the cons that came after me.

But I was finally free of the system. I could now leave the UK and meet up with my friends, teach English and enjoy life… or so I thought.

Chapter 5

What a Surprise!

My confidence was up. I was off to Asia, and the past three years had somehow become a blur. The question was, had I learnt anything from my long-incarcerated experience? Does crime pay? It's an age-old question, and I wasn't sure of the answer. However, when it came to smuggling drugs, the hours were good, and you got to travel a lot! All said and done, though, that was behind me now. I was focused and ready for whatever life had to throw at me, and I wanted to see if I could catch it.

I was packing my bag, and it all smelled wonderful, new and fresh—the new sleeping bag, the new T-shirts, the new socks. "Here we go," I thought, "I'm out of here." I had been suffocating; I could hardly breathe. The sight before me—tickets, passport, maps and a crammed backpack—put joy in my heart.

It was sad to say goodbye to my sister and her family. Spending the weeks and months with them had been a special time for me; it really helped me to adjust to the outside world, so I wished them well and left for the airport.

What a Surprise!

At Terminal One at Heathrow, the aroma, the noise, and the smell of freedom had me buzzing, and I couldn't wait to get on that plane. The airport was busy, with the clickety-clackety of luggage wheels rolling over the hard tiled floors, that unmistakable sound you only hear in airports. I checked my luggage in and wandered off to passport control. The airport was cavernous with high ceilings, and it seemed to stretch on for miles. Every sound echoed throughout the whole building. It was vast and full of the hustle and bustle of people on the move.

I made my way through passport control and into the departure lounge. The Americans still hadn't blown up the Twin Towers yet, so security was minimal, with no long queues and no taking off your belt and shoes. Just a nice slow, easy pace, and there I was in the departure lounge, with people everywhere, many of them looking stressed, with kids running amok, and people having an early morning pint—8 am and downing a beer! The area below the big screens with times of the departures and arrivals was the hub for many people, all staring up with anticipation and concern as though they expected their flights to be cancelled. My plane was due to leave in two hours, so I sat at a bar and watched the world go by. I even had a cheeky beer myself.

I was in a reflective mood; prison seemed like light years away. Time had passed so quickly—India, the heroin smuggling, getting caught. I certainly wasn't going to get involved with that sort of caper again. My friends had cracked it; they had etched out lives in Asia, getting up to all sorts of exciting things, enjoying life and teaching. I couldn't wait to catch up with them. Hong Kong, here we come!

Hong Kong was built on the opium trade. The Brits had imported opium into China from India, with the help of The East India Company, which was the largest corporation in the world in its day, with an army of no less than 260,000 soldiers. It was a powerful company with the ability to disrupt the economies of nations, which they happily did, especially China's. The portal to China was the port of Hong Kong, which the Brits still controlled. I was off to a country built on the drug trade! I didn't see the irony at the time, and I couldn't see what was coming.

It was an overnight flight in economy class: no leg room, tossing and turning without ever quite getting comfortable. I didn't get a lot of sleep.

The plane made its final descent into Kai Tak Airport. What a spectacular landing, right into the heart of the city. Kai Tak Airport was built on the mainland, Kowloon side. The geographical layout of Hong Kong includes Hong Kong Island, Kowloon on the mainland coast, and the New Territories, the land mass stretching up from Kowloon to the border of China.

The airport itself was built back in the early 20th century, but as it evolved, it became the busiest hub in the world. As the runway reached right out into the harbour, pilots were specially trained to land at Kai Tak. All planes were manually landed under the pilot's total control—no autopilot, just pilot skill.

On its descent into Hong Kong, beyond the hills, the pilot was immediately confronted by skyscrapers. At this point,

What a Surprise!

the pilot could see the checkerboard strip in the distance on Tsai Hill, using this as a reference point. The pilots had the highest skill levels and referred to the Kai Tak landing as the "checkerboard approach". As a passenger, it was breathtaking; the plane descended, passing the windows of apartments where people were quite visible, watching their TVs. What an entrance. It was by far the most exhilarating landing I've ever witnessed.

The runway was short, so as soon as the plane touched the ground, the pilot engaged the thrusters; the plane had to be halted before it ended up going off the end of the runway and into the sea. The power and pure energy of the thrusters forced the passengers back into their seats, crushing the wind from their lungs; it felt like a rollercoaster ride. I flew in and out of this airport many times, and it was always the same: scary and exhilarating all at the same time.

Alighting the plane, I was immediately hit in the face by a wall of stifling air. It was hot and sweaty, though inside the airport, the air con was a welcome relief. I made my way through passport control, picked up my luggage, and was out, into the heat and the sun of Hong Kong; it felt glorious!

What a sight for sore eyes when I spotted Cody with Mack. Mack hadn't changed. He was always smart, and here he was, wearing a polo shirt and chinos with an expensive-looking pair of sunglasses. I liked Mack; he always had an air of confidence about him. He could also come across as all "sweet and innocent", like butter wouldn't melt in his mouth, which was deeply misleading because he could give

The Rocky Road

as good as he got. He was an opportunist, and even at a young age, he had business acumen. He looked healthy and happy, and he was obviously still full of confidence, beaming with a grin from ear to ear.

They were both pleased to see me, and my first impression proved to be correct. As we spoke, they had a self-assurance about them that was way beyond their years. As we strolled over to the taxi rank, they talked of all things Hong Kong; joy and positivity were exuding from every cell of their bodies. They were a joy to be around from day one.

The taxi ride back to their place was full on, and the questions came thick and fast: "What happened?" "How did you get caught?" "What was the bird like?" "How's Croxley?" "Who's doing what?" "Is the weather still crap?" "How is everyone back home?" And on the questions went. We had a lot of catching up to do.

They had a nice flat just outside Kowloon, at the top of a seriously steep hill! They lived with another guy, Phil, who was also from the UK. He worked on local TV, a big jolly sort of guy. The questions were still coming as they asked if I smoked hash, which of course I did, so as soon as they got me settled in, we had a joint. The boys had this concoction of grass and oil, which they called "the bullet". These guys were no different from any other smokers from around the world: if you had a smoke that could knock your socks off, the best thing you could do was to share it with friends and watch the fallout. After a couple of tokes on this unusual concoction, the results came thick and fast. I couldn't talk, I couldn't move; I was shitfaced and paralysed. They thought this was

What a Surprise!

really funny, and they danced around the room, making fun of me, having a laugh at my expense.

When the hit from the bullet finally eased, I asked about the other lads, Keith, Monty and Sebastian. Sebastian was living in Bangkok, and Keith and Monty were in Taiwan.

Cody and Mack had established themselves as English teachers in a language school in Mong Kok, which they said they would take me to the next day. Over the last three years, they had taken jobs in the film industry, working as extras, trying their hand at import and export, ducking and diving, and making a living doing anything and everything.

But they saved the best until last. They told me they had also been moving "stuff" around Asia. The term they used was "milk runs". They would take clothes, jewellery, watches, cameras, you name it, from one country to another. They had contacts that would pay Westerners good money to bring clothes and jewellery from Hong Kong to Taiwan. Taiwan was very expensive compared to Hong Kong, so loading up a Westerner with a suitcase full of clothes and getting them to wear expensive watches and jewellery was very profitable, with no risk. You got paid a few hundred dollars with a free return flight. They had other scams going on, too, like taking gold up to India. That was a bit riskier, and you had to hide the gold up your backside—think of the weight of that hanging out of your arse! On return trips from India, they would bring back hash. So, for me, it was out of the frying pan into the fire!

As it turned out, everyone had a little bit of action going on in one place or another. Sebastian and his mate Nigel were the creators of the bullet. Two upper-middle-class boys pretending to be gangsters. They had certainly created a great product, but neither of them needed to do it. They were both from wealthy backgrounds, so their parents almost certainly could and would have looked after them for the rest of their lives. It was more of a game to them than a matter of survival. Sebastian had this ability to tell untruths as much as possible. I did wonder sometimes whether he actually knew reality from fantasy.

Keith and Monty had chosen Taipei as their home due mainly to the Taiwanese girls liking Westerners; they were horny bastards, and they loved the Chinese girls. These guys were running the bullet through Taipei. The bullet was popular with the expats in Taiwan, and they had a thriving business.

Back in Hong Kong, Cody and Mack were in their element, and life was good; they weren't rich by any standards, but they were cruising along, living an easy life. They put me up, letting me sleep in their front room.

On the first morning, I got a taste of life according to Cody and Mack. One of these two guys would be up, making noises and looking for the choc box (the home of the hash), then a spliff would be made, and we all had a good draw on it and crashed again for another couple of hours. At about ten, we would stir and go about our business, brushing teeth, showering, getting dressed and eating breakfast. Mack and Cody found a bottle of Optrex eye drops and began putting drops in their eyes.

"What's that for, guys?" I asked.

"Come on, Dick, put some of this in your eyes. It stops them getting bloodshot." I obliged, and then we smoked

What a Surprise!

another spliff! The two guys stood looking at each other like a couple of cowboys about to have a gunfight. Cody said, "Do I look good, Mack?"

Mack said, "Yeah, Cody, you look great. What about me?"

"Yeah, cool, man. Let's go." The odd couple! They were really funny.

We made our way down the hill from their apartment to the train station and jumped on the MTR, the Hong Kong Underground. It was humid, hot and sweaty, and the pace was slow, stoned-out-of-your-head slow. The sunglasses were a must, a disguise, really. Because, for all the Optrex in the world, we would have looked shitfaced without them.

The train pulled up, the doors slid open, and we got that slight rush of cool air from the train's air conditioning. Stepping onto the train was like stepping into another dimension; it was cool, almost cold, and not very busy. It was truly refreshing, like a long ice-cold glass of water on a sunny day.

We were heading for Mong Kok, where the guys taught English. Mong Kok was known for shopping, clothes, trainers, and general bric-a-brac. There were plenty of restaurants, but it was the cheap shops that it was famous for.

As we got closer to Mong Kok, it became hugely busy on the train. The guys took no prisoners and softly but surely shoved their way through the heavy throngs of people.

Hong Kong is a 24-hour city, and during the day, there were a lot of people. The guys seemed to enjoy the circus that was going on around them, stoned in the middle of the mayhem! I caught Mack with a wry smile; I think he was

The Rocky Road

enjoying watching a friend from back home dealing with the Hong Kong way of life. It was mad, but I was enjoying the experience. Again, I was in a new culture. The smells, the colours and the noise were exhilarating, to say the least.

The lads took me down to the language school. They introduced me to the lady who owned it, and we wandered into a class. I was quite taken aback by the reaction of the students when they saw Mack and Cody. I felt like I was in the presence of a couple of celebrities as the students became really excited and animated, jostling for their attention. It was noisy, with about twenty students giggling and talking all at the same time. It was a joy to watch my two friends joking and laughing with everyone in the school. They looked happy, content, and very much at home; this was definitely their domain.

We left the school, jumped back on the MTR, got off at Tsim Sha Tsui, and made our way to Ned Kelly's bar on Ashley Road. Cody and Mack knew how to get across town, going through shops and hotels, into shopping malls, onto walkways, all under cover and all with air con. They knew this city like the backs of their hands and had worked out these intricate air-conditioned pathways right across the city.

Ned Kelly's was an Australian bar (and still is) that served good old English or Australian fare: bangers and mash, steak and kidney pie, fish and chips, a real home from home. It was mostly full of Western expats. In the evening, it was a jazz bar with live music.

We arrived at Ned's and ordered food and a cold beer. The guys were keen to know what I thought of their chosen

What a Surprise!

home. I thought it was spectacular: out-of-this-world spectacular. Three lads from back home in Croxley Green in Hertfordshire sitting in a bar in exotic Hong Kong. I was still not taking on board what they were really up to, but more of that later.

The guys gave me a whistle-stop tour, getting me orientated with my new environment. We jumped on the Star Ferry over to Hong Kong Island. The ferry was a four-minute ride; it's roughly 1000 metres from the mainland to the island, and the ferry ride is the most stunning commute ever. Both the island and the mainland shoot up out of the ground. The terrain on Hong Kong Island is hilly and land is limited, so it comes at a premium. Because of its limitations, everything was built upward. Huge glass monoliths peppered the skyline. The Bank of China Tower was just being completed and rose above everything. The island was the financial capital, where serious money could be made.

We went up to the peak, a 550-metre-high hill overlooking Hong Kong and beyond. We jumped on the tram to the top—the view was breathtaking, and you got a true perspective of just how extraordinary this place was—a mass of skyscrapers jutting out of the earth. It was a tightly-knit area of human development, with five million people living on top of each other in this 428 square miles of urban development.

We whiled away the day chatting about old times. There was definitely an air of confidence with these two, not arrogance, but true confidence, like they owned the city, and they were comfortable here.

The Rocky Road

The next evening, they had arranged to take me out for dinner with some of their friends on Lantau Island, out in the bay. We took a small boat from the Central Ferry Pier. The sun was going down, but it was warm with that sea-salt-taste smell in the air, and the breeze was welcoming after a long day in the heat of the city. We docked and made our way to a seafood restaurant. The Chinese love to eat out, so you are spoilt for choice when it comes to restaurants. This one overlooked the bay, so the view was beautiful, and the food was, well, different, but delicious. We sat at a huge round table with a centre that was independent from the outside, so you could spin the centre around to grab what you wanted. The food arrived; there was enough to feed a small army: barbequed whole fish, prawns, vegetables that I didn't recognise, battered things that I didn't recognise, and dips and sauces that I didn't recognise. The table was fit for a king, and everyone got stuck in, with a lot of chatter and a general banging of bowls and dishes. Eating in Hong Kong is a noisy affair.

The guys encouraged me to eat with chopsticks, more for their entertainment than anything else. However, it didn't take me long to work them out. By the end, the table was demolished, napkins screwed up and strewn around, and just a general food mess with sauce stains and bits of discarded food all over the white tablecloth. If you ordered fish, you got the whole fish; there was goodness within the bones that the Chinese understood, so they would never cook fish off the bone. Consequently, you would spit the bones out onto a side dish. Sometimes, you missed, and it ended up on

What a Surprise!

the table. The fallout on our table was colossal, but I was led to believe this was the ultimate compliment to the chef and the restaurant. There was, however, a rather forlorn-looking fish left over, with every bit of it eaten apart from its head. Mack informed me that they had left me the delicacy, the sweet bit, the part all the Chinese loved to eat—the eyes and the lips. The other people with us were Chinese, so it would have been rude not to have eaten them. So I ate the eyes, which were a little crunchy, and the lips, which were soft and squidgy. Mack and Cody were laughing their heads off. I had had my pants well and truly pulled down and given a good whack on my arse. Cheeky bastards!

Hong Kong was as busy at night as in the day. Nathan Road was the main thoroughfare running from the water's edge near the ferry through Tsim Sha Tsui and up to Mong Kok. This was a busy road, mostly shops and hotels, and at night, it came alive. So many people, and red taxis, and it was lit up like a Christmas tree. An incredible sight!

The time with these two in Hong Kong was a blast, with great hosts and great friends. I spent a couple of weeks with them, and then they shipped me off to Taiwan to meet up with big Keith and Monty.

I flew into Chiang Kai-Shek airport in Taipei and got a taxi to my hotel. Taipei looked totally different from Hong Kong; it was somehow drab, slightly dirty, and overcast, a bit like England on a bad day. The hotel was fine, but nothing to write home about. I phoned Keith to let him know I had arrived, and he said he'd pop down. He lived in Yangmingshan National Park, up in the mountains overlooking the city. He had a way to ride, so I grabbed a beer in the bar downstairs. Keith turned up with Monty. They were like a married couple, with Keith being the husband and Monty the wife!

Again, it was great to see some familiar faces from back home. I had gone to school with Monty, and Keith was a friend who I used to get up to a little bit of skulduggery with. Monty was a simple guy, not someone you would call super bright, but he could speak Mandarin, so he was far from stupid. Keith, on the other hand, was borderline genius on the edge of insanity. He was six-foot-five, slim, with tattoos on his neck—I bet the Triads loved him! He was an intense guy who could be quite intimidating. He had this uncanny ability to read your mind, which was really disconcerting. He was a hothead, blowing up at the flip of a coin. He was very entertaining, but not if you were on the end of one of his verbal bashings. He also had a true loyalty to his friends but demanded the same loyalty in return. As you can imagine, this wasn't always easy, as the demands could be high. He also spoke Mandarin.

They liked it in Taipei because of the girls. I hadn't realised what a horny pair of bastards they really were; everything with these guys revolved around getting laid. They looked fit and healthy, probably due to their "unhealthy sex lives". It had been well over three years since we had seen each other, so we gave each other big hugs. Keith's opening line, which was typical of him, was, "What the fuck happened to you, Dicky?"

I said, "Long story, Keith, long story. I'll fill you in."

What a Surprise!

Keith held my brother Dave in high esteem, so he was crushed after I told him what happened, and he couldn't believe it. Big Dave! It was a crushing blow to him.

So these two urchins lived here in the capital of Taiwan. We ate food and talked for hours, lots of drink, plenty of food and laughter, lots of laughter. They were making a living selling the bullet (Sebastian's grass oil mix). These two weren't rich, but they had a good life; Monty would supplement his dodgy dealings with teaching English: not anything academic, just the spoken language. This amused everyone because he couldn't speak English very well, even though he was English.

For all his intelligence and self-assurance, Keith didn't have the confidence to take on such a role, so he relied on his illicit earnings from drugs.

Both had motorbikes. Taipei City was heaving with trucks, cars, taxis, buses and, most of all, motorbikes. At the end of the evening, I went back to my hotel, but I arranged to meet up with Keith the next day for breakfast.

Keith picked me up on his bike first thing, and we went for some food. After that, he wanted to show me his home, so we jumped on his bike and sped off up the mountains. It was a stunning ride through the forest of the National Park until we got to this secluded little turn-off, and there we were in a relatively small clearing, where three or four chalet-type buildings stood. This was where Keith lived; it was situated in the most idyllic location, with a panoramic view over the city. It was completely isolated, which was perfect for someone like Keith, who really didn't like people. You could see why he lived here; the isolation and solitude were all-encompassing, and it was perfect.

We spent the day chewing the fat and smoking joints; it was a memorable, laid-back day. Keith played guitar while I listened. We ate more food and talked about life. In a few days, he and Monty were heading off to Thailand for a "short, good time", as they liked to put it and also to pick up some bullet from Sebastian. A "short, good time" meant frequenting the red-light district in Bangkok, so girls, girls, and girls. Keith insisted I came along; we would stay at Sebastian's in Bangkok. Keith told me at this point to be wary of Sebastian, as he had turned into an untrustworthy character. Funnily enough, the boys back in Hong Kong had told me the same thing. Obviously, Sebastian had upset everyone, but I didn't know why, and no one would tell me. I was left to work that one out for myself.

Time whizzed by in Taiwan, and the next thing I knew, we were off to Thailand via Hong Kong. Flying around South East Asia was relatively cheap, and the service on the aeroplanes was exceptional. They had the best airlines in the world: Cathay Pacific, Thai Air, Qantas Airways, and Singapore Airlines; they also had Aeroflot, the Russian carrier. Aeroflot flew in and out of Asia, but they're a whole different story when it comes to comfort and service.

We arrived in Hong Kong and went straight up to see Cody and Mack in the New Territories. Keith was a funny guy, which came out most when he was with his friends. The same applied to Cody and Mack. Keith had this habit of taking the palm of his hand and tapping you on the

What a Surprise!

forehead, like an open-handed Kung Fu thrust straight onto your forehead, playful but precise, bouncing off your third eye, a "Bod" as he liked to call them. Even at an early age, Keith was starting to lose his hair. Mack was aware of his own frailty when it came to hair loss, as was Cody. It was a running joke with these guys whenever they met up. Keith got hold of Mack, gave him a Bod, called him some unrepeatable names and pulled his head down so he could see the top of his head. He would make a few comments and then ask if Mack had discovered any new cures for hair loss. Lots of banter ensued: comments about clothes, footwear, digs at each other's weight, and generally, everything about life. I don't mind saying, it was a joy to witness; it was straight out of a Monty Python sketch; they were a crazy bunch, dead funny!

In the 80s, if you lived in South East Asia, Hong Kong was the only place to get anything done—passports, visas, legal matters, and anything involving paper and authority. Keith and Monty spent a couple of days busying themselves with visas and whatnot, and then we hopped on a plane and went to Thailand.

We were flying business class on Gulf Air, which was cheaper than Thai Airways economy class. It was a no-brainer; the lads from England had worked out the best routes, the best airlines, and the best class; they had it all well and truly sorted. I just piggybacked on their knowledge, so it was a breeze. This was my first experience in business class: leg room, comfort, food, service... how the other half lived! My next lesson was making use of the hospitality and getting

The Rocky Road

hammered on good Cognac. I was told this was a must when flying in Asia, so we set about getting absolutely smashed. By the time we got to Bangkok's Don Mueang Airport, we were drunk, but still standing.

We got a taxi and made our way to the Miami Hotel, just off Sukhumvit Road. It was an established hotel from the days of the Vietnam War, with clean rooms and friendly, honest staff. I thought we were staying at Sebastian's, but Keith and Monty wanted to go out on the town first. Sebastian lived way out near Lampang University, but these guys wanted to be in the middle of the city, near all the action.

We went to our rooms, showered and got ready to go out. Not far from our hotel was Nana Plaza, a relatively new place; it had a restaurant come go-go bar called Woodstock and another restaurant called The White Rabbit, and there was also a snooker club in the corner. The Woodstock had a unique menu; they had a sandwich called the "All Along The Watchtower", in honour of Jimi Hendrix, which was one foot high; obviously, it was the first item I ordered. I couldn't eat the whole sandwich, but it was a thing of beauty. Woodstock was owned by a couple of Australians, so the food was all burgers and chips, lamb chops, and so on. We ate and then wandered next door into the go-go bar, where half-naked girls were dancing on stage with half-naked girls serving at the tables and bars. "This is it, Dicky. Welcome to Bangkok." The experience was surreal, with loud music, huge mirrors adorning the walls, and a giant disco ball sending shards of light bouncing around the bar. It was a stimulus overload. Then we got drinking, and it became even more of a stimulus overload.

What a Surprise!

We hung around the bar for an hour or two, and then the guys said we were off to Patpong, the heart of the red-light district, where the real action took place. We jumped into a tuk-tuk and sped off into the night.

Riding through the traffic of Bangkok in the early evening was a blast. Tuk-tuk drivers are crazy motherfuckers, and the faster he went, the more we laughed, and the more we laughed, the faster he went! The evening was warm; even in short-sleeved shirts and shorts with the wind rushing by, we never felt cold. The smell of the pollution from a million vehicles and the noise was intoxicating. We raced through the streets without a care in the world, and then the tuk-tuk driver put on "The Boys Are Back In Town" by Thin Lizzy! We all laughed as the city lights came on and Bangkok came alive.

Eventually, we ended up in Patpong, the numero uno of Bangkok's sex industry. The guys gave me the heads-up on the ladyboy situation: "Deep voice, large Adam's apple and big feet; keep your eye open, Dicky." It was difficult to spot who was a female and who was a boy. The King's Castle Bar was notorious for ladyboys, so we steered clear. We headed over to the King's Corner, which had a disco upstairs and a go-go bar downstairs. We went straight upstairs to the disco, which was just a mass of partygoers, loud music, sexy-looking Thai girls, and some really odd-looking older fellows. It was like a perverts' reunion. The girls liked the older men because they paid, but they weren't as keen on the young ones. As the girls said, "Too young, you handsome man, you no good, you no pay."

The Rocky Road

Again, there were mirrors everywhere. It had a small dancefloor in the centre and comfortable seating around the edges. We sat around for a while just checking the joint out, and the guys were giving me some pointers. If you wanted a girl from the bar, you had to pay the bar fine, which was about 100 baht (two pounds sterling). You could then take the girl and negotiate a price for whatever you wanted. The cost would be anywhere between 400 and 500 baht (eight to ten pounds). It was a strange, unworldly situation; every girl had a price. When I voiced my concerns to Keith, he said it was the Englishness in me and that once I had been out here for a while, it would all seem normal. I found that hard to believe.

Men are fickle creatures led by their penis, and these girls knew it. The men came here and thought it was all one-way traffic; they had the money, they had the control, and they were smarter than the girls. The reality was that many of the girls were highly clever and astute. Once I got to know them, I got to see things from a different perspective. Needless to say, I was as fickle as any man, and I had a fun evening. It's an experience: no love, just urgency. A girl stayed the night with me, and in the morning, she tidied my room and folded my clothes, but it left me cold and empty!

In the morning, we went next door to the Ambassador Hotel, which was without doubt the best place in town for breakfast. It had a spectacular eat-as-much-as-you-want buffet for 100 baht. It was gluttony at its best.

After breakfast, we headed off to see Sebastian in the suburbs of Bangkok. He lived in a village, not quaint like one

What a Surprise!

would imagine, but a concrete mass, mainly influenced by the Americans. It was laid out in a grid pattern, with concrete roads and high kerbs that looked ridiculous. The houses pretty much all looked the same, all concrete structures and flat roofs, like a modern-day dystopia (or an environmental disaster!). It wasn't attractive, but his house was a big, old, detached property with a large carport to one side, a good-sized garden and a glorious mango tree that hung over the house. He also had papaya trees in the garden. The house looked like Fort Knox with this big solid steel gate at the front.

When we got out of the taxi and banged on the gate, Sebastian came down to let us in. He had all the suave arrogance of some sort of colonial lord, dressed in a princely-looking dressing gown, and his hair was all slicked back. He knew I was coming with the boys, so when he opened the gate, he smiled in a courteous sort of way, shook my hand, and said, "My God, man, how are you?" He was straight out of a P. G. Wodehouse novel, like Bertie Wooster answering the fucking door. He exaggerated his articulations as he headed back up the garden, flailing his arms about like a wild, demented John Cleese. "Come in, chaps, come in," he said.

He was a complex fellow who based himself on Keith: a pseudo-Keith! But he was never able to get it right. Keith was genuine and honest, and Sebastian was quite the opposite, fake and untruthful, a twisted version of the real thing. It has to be said, he was also rather slippery, but a good host. We went up to the house and chucked our bags on the floor.

Sebastian shared the house with his business partner, Nigel, who was Canadian, and a girl called Kelly, who was an American; she looked like a man, talked like a man, and walked like a man, the same as a duck. Rumour had it she was having an affair with Sebastian. Nigel was a Canadian who may or may not have been having an affair with Sebastian as well. The rumours were rife about that. Nigel gave off a pleasant vibe: very talkative, very articulate, a nice guy. Sebastian and Nigel were in the import/export business, moving Thai artefacts around the world. Legitimate businessmen... yeah, alright! Nigel, as it turned out, came from a similar background to Sebastian, one of wealth! Sebastian's dad was a director of one of the biggest banks in the world, and Nigel's mum was dating the CEO of one of America's most prestigious banks! A couple of bankers' children, out in Asia, just shooting the breeze and playing the game.

Keith wanted to get straight down to business; these two import/export tycoons were the brains behind "the bullet", the grass oil mix that blew your head off. So they weren't just bullshitting; they were definitely in the import/export business! Keith had some complaints about the quality of the last batch he had bought and was trying to negotiate some sort of reimbursement or, better still, all of his money back. The Chuckle Brothers (Nigel and Sebastian) were the kings of flannel and were batting their corner, trying to convince Keith that the last batch had been good, and somehow, Keith was mistaken.

Watching this was nerve-wracking; I could see Keith was on the verge of blowing. He tolerated their nonsense

What a Surprise!

for quite some time and then said that if they didn't stop with the bollocks, he was going to beat the fucking pair of them. They had to either honour the deal, or he would not be held responsible for his actions. For all the bullshit these two could muster between them, pain was not something on their agenda, so they relented to his terms.

Keith and Monty didn't want to hang around at Sebastian's; they were on holiday and desperate to go down to the islands. The next day, all three of us got bus tickets and headed off to Ko Samet, a tiny island off the coast of the province of Rayong, some 220 km south of Bangkok. So we hopped on to a rickety bus and spent an uncomfortable three to four hours all the way to the ferry port, with Keith cursing nonstop. When we got to the coast, it was lovely and sunny, and the sea was crystal clear. We climbed aboard the ferry, which was more like a fishing boat, and it smashed its way through the waves all the way to the island.

Ko Samet was a small, almost untouched island with beautiful beaches and just a handful of beach bars; accommodation was an array of small huts dotted around the island. As a holiday destination, it was relatively new for the foreign tourist, but locals had been visiting here for decades. Until 1981, no overnight stays were permitted. The government had designated the island a national park, so it had restricted development. This kept the big boys at bay, and the natural beauty was preserved.

We spent the next ten days just smoking joints and eating lovely food. It was good to see Keith chilled, but Monty didn't have much trouble doing nothing; in fact, it came easy to him. Keith and I spent many a long evening putting the world to rights. He gave me the whole history of how the lads had upped sticks and left the UK; at least, the version according to Keith! Over time, I would get to hear each and everyone's version; they were all different and all interesting at the same time.

It went something like this. When the boys arrived in Hong Kong, they worked in the film industry and then found teaching, and then it was the milk runs, gold runs, and finally, a little drug running. They stayed as a group for some months, but Keith was overbearing and controlling, so they had to find a way to separate themselves from him, not throw him away; they all treasured his friendship, but they couldn't live with him. In the end, the guys got control of the situation and convinced him that Taiwan was the best place for him, so he took Monty and moved there. Which brought us to where we were: Monty, Cody, and Mack still taught English, with other revenue streams. Sebastian pretended to be a successful businessman but was really selling the bullet, and there was a suspicion that Sebastian and Nigel were running smack out of Thailand. Keith didn't like the heroin business; he thought it was dirty, and the rest of the boys felt the same. Mack had his fingers in some pies but kept his cards close to his chest; however, he and Cody always had teaching at the language school to fall back on. I think it was more of a social event than work though.

I was still buzzing from actually being in Asia; I had to pinch myself on occasion as I sat there with my mates, listening to story after story of their escapades. I wasn't much

What a Surprise!

interested in getting involved with any of their ducking and diving; prison was still raw in my mind, and I didn't fancy that again. The only problem with me was that I tended to be easily led—led by my own stupidity—and then fall over. I tended to fall over a lot!

The week soon passed us by, and we headed back to Bangkok. I went to Sebastian's house while Keith and Monty disappeared off into the lights of Bangkok to pick up their friend, who would take their product back to Taiwan. In the game, he or she was referred to as a donkey, someone you paid to carry contraband for you.

I spent time with Sebastian and Nigel; they were good company and great fun to be around. They liked being busy, busy doing something or nothing, mostly nothing. They both had motorbikes, Honda MTX 125rs, jacked-up trial bikes that were noisy and fast, just the sort of transport for one of the most congested cities on earth. On the other hand, as a *"farang"* (white European), one stood out on these contraptions like a sore thumb; the bikes stood tall and had brightly coloured paint jobs. Good for getting around town but not the best mode of transport for a drug smuggler trying to stay under the radar. Many years later, a friend who had visited me in Bangkok said that the first time he saw me riding one of these bikes, he said to himself, "Now there's a drug smuggler." I must have looked a sight; it's just a shame he didn't tell me at the time!

Life was good in Thailand. I loved the people, and they seemed to love me back. As a *farang*, I was considered wealthy even if I wasn't, so they deemed me fair game for a scam or ripping me off. In my lop-sided way of thinking, I considered that fair enough; someone ripping me off with a smile on their face I could deal with. It could be worse, and I could be seen as a cash cow and be held up at knife point and robbed, which would not be so good.

Of all the places I had visited in my short time in South East Asia, this was the place where I wanted to live. For that to work, I would have to figure out how to make a living without breaking the law.

I stayed with Sebastian and Nigel much longer than anticipated. They were slippery characters, and they were moving a lot of the bullet around the world. I always had a penchant for villains; the bigger the villain, the better I liked them, and for some reason, they liked me back. I think there was a mutual respect going on. I liked breaking the law, and so did they; we all wanted to make money, and we didn't want to be working too hard, which happened to be the philosophy of all the lads in Asia.

I spent the next few months just mooching about from Hong Kong to Taiwan and back to Thailand. The lads were good to me; they all put me up when I arrived in their countries. I was freeloading, and I knew it, but I got to see my mates, and I got a real insight into their lives. Everyone was content. There was some risk-taking, of course, but generally, everyone was living a life of choice and not doing the rat race thing.

When Christmas came round, I decided to tag along with Keith and pop back to the UK. I had a return ticket, so I thought I would use it to go back home. Cody and Mack

What a Surprise!

thought I was crazy. I had only just got there, and now I wanted to go home? I had no answer to the question; I just felt compelled.

England was bitterly cold and damp, so I didn't stay home for long. I spent Christmas at one of my sister's, but I was a bit of an irritant to her. I was over-excited from the last six months in Asia, and when I would talk about my experiences, I could see the shutters coming down as I spoke of far-flung places that meant little or nothing to her. Soon, she was showing all the signs of being bored with me. Welcome home!

England was drab, so I felt oppressed, and I wanted to get out of there as fast as I could. It reminded me of an open-air prison. Asia, on the other hand, was like the Wild West: yet to be discovered by most and holding the keys to freedom!

The trip to England was short. Keith hated it as much as I did, so we got on a plane and disappeared back to where we had come from. This time, I had a one-way ticket. I had no thoughts of returning to England.

Coming into land at Kai Tak airport, just missing the buildings again on the way in, the excitement was still there. Leaving the airport, the blanket of heat that crashed into my face and the smell of aviation fuel and car fumes filled the air; it was uniquely Hong Kong.

I was back in South East Asia, spending time with the boys in Hong Kong. Everyone was in town apart from Sebastian, so Keith, Monty, Mack, Cody and I got stoned and listened to music and enjoyed each other's company.

Keith went home to Taiwan with Monty, and I wandered off to Thailand. I could stay for ninety days without

The Rocky Road

a visa, so I decided to hang out with Sebastian and Nigel for a while.

Arriving at Don Mueang Airport, I found it had none of the razzmatazz of Bombay or Hong Kong; it was just an airport, with no turbulence and no skyscrapers. It was, however, Thailand, and I loved arriving there. I already considered it home. I grabbed a taxi and headed for Sebastian's.

While I was away, these two likely lads had been busy trying to set up an import/export business, focusing their attention on the local handicrafts market. They asked me along to one of their meetings with a successful Thai businessman. These two could talk the talk: quotas, tariffs, import duties, carrier costs, and so on. I sat and watched these two likely lads spin their web. The meeting looked like a success, with lots of smiles, plenty of handshakes, and slapping each other on the back; what more could you ask for. After the meeting, a decision was made to fly up to Chiang Mai on a fact-finding mission, looking for products to source. They invited me along on this mission; it sounded like a lot of fun.

Arriving in Chiang Mai, we found a nice, simple hotel, booked in and dropped our bags off. The first thing we needed was motorbikes; we tracked down a local hire shop and did the deal, and now we were free to roam. We went out and got drunk that evening, then bright and early, with a tinge of a hangover, we left the city and headed out into the countryside. Chiang Mai was the epicentre of the Thai handicraft world. Nigel was learning to speak the language—his grasp was already pretty good—and he took this opportunity to expand his vocabulary. The language is not easy for

What a Surprise!

Westerners to learn as it is a tonal language, five tones in all, and it's extremely difficult for the Western ear to distinguish them.

Nigel was superb, and really enthusiastic, with loads of energy and nonstop talking. We went off and found some factories: long, thatched open shelters with around thirty women carving and weaving crafts of all shapes and sizes. The best known was the Chiang Mai Baby, a carved chubby wooden infant!

We spent two days going from one of these tiny little concerns to another. Nigel would do all the talking while Sebastian and I would drink green tea and soak up the experience. Nigel's enthusiasm for the language was inspiring; he voiced his concerns on many occasions about his lack of confidence, doubts about his pronunciation and the wrong tone, but from the perspective of a non-speaker, his grasp of the Thai language was extraordinary. He spoke it with joy and gusto; all Sebastian and I had to do was sit back, watch and listen.

On the last day before Sebastian returned to Bangkok, we went on a beautiful long bike ride around the hills of northern Thailand; we had no crash helmets, and the hot air was like a hairdryer on full blast. The roads were empty, and we just rode and rode. In the afternoon, we came across this long, straight stretch of road, perfect tarmac with no potholes, and paddy fields on the left stretching as far as the eye could see; on the right, there was jungle. It reminded me of the tuk-tuk ride from Panjim to Colva, way back in India. As we rode along, we passed an old man sitting on a rocking chair smoking a pipe by the roadside. There was nothing else around, no homes, no shops, and no people. Nigel shouted for us to pull over.

"Did you see that old guy?"

"Yeah," we said in unison.

"What do you think he's doing? There's nothing here, with nothing for miles; let's go back and talk to him."

"OK," I said.

Nigel wanted Sebastian and me to ask questions so he could translate them into Thai; he thought he would struggle to think and translate at the same time. So we went back to the old man sitting on a rocking chair in the middle of nowhere. We pulled up, got off the bikes and wandered over.

"Ask him where he's from, Nigel," Sebastian said.

So Nigel started chatting with him.

"Come on, what's he saying, Nigel?"

They stopped talking for a moment. It seemed this old chap was from a village some miles away in the forest.

"Well, what's he doing sitting here, Nigel? Look, there's nothing here. Does he want a lift home or what?"

They carried on chatting for some time. The old man was laughing and smiling; clearly, these two were having a ball. The old man was a small, wiry fellow with a pointy beard and slightly hooded eyes; he was puffing on a bamboo pipe between answering Nigel's questions and rocking back and forth in tune with the flow of the conversation. Sebastian and I wanted to know what he was doing, so we started badgering Nigel for the answer. He was enjoying the banter with the old guy and completely ignored our pleas. Then, it all went silent, and he turned to us.

What a Surprise!

"Well?"

"He's watching the rice grow!"

"Fucking hell, why's he doing that? Come on!"

After more discussions, Nigel turned to us and said, "He says there's a particular point in the growth pattern when the grain hangs over, and it turns golden yellow in colour; he's the only person in the village who knows when the time is just right. When that time arrives, he calls in all the girls from the village to pick the rice."

Nigel talked some more with the old guy, and as we were leaving, we heard him say the familiar, "Sabai," which means life is good and he wished us well! From what Nigel could work out, the old man was 89 years old and had been watching the rice grow for the past thirty years. The old man of the sea, but his was a sea of rice, not the big blue one!

Sebastian left the next day, so Nigel and I hung up our scouting boots and got absolutely wasted for the rest of the week. This was a familiar theme with these two; when one wasn't watching the other, the other would party—like a proper married couple!

* * *

My money was dwindling, and I was starting to think about work and looking at my options. Life was always busy at Sebastian's due to the comings and goings of the criminally-minded traveller. The scams across Asia by this band of merry men were incredible. One chap had made his way from Thailand all the way back to the UK by land with nothing but a pocket full of dodgy credit cards and a good dose of confidence. He achieved his goal... and then returned to Asia!

Jerry turned up at Sebastian's one day. He was in his mid-twenties, a smart dresser, clean-shaven with a mop of golden blond hair, a bit of a Brad Pitt lookalike. He carried himself well, another confidence trickster. He had this camp, mincing thing going on. He was gay but hadn't realised it yet. Monty happened to be in town at the same time, so all three of us met up in Patpong for drinks.

Jerry had been hanging around Bangkok for a couple of years, running dodgy traveller's cheques and using stolen credit cards. It seemed everyone had some piece of illegal action going on. He got talking to us about the credit card scams he was running out of Singapore with a guy called Chinese Gow. Gow took two or three *farang* to Singapore with fake passports and a ton of credit cards and worked the city for the weekend, buying Rolex watches, jewellery, and other expensive items. The pay was good, three grand for the weekend, and as Jerry assured us, you never ever got caught. How does the saying go? "If it sounds too good to be true..."

The last thing on my mind was doing anything to jeopardise my freedom, but to be honest, the gig did sound "too good to be true". The conversation went on through the night. Monty was up for it, as he hadn't been to Singapore yet, and it seemed like a great chance to see that country. I wasn't having it, but by the night's end, they had convinced me it was a good idea with "no risk"! So Jerry put the wheels

What a Surprise!

in motion and organised it. A month later, we were on a flight to Singapore.

We met Gow, a dodgy little character. He was small with tiny beady eyes that constantly darted around the room; he was unable to maintain eye contact—not a good sign—but he again assured us that there was no risk. I kept hearing that! The basic outline of the scam was to shop until you dropped with stolen credit cards; Gow would be our lookout man. What could go wrong?

Singapore sits just off the Malay Peninsula, almost bang on the equator. It's a massive trading post established by Stamford Raffles in 1819 as part of the British Empire. In WWII, it was occupied by the Japanese, who returned it to the Brits in 1945. It became independent in 1959. Today, it has a reputation for money, honesty, and human rights; three things that don't really go together. Singapore was super clean with a low crime rate. It was orderly, the roads were spotless, and everything shut at midnight; it was like a sanitised shopping mall. As a result, it had no character; it was a clean version of Hong Kong. All the history was being replaced with glass and steel monsters, buildings with no character and no sense of human life.

That evening, Gow took us out for an expensive meal at the Hua Yu Wee seafood restaurant. We joked and laughed through the meal. It was obvious that we were all full of false confidence; the laughter was fake, and the fear was real.

The next day, we met up in one of the hotel rooms for a briefing. Gow gave each of us an Amex Gold Card with different names, plus a passport that corresponded to the names on the card. He said we had to copy the original signatures on the backs of the cards; fucking hell, no one had told us we'd be forging signatures back in Bangkok! Anyway, we set about our task, and when Gow was happy with our ham-fisted attempts at forgery, we went off to Orchard Road, the main drag, with all the malls and upmarket shops. There was no internet, no electronic swiping machines, and no mobile phones; there was just a swipe machine with carbon paper that took an imprint of the cards. You signed the receipt and were good to go, with no checking, and nothing like the electronic world we now know.

Being a white European, you were instantly classed as rich, so if you were white and European and you were in a shop, it was because you could afford it, so you had their trust. The first thing to do was to test out the cards.

To play the part, you had to look the part, so we headed off to a few swanky menswear clothes shops. Jerry had been here before, so he volunteered to demonstrate how easy it was. We found a beautiful men's clothes shop, and he wandered in. Twenty minutes later, he came out with an Armani suit on—casual but smart—handmade leather penny loafers and a great big grin. He had gone into the shop rather sheepishly, but he came out not only looking like Brad Pitt but also dressed like him and exuding the same confidence: look the part, feel the part, as they say.

It was my turn, so I gathered all the false confidence I could muster and went into the next clothes shop. It was lovely, full of the most exquisite clothes, and clean and air-conditioned, and the staff were very professional and only too pleased to accommodate your every whim! It was a

What a Surprise!

nerve-wracking experience though. I got talking to the staff, and by the end, we were like old friends. They gave me good advice on what suited me and what didn't. I was inspired to go for the Jerry look: Armani suit, soft shoes and a Fred Perry shirt, the casual but smart look, and, let's not forget, the loaded look. In the end, I paid with my dodgy card, ripped off my new shop "friends" and left. I came out of the shop to a round of applause. It was extraordinarily scary, but the rush of getting away with it was quite addictive. Monty went next and bought—you guessed it—an Armani suit. We looked the part now—the three wise monkeys—and off we went to shop till we dropped.

Next, I went into the jeweller's with the explicit task of buying a Rolex Oyster Perpetual Motion, a diamond-encrusted ugly old monster of a watch with a massive price tag. I went through the whole process, trying them on and looking at the different styles, and in the end, I found the one that suited the bill, a five-grand garish thing. The assistant packaged it all up, took my card, and then decided to ring the bank. This was not good. Gow was in the shop, and he had no signs of panic, so I stood there like a lemon, waiting for the cops to turn up and arrest me. The minutes felt like hours, and then the shop assistant appeared with a beautifully presented bag with my watch inside and the receipt. With a big smile, he said, "Thank you, Mr Ramadada. Everything is good, have a nice day." He shook my hand, and I left the shop. No cops, no jail! But Jesus, that had been scary.

I wore that watch for the whole trip, for that little extra pizzazz. The other two did the same with their expensive watches, and after that, we thought we were indestructible. As the weekend progressed and our confidence grew, we just shopped and shopped. At lunchtimes, we frequented the best restaurants, eating the best food and drinking the best champagne. We would fight over the bill, each forcing their generosity on the other by insisting on paying. The winner got out their credit card and paid the bill. We were like children whose parents were away for the weekend.

The scam was a success. We got on the plane to leave, exhausted but exhilarated. We had pulled it off—the Singapore Heist! We got absolutely smashed on the flight back to Bangkok. We were loud and boisterous, like schoolboys, and probably ruined the flight for all the other passengers. We didn't care—we were too busy enjoying ourselves—so we were rude and arrogant, and we should have got arrested just for that!

It was hard to come down off the high of Singapore, so we went out partying for days. These two were far more familiar than I was with the nightlife in Bangkok. When the night drifted into the early hours of the morning, Patpong slowed down, and the girls who hadn't seen any action drifted off to other places to find punters. Monty and Jerry knew that one of these night-time haunts was the Thermae, right next to the Miami Hotel. In the daytime, it was a coffee shop; at night, it was the last stand saloon for the girls looking for a late-night punter. It was dark and dingy, so it attracted all the creatures of the night, and Monty loved it! I grew to love it too; it was truly seedy, with its unique smell that went with the ambience. It was a dive, but somehow attractive.

What a Surprise!

I spent a lot of my time there over the years. These two also introduced me to the Malaysia Hotel in the heart of the so-called backpacker's area; Soi Ngam Duphli and Soi Sribamphen were the roads that made up the area around the hotel. As rumour had it, Charles Sobhraj had spent many years around this area, looking for backpackers to kill! This area was notorious for Western criminals. If you were short of cash, this was the place to go, as there were plenty of people here smuggling drugs all over the world, and they were always in need of a donkey or two. I liked this area so much that I moved there later.

So we partied for two nights, then Monty went home, and Jerry disappeared to wherever. I saw Sebastian on the odd occasion, and Cody, Mack and Keith would pop into town. Then we would all meet up and party and maybe go to one of the islands.

One time, I popped over to Hong Kong to see the boys, and they had a friend staying over called Ossie. I knew him from the past. When I was 16, I had bought a Garelli moped from him. It was the fastest moped in town, a real memory piece. Funnily enough, all of us were involved in the moped days of Croxley Green and Rickmansworth, tearing around the towns and villages on our bikes, causing mayhem and upsetting all the locals with the noise and general lack of respect. Harmless fun, or not so harmless; several of us had terrible accidents, and there were many injuries. Anyway, Ossie, the Garelli moped man, was over to take the bullet back to the UK; he was a funny little guy with a liking for booze; he was also a liability.

The Rocky Road

Cody and I talked about the Singapore gig, which Ossie already knew all about—news travelled fast in Asia. We got talking, and he said Ossie possessed a gold Amex card, so we decided to proposition him with a "Singapore scam", but this one would be called the "Hong Kong scam". We thought maybe he would be up for a little skulduggery while he was in town. We were right. Ossie was up for anything, and he agreed with our plan, so we packed him off to Thailand, less one gold Amex card.

Cody and I hit the streets of Hong Kong and went shopping all day Saturday and all day Sunday. Ossie agreed to report his card missing on the Monday. Cody had a fence in Hong Kong, so we had somewhere to offload all the goods in one hit. It was a gruelling weekend, and when we were done, and the dust had settled, Cody and I flew to Thailand to meet up with Ossie, who was staying with Sebastian.

Everyone was there when we arrived at Sebastian's house: Monty, Keith, Mack and some French dude. Everyone was in high spirits, joking, laughing, and dancing round the house to Bobby McFerrin's "Don't Worry Be Happy". The spliffs were fired up, and the music was blaring out. Then Keith threw a wobbly, and the mood changed instantly. Sebastian said something innocuous, and Keith went off on one. This was normal; Keith was a livewire, and everyone was used to it. It killed the vibe, though, as Keith was ranting and raving and intimidating everyone in the house. Then, after a while, he calmed down, and Cody took him off for some breakfast. The dark clouds in the house left along with Keith, and calm was restored.

What a Surprise!

It was a fun week; it wasn't often that I got to see all the lads at the same time. However, as the week drifted on, everyone headed back home. I again stayed at Sebastian's for a week or so. Kelly had moved out, and I commandeered her room for a short period. Things at the house hadn't changed much; there were people in and out all the time: Australians, Americans and the French guy who had been there when Cody and I had arrived from Hong Kong. His name was Edward (pronounced Edwwwaaaaard). He was a flamboyant guy with that French confidence and nationalistic attitude; the French are very proud to be French, a quality I admire. He was good fun and supposedly a model; I wasn't sure what he modelled. He was there to donkey the bullet back to Taiwan for Keith and Monty—so much for the modelling.

Nigel was into parachuting and, more importantly, base jumping, which entailed jumping off buildings and cliffs with a parachute on. Consequently, many parachutists passed through the house. Some came to teach, but they all wanted to base jump. One Australian named Brin was there to coach the Thai army in parachuting, but first, he wanted to jump off the roof of the Baiyoke Tower, a well-known tower block in the heart of Bangkok.

Over the next few days, a big gang of us scouted the building, working out how to get on the roof and the best side to jump from. A friend lived in the apartment block, so one morning, we all converged on his apartment. We sat around for a long time. I wasn't quite sure what was going on. Brin was in the corner with his parachute on, looking chilled out and not particularly talkative; everyone else was smoking dope and trying to work out the best way forward. The roof was out as it was securely locked, so Brin said he would jump off the balcony. Everyone started to get excited, and bodies with cameras disappeared outside. The general excitement in the room escalated, and then Brin stood up, went over to the balcony, and, as casual as you like, threw himself over the side. I had never seen anything like it; the guy had just jumped off the balcony. We all rushed over to see what happened, and there he was, floating down to earth with his parachute open. There was lots of hooting and hollering as he landed, and then he was back in the room with his eyes out on stalks, bloodshot and crazed. He sat down and said he hadn't considered all the telephone cables and had nearly died. Someone skinned up a joint and gave it to him. He just sat there, not saying a word, staring into space and chomping on a joint.

Not long after, he disappeared to one of the king's retreats to await instructions from the Thai army.

Life was a little too crazy at the house, so I decided to go and visit Keith and Monty in Taipei. Taipei always felt dirty to me; there was lots of pollution, and I also got an upset stomach whenever I visited there. I just never felt clean in Taiwan due to the climate and the dirty habits, like the way the Chinese liked to throw their rubbish out of their windows. It was a filthy habit, going back to the Middle Ages. So I went and stayed with Keith up in the mountains, where it was relaxed, and the views were spectacular.

What a Surprise!

He had a neighbour called Carol, a frustrated American housewife. The lads were convinced she was gagging for it and would flirt with her, and she seemed to enjoy the attention, so maybe they were right. I've never been good at reading the signals that women give off. To me, she behaved in a completely normal way. I couldn't see what they could see, if there was anything to see. She never shagged them!

I spent a good amount of time up the mountain. I would go walking. One morning, while I was out, Carol happened by in her car, and she pulled over to ask if I wanted to go into town with her to meet some ballerina friends she was having lunch with. I wasn't exactly doing anything, so I jumped in her car, and off we went. I said I didn't exactly feel dressed for the occasion, in my vest and cut-off jeans, but she said it was the perfect outfit for the occasion!

We arrived at her friend's house, which was way out in the suburbs. Carol knocked on the door, and a rather effeminate young boy of about 18 answered. He was obviously gay, and he took us inside to the dining room, where there was another gay boy—his boyfriend—an old woman, a girl of about 10, a young Chinese couple, Jin and Hok, who were about 20, and this absolutely beautiful Chinese lady, maybe seven or eight years older than myself, who I was sitting next to. The meal was a couple of hours of eating mixed in with the two gay boys trying to flirt with me and giggling endlessly. I could see what Carol meant now by my dress being perfect. I resembled some sort of Freddy Mercury lookalike. It was entertaining, but men are not really my thing. I was more interested in the lady I was sitting next to. She was

The Rocky Road

stunningly beautiful and, as it turned out, a ballet teacher, and I took her number. She invited me to her dance school, so we arranged to meet the next day.

I arrived at the studio to be met by these rather long-limbed girls with extraordinarily extended necks and long arms: odd-looking creatures but beautiful all the same. They looked like ET with pretty faces. In among these young girls was Chia, this graceful beauty, the teacher and owner of this prestigious school, and the woman I had come to meet. The young students followed her every command. It was effortless; she had grace and power, which was beautiful to observe. I caught her eye, and she came over to the door where I was standing. There was an audible silence in the room; everyone carried on with their warm-ups and dance routines, but all eyes followed their teacher as she made her way to this foreign man and gave him a peck on the cheek. I felt myself flush at the attention and the intimacy of the situation. She smiled and said she would only be ten minutes if I didn't mind waiting.

Her studio was a classic example of a time gone by with wooden floors and mirrors from floor to ceiling on every wall; it was like a dusty old room without the dust. Chia finished her tasks, and we went for some noodles. When we sat down at the table, I asked a couple of questions about her life, so she talked and talked about a messy separation and her dance career. Her father was a retired colonel who lived in the south, in Kaohsiung City. She was very open and mesmerising. I told her I was an English teacher, and I was looking to move to Taiwan.

What a Surprise!

As we sat and talked, I felt myself falling in love with this creature. She was beautiful. I think she got the message and put me down gently. She wasn't ready for any relationship as she was still struggling with her marriage breakdown and needed time. Soul-destroying stuff. But she asked if I would like to meet her father in Kaohsiung. I took her up on the invite, and the next day, she saw me off at the bus station. Her father met me at the other end in Kaohsiung; he was smartly dressed, quite old and short, and had that military stance with his square shoulders and chest all puffed out. He spoke good English with a strong American accent. We went back to his home, and he showed me around. It was a nice single-storey house. He took me to the room I'd be staying in, and I left my bags. He was very talkative, with lots of questions. We talked for some time, and then I made my excuses; it was already late and I needed sleep.

The next day, he took me on a sightseeing tour. Kaohsiung was the second largest city in Taiwan, and it had one of the largest ports in the country. It wasn't pretty and it wasn't ugly; it was just another city. I didn't see any other foreigners here, and I was drawing a lot of attention; people would come and stand next to me to have their pictures taken. The colonel seemed to like all the attention; whenever we got out of the car for a walk, the people would start staring, and he would grow by a few inches. We had a great day together, and then we ended up back at his house at four in the afternoon. He made a little egg noodle and brought out a bottle of his homemade plum wine.

As the day disappeared and the afternoon drifted into the evening, another bottle appeared; as the wine flowed, we

The Rocky Road

began telling each other funny stories. We were pissed and getting on like a house on fire when there was a knock at the front door, and in came one of his old friends, who took up a seat at the table. His name was Wong, and he was fascinated by me; he had never met an Englishman before. Like the colonel, he spoke with an American accent. It was a bit off-putting to think the Yanks had got here first and taught these poor, helpless people a bastardised version of English. Anyway, Wong had his fill and was gone, but as soon as he was gone, there was another knock on the door, and the colonel got up to answer it, looking excited, and slightly wobbly. He came back with another guy who had never met an Englishman. When he left, another one turned up, then two more, and it went on like this for two or three hours.

When we had a 15-minute breather with no visitors, we talked about my desire to find a teaching position. I thought maybe Kaohsiung could be an option for me. As we talked, a Chinese guy in his mid-30s came in and sat down. I didn't hear a knock; he seemed to appear out of nowhere.

He spoke perfect American English; just about everyone else who had stopped by spoke a type of Pidgin English, but this guy's English was better than mine. We had a long chat about the English language. I was drunk and gave him my best drunken wisdom on the subject, beginning by explaining the pitfalls of learning American English instead of the Queen's English. I began mimicking the different accents of the Americas, the southern drawl and so on. I was pretty good at it, too, even though I was drunk as a skunk and nearly falling off my chair. I basically took the piss out of

What a Surprise!

him, explaining how he couldn't speak English properly; then he left with his American accent and his tail between his legs. The colonel and I were roaring with laughter, merry and drunk. I asked him who that had been. He said it was his son-in-law, the English teacher from the local army base, and he had come over to interview me and maybe offer me a job! Needless to say, I didn't get the job, which was embarrassing.

I spent the next week hanging out with the colonel before I went back up to Taipei to see Keith and Monty. I didn't stay for long and headed back over to Hong Kong to see Mack and Cody. Cody had a gig if I wanted it: going up to South Korea with some jewellery, watches and clothes. It paid OK, and there was, of course, "no risk". In fact, it wasn't exactly breaking the law. So before I headed off to Thailand, I made a quick detour up to South Korea.

I spent a day or so in Seoul before heading back. Before I left, I had a list of things to buy: Reebok boots, Levi jeans and other items for Cody and Mack. It was cheap even for South East Asia, so I did my bit, dropped off the merchandise to the boys in Hong Kong and went back to Bangkok.

I'd given Sebastian a call before I left Hong Kong, and he invited me to stay at his place. Before I headed over, though, I decided to stay in the city at the Miami Hotel for a few days. I needed to get my breath back. I was ducking and diving again, surviving in Asia and breaking the law. The fact that I was a white European gave me the edge across this whole region. The police in Thailand gave you a wide berth. By contrast, the Bangkok tourist police were all-powerful and were there to protect the tourists as tourism was big business, and

The Rocky Road

the government didn't want to buck that. So, I was a protected species! However, if a tourist did get caught breaking the law, they could be brutal, from the police on the street right through to the judiciary. Prisons in Thailand were notoriously horrific, the last place you wanted to end up. On the other hand, if you were clever enough, there was always a chance to buy your way out of trouble. Sebastian and Nigel had the great misfortune (or fortune) to have experienced this first-hand.

Nigel was also heavily involved with the skydiving fraternity; anyone and everyone who was a skydiver coming to Thailand stopped off at Sebastian and Nigel's. It was like an outpost for skydivers. Many of them were in Thailand to train either the army or the police, as both had parachute regiments. So these parachutists would stop over at the house; they were all smokers of the dreaded weed, and they would stay for a week, getting smashed before taking up their posts. And they were all crazy! Because of this connection, Nigel was friendly with the Chief of Police and Tod, one of the personal bodyguards to the king; both had skydived with Nigel.

The one with the most kudos was the king's bodyguard, as he was one step away from God. Nigel and Sebastian carried his personal business card with them at all times as this could potentially get them out of all sorts of trouble, like the trouble that came along when Nigel broke one of the cardinal rules: never carry anything incriminating when out riding on your motorbike.

Being a foreigner on a motorbike was seen as a cash cow. The cops would pull you over and give you an

What a Surprise!

on-the-spot fine for some bogus misdemeanour—basically a bribe. It was usually only 100 baht, and then they would let you be on your way. However, on this particular day, Nigel decided it would be more convenient just to jump on his bike and drop off a couple of kilos of the bullet across town. It just so happened that, on this day, the cops were having a self-funding day; about eight of them had posted themselves at a major crossroads, pulling over cars and bikes to check their insurance, etc. The police generally rode their own personal motorbikes while at work. The quality of motorbike dictated which police officer took the bribe—the more expensive the bike, the bigger the bribe.

So, on this fateful day, Nigel rode straight into one of their traps with a bag full of drugs. He got pulled over, and the cops searched him, so he was in trouble. Nigel had a good grasp of the Thai language by this point and listened as the cops decided what to do with him. He never gave the game away, keeping to the English language. As they talked, he called them over, separating them from the other police officers; he wanted to keep this to himself and the two cops as if they beckoned the other cops over the implications were enormous. Nigel asked them if there was any chance of solving the problem there and then and produced Tod's business card: the king's bodyguard! The colour drained from their cheeks as they digested the implications; this man had the power to get them sacked and more. They asked Nigel how he knew this man, and Nigel said they were good friends, and if they called him, he would be able to help and resolve the situation… or was there some other way to sort this out? The cops had a little discussion among themselves and said that if he gave them US$ 3,000, that would be the end of the matter, and he could be on his way. Nigel agreed the price and messaged Sebastian on his pager, saying he needed the money, and he needed it now. Sebastian sped over with the money, which they handed over to the cops, who quite graciously accepted the bribe. Nigel kept his drugs and rode off. English cops would at least have confiscated the drugs, and no doubt kept Nigel on a leash forever more. In Thailand, when the deal is done, the deal is done, and that's it: no leaching, no blackmail, no being forever more in debt to the police. The Thais did the deal, and the person disappeared into the ether. As they say, "A better people you couldn't buy!"

Anyhow, I was in the Miami Hotel thinking things through, like a butterfly floating along, not knowing what I wanted or what I should do. It seemed like the wind was blowing me along. I had money, but I didn't have any roots; I was just existing. Looking back over the past year or so, going from having had all the right intentions, wanting to teach and do my best, to not doing my best and having all the wrong intentions. I thought about my options in my life. Where was I going? So I boxed up all my thoughts, regrets, and doubts, put them in a neat little box, hid them in the furthest recesses of my mind and forgot all about them. Then I went to Sebastian's house.

Sebastian was having a moment himself; he was talking about moving to Hong Kong and wanted to offload the business, and more importantly, he wanted to offload it onto

What a Surprise!

me. I wasn't that interested; I was OK for cash, and what he was offering wasn't something I wanted. He badgered me for some time, and then Keith turned up. Keith always had a short fuse with Sebastian; he wouldn't have tolerated that sort of behaviour, so Sebastian packed his pestering in. I discussed the offer with Keith, who advised me to be careful of Sebastian. He said he was a duplicitous character, and he didn't trust him at all. Cody turned up, and he gave me similar advice. Then, the house began to fill with people. Sebastian became the definitive host and didn't bother me any more with his proposal. One person who turned up was Carter Matheson, a Jack the Lad from Borehamwood.

Carter was an old friend of Sebastian, Cody and Mack; they had all been involved with the scooter-racing scene back home. Carter was in Thailand to pick up some bullet and smuggle it back to the UK. Carter and I hit it off straight away; he was over-confident, had an opinion on everything, which he didn't mind sharing, and already gave off the air that he owned the place. He was sticking around for a few weeks, so we hung out together. He introduced me to his guys, the donkeys. By the time I met them, they were fully immersed in the delights of Thailand. All three of them were buzzing with excitement. Carter liked the hedonistic way of life, and his two friends seemed to be the same. All three were living on nervous energy. The process was always the same: they came to town to smuggle drugs, they hit the town hard for two weeks, and then they were gone. Carter calmed down after the initial shock of drugs, booze and the abundance of girls, and we went off to the beach for some peace. Before we left, Gow approached me

The Rocky Road

to go back to Singapore, so I asked Carter if he fancied it. To my surprise, he was up for it.

Cody and Keith were with us, so I asked them for their opinion about one more trip to Singapore. They advised me not to go. They said the net was closing in. Traveller's cheque and credit card fraud had been exhausted in Thailand, and they said Singapore was the same. Of course, I ignored their advice. I was fully immersed. I was aware of my failings; I took risks, unnecessary risks, and these guys would often steer me back to reality, giving me a whack round the chops and bringing me back down to earth. However, on this occasion, I ignored them. I don't know why; it was the best advice I had ever received from them.

After sunning ourselves for a week, we headed back to Bangkok, where Gow had already put the whole gig together. We spent the night at the Miami, and the next morning, I was flying back into Singapore. I had convinced Carter that it would be a breeze. I had even found myself repeating the ridiculous notion about there being "no risk".

That evening we had dinner and a few drinks at the hotel in Singapore, practised some signatures and got an early night. I felt uncomfortable, though I couldn't put my finger on why. There was just this feeling eating away at me; maybe it was the words of warning from the lads back in Bangkok, but I couldn't shake it off. Dark clouds were looming; I could feel it in the air!

In the morning, we had breakfast, and then we went off shopping. I was back on Orchard Road where it all started, with the swanky Armani suit and the buzz of getting away

What a Surprise!

with it! Gow had another spotter with him, so I went with Gow, and Carter went with the other guy. Gow and I entered this very chic-looking jeweller's. Like most of the jewellers, in town, they sold top-end watches, and we were there to purchase the best that they had to offer. The assistant was young and amiable, and we talked watches and my preference for the Rolex. I chose the most expensive watch possible, and he went off to process the payment. Another assistant offered me a chair, so I sat for a while. He was taking his time, but it seemed like nothing to worry about. I sensed Gow was still in the shop even though I didn't look up. I really wasn't concerned until I noticed a rather large security guard appear in the doorway; he was at least six-foot-three and a good 260 pounds, a mountain of a man. At that exact moment, an Indian woman strode into the shop. She was smartly dressed in a trouser suit and shiny shoes with this long black flowing hair. She looked stern, almost angry, and purposeful.

She stopped next to me and said to the assistant, "I'm from American Express. You have a Mr Jones here?" The shop assistant nodded to me. The lady said, "Are you Mr Jones?"

"Yeah," I said as I stood up.

"We seem to have a problem with your card, sir," she said. "It has been reported stolen."

"I don't think so. I'm Mr Jones, and I haven't reported my card stolen," I said.

The game was up. I took in my surroundings: there was only one doorway in or out, and the big security guard was blocking the way. The dark-haired woman was shouting in my face, saying something at me, but I couldn't hear her; I was busy assessing the situation. The two shop assistants? They were harmless. The woman from Amex? Not a problem, though she was still shouting, and I still couldn't catch what she was saying. The security guard was the real issue. My odds looked slim. I wasn't just stuck in the shop; I was also stuck in the shopping mall. What were my chances of getting out of there? Slim to none.

This assessment took a fraction of a second. Then, before anyone could take stock of the situation, the Amex lady was on her back on the floor screaming, and I was heading for the door. The guard proved to be as much of a problem as the lady, and he also soon found himself lying on his back, bewildered and not quite knowing where he was, and I was gone, down the stairs, out of the mall and onto Orchard Road. The heat and the humidity hit me in the face, the sweat pouring off me.

No place to go and no place to hide. I had these big clodhoppers on my feet, and I could hardly run. It was like a scene from Benny Hill where Benny gets chased by all the gorgeous girls, except these weren't gorgeous girls, they were great big bruisers in uniform, and they weren't about to tickle me, they meant business. With the theme song from Benny Hill ringing in my ears and half a dozen uniformed guards on my tail, I headed to another shopping mall across the road. I thought if I could just make it in there, I could mingle with the crowd and hopefully lose them.

So, my legs somehow took me in the direction of the glass double doors and into the vast mall. It had a huge water fountain and an enormous marble angel towering over the

What a Surprise!

shoppers. Glass-walled escalators reached up into the heavens, and chrome and glass lifts full of people seemed to hang in the air. All of a sudden, I was freezing cold; the air-con in the mall was up full blast. I could feel the cold sweat running down my back; I was hot and clammy and shivering.

The mall was busy, so I slowed down to a walking pace. Puffing and panting with a bright red face and saturated in sweat, I tried to make myself look inconspicuous. However, my Persil white shirt and glowing red face did me no favours, I must have looked like a red beacon glowing in the dark.

I was so busy trying to look casual that I hadn't noticed the mall guards; they had been notified of my imminent arrival and jumped me. I was forced to the ground as the guards piled in. As one guard after another sat on me, the air went out of my lungs, and I gave up. I was captured.

I was now on my back with half a dozen guards on top of me. I was lying there in the middle of the mall, on the highly polished granite floor, with the angel in the fountain staring down at me: the Angel of Doom! They roughed me up a bit, then handcuffed me, and then they all stood around, clearly not knowing quite what to do. I don't think it was an everyday occurrence to catch a European this way.

Once everyone had calmed down, they proceeded to take me outside. One of the guards was being overzealous and nasty. He gave me a dig in the kidneys, so I told him to fuck off. He was standing inches away from me, and I said if he did it again, I'd fucking beat him with my fucking head. He had a look of disbelief in his eye, but he weighed up the situation and backed off; I had meant what I said. I was not

The Rocky Road

happy. Being captured was one thing, but getting a whack in the kidneys was another.

For some reason, I wasn't overly concerned with the situation. The guards didn't bother me. I was more bemused than worried; the worst they could do was stick me on a plane and deport me, or so I thought. Then the police arrived, and they cuffed me and took me away.

Chapter 6

Singapore Justice!

When I arrived at the station, much to my surprise and disappointment, Carter was there too, handcuffed inside a glass-panelled room. There were a number of police officers around him, and as I passed by the room, we made eye contact, and, with a look, we acknowledged each other and the situation we were in. The cops all spoke English, which was a Godsend and a surprise; it turned out that English was the first language in Singapore, so no language barriers! They brought Carter out of the room and stood us next to each other. One of the cops said, "Right, you two obviously know each other. Where are you staying in Singapore?"

Carter knew the cue. He was from Borehamwood, a notorious town where, back in the 60s and 70s, they dumped all the more undesirable families from London. Borehamwood was rough, and Carter wasn't averse to a scrap, he'd been in plenty of scrapes with the old bill. We looked at each other and shrugged our shoulders. "Can't remember," we said.

The Rocky Road

The cops seemed nonplussed by our answer. One of them said, "You need to tell us where you're staying."

"Sorry," I said. "I can't remember; it's the truth. Honestly, I can't remember. What about you, Carter, can you remember the name of the hotel?"

"No," Carter said, "I have no idea."

Playing dumb didn't get us far though. One officer said, "Let me tell you something. Singapore is not a signatory to the European Convention on Human Rights; we can do whatever we want with you." Then he beckoned us over to an open door. This room was, to all intents and purposes, a giant fridge. The police officer said, "This is one of our interrogation rooms. If you like, we can strip you naked, turn the freezer on and question you in here. Or you can just tell us; it's only the name of your hotel. Well, what do you want to do, then?"

"Oh," one of us said. "I think it's the Hilton."

The cops bundled us into a car and took us to the Hilton. At the hotel, we caused a bit of a scene with two handcuffed foreigners being marched to the reception desk and retrieving the keys to their room. All eyes were on us, staff and customers alike. In the room, the cops started pulling the place apart. I still wasn't intimidated by it at all. I had a sense of calm that didn't match the situation. I was standing next to the TV, and a tray with packets of nuts was on top of it. I noticed the corner of a credit card poking out from under the silver tray. While they were rummaging around in the room, I said, "Don't mind if I grab a bag of nuts, do you?" I grabbed a packet and knocked the tray

~ 164 ~

Singapore Justice!

covering the card. One of the detectives shouted, "What's he doing? What's he doing?"

One of the others came over and asked the same thing.

I said, "Just grabbing some nuts, take it easy." He looked at me with this cold, stern look that only the Chinese can do and lifted the tray. Lo and behold, there were half a dozen cards. Gow had gone to our room, put the cards under the tray and disappeared into the night. What a bastard! In all the confusion, I saw Carter bend down and take something out of his bag. I didn't know what he was playing at, but no one else noticed.

They took us back to the station and threw us in separate cells to cool off. I was back in the clink, something I had sincerely promised myself I would never let happen ever again. It's hard to explain your own stupidity, so I won't bother. Here I sat, awaiting my destiny with yet another judge, but first, I had to deal with the cops.

Carter and I had already been threatened with the fridge treatment. What sort of country has a refrigerated room built in the police station? Obviously, these cops meant business. Sitting in the cell, I was lost in thought. I had fucked up again, and now I had to think of a way to get us out of this mess. As I was mulling over my options, I heard the familiar sound of the jailer's keys. That brought me back to the present and the reality of my situation. I was back in a cell and back in the shit!

The door opened, and this tiny little Chinese man stood there and beckoned me to go with him. "Come, come," he said, with this heavily-accented Chinese English. It was

The Rocky Road

somehow comical; he was like a Chinese version of Manuel from *Fawlty Towers*. He took me to his office to interrogate me.

It was odd that there was just one cop; in the UK, there would always be two cops, and the good cop, bad cop routine. Somehow, that didn't apply here. We couldn't have been that important, I guess. He sat me down and made his way round to the other side of the desk. As he sat down with a heavy thud, he introduced himself as Sergeant Won Hon Kok. This was not going to go well; his name was "cock", for fuck's sake. He had my passport open on the desk and asked if the person was really me. Was this my real passport? Was that my date of birth? Are you English? Yeah, yeah, yeah. He was a crazy-looking dude with black hair and beady little eyes, one slightly out of balance. It was disconcerting and hard to focus on him; which eye do you look at?

Won asked me some casual questions, then said, "Why you in Singapore?" I had to dig deep now, so I gave him the story: Carter and I were sent to Singapore by a gang of villains, gangsters from Thailand. We were down on our luck in Bangkok, so we borrowed money from some locals who turned out to be gangsters. These gangsters had stolen our passports and said that if we didn't do what they said, they would kill us. They had shipped us off to Singapore with this thug called Bow, a violent, ugly man with a huge scar down his right cheek who would beat us if we didn't do what he said. Won Hon Cock spoke Pidgin English and kept saying, "You do this wight; you do this wight." He wanted me to admit to the crime, but I carried on with my story of woe.

Singapore Justice!

Over and over, he kept repeating the same mantra. The more he repeated himself, the stronger the accent was. "You do wight, you do wight."

It was hard to understand him, but I persevered, nonetheless. I said we had been tortured and that the Thais would kill us if we were sent back to Thailand; I tried to convince him that I was really scared. He was becoming hot and bothered, all sweaty, with flushed cheeks. I wasn't sure I was getting through to him, so I just pushed on a bit more with this fantasy tale. We spent a couple of hours talking. By now, I wasn't sure who was interrogating who.

I span him up in the air for a good hour, and then he became agitated and looked tired and defeated. After some time, he had had enough of me. I may have laid it on a bit thick. He stood up and said he was taking me back to the cells. As he led the way down the corridor, I noticed he had this walk where he dragged his feet, and it reminded me of school and walking down the corridor with the teacher shouting, "East, stop dragging your heels, boy. Pick up your feet." So I followed this man dragging his heels, with an impulse to shout, "Kok, pick up your feet, boy." Instead, under my breath, I whispered, "Pick up your feet, man," whereupon the sergeant turned and said, "What you say? What you say?"

"Nothing, nothing, just talking to myself," I said. He looked tired and worn out, but I wasn't out of the woods yet. I needed to get a message to Carter so he could corroborate my story. Before we left Won's office, I asked if I could have a pen and paper, and he happily obliged.

The Rocky Road

We made our way to the cells and Won Hon Kok handed me over to the jailer and left me. I asked the jailer, "Do you mind if I write a note for my friend?" He was also very obliging and let me scribble some words down. I quickly wrote: *We were held by Thai gangsters tortured and we were made to go to Singapore or be killed.* I folded the note, and the guard then led me down another corridor with cell doors on either side. Carter must have heard me talking to the jailer; he called out to me. So, I said, "Do you mind?" and pointed to Carter's cell. He left me outside the cell door and said, "Be quick." I hurriedly told Carter the fabricated gangster story and slipped the note under the door. Carter then told me that he was as high as a kite. He said he had brought some bullet with him from Thailand and that he had swallowed it. He didn't have a chance to explain himself before the officer was back and beckoned me to my cell. He opened the door and unceremoniously slammed it shut behind me.

Back in the cell, my mind was all over the place; Carter had swallowed a whole bullet? The chances were that he was going to have an episode. I was fully expecting a knock on the door and someone telling me he had been taken to the hospital. The knock never came, and after a fitful sleep, I was taken for another interview with Won Kok. At this point, he informed me that they were taking Carter to the hospital, so it seemed my worst fears had been realised. But then Won Kok said Carter had something wrong with his penis. That left me somewhat bemused and confused, but, of course, he had caught a dose from a whore back in Bangkok.

Singapore Justice!

I had injured myself in a motorcycle accident just before we left Bangkok, and it was healing nicely, but I convinced Won that I also needed to go to the hospital. He resisted my pleas, but I badgered him and badgered him until I could see I was sending him slightly crazy. In the end, he relented and allowed me to go. So that afternoon, they came and collected us both—three cops with guns, two prisoners, one with an injured knee and the other with an injured penis.

They cuffed us together and marched us off. Carter said he was still tripping; he looked stoned, happy and carefree. I'm not sure he knew where he was. The cops were on our case, so Carter still couldn't explain himself.

They took us to this state-of-the-art hospital, all hi-tech with lots of shiny knobs and beautiful plants. The nurses were dressed like Florence Nightingale with neat-looking nurses' caps, frilly short sleeves and knee-length dresses. They looked smart and somewhat sexy. One of the cops went over to reception while the other two held onto us. The officer came back and said they wouldn't accept us as patients, being criminals and all. We had to be taken to the public hospital; so we moved on.

This was completely different; nothing shiny or cleansed, and definitely no plants or sexy nurses, more spit and sawdust, like an old saloon bar from a black and white movie. The staff looked tired, all worn out and with bad attitudes. It was something like the NHS, with its underpaid staff and lack of funding. We managed to get accepted, though, and the doctor would see Carter and the nurse would dress my "massive wound". We made our way to the VD clinic, still handcuffed to each other. We drew far too much attention with the cuffs on and the cops with their guns exposed. The VD clinic was even more destitute, with a waiting room full of ladyboys and prostitutes, though Carter felt right at home! When the time came and they called him into a cubicle, I asked the cops to uncuff me from him. I didn't want to be handcuffed to a guy who was having his dick examined. The cops thought my request reasonable, so they obliged and handcuffed me to a chair that was bolted to the floor while they took Carter away to a room for men with festering dicks.

When they had finished poking about with his appendage, he returned to the waiting room, smirking like a Cheshire cat, still high as a kite. How the cops couldn't see it, I shall never know. Having drugs in your system was a criminal offence in Singapore; if they had suspected he was high, he would have been in big trouble. As it was, he had already got away with smuggling the drugs into the country.

The nurse dressed my wound; it was a beautiful dressing and well worth all the trouble. The cops appeared bored with the whole episode, with one or the other disappearing off for a fag every ten minutes. They looked relieved once we had been seen to. They took us back to the police station and handed us over to a withering Won Kok.

By the next day, Carter was straight, and they took him off for questioning. On his way back, he stopped at my cell. There didn't seem to be any logic behind their system; we were two co-conspirators, and we were being allowed to freely conspire between interviews. Won Kok also deliberately left my statement out on his desk while questioning

Singapore Justice!

Carter. Carter could read every word and repeated my version of events. Once he had our statements all typed up and they corroborated, which they obviously did, he then decided to interview us together. Won Kok wanted this to be an open and shut case; no complications, slam dunk, a job well done.

In the coming days, Carter got on well with him. He liked Carter, but he really didn't like me at all. However, I wasn't intimidated by the situation; I had been in far worse trouble than this. Won Kok sensed my lack of respect and tended to ignore me in the interviews and concentrate on Carter.

I was still surprised by my own attitude; I should have been devastated, and somewhat broken. Here I was, halfway around the world, with opportunity abound, and I was banged up again. Any sane person would have been broken. For me, it couldn't have been further from the truth. I had turned up in Hong Kong with the best intentions in the world and blown it within months of being there. What a dickhead!

I was living this exotic life, with beautiful beaches and beautiful girls, playing the big fraudster with my designer clothes and flying around first class. And now, I was in this situation. This was, as they called it, "an occupational hazard". I was a long way from home, but the rules were still the same; it was a "them-versus-us" game. They had to use as much cunning as you, and in many respects, they were better at this game than you; they played this every day, whereas you only had to play it when you got caught.

Won had us in his office, asking the same old questions over and over again, but now Carter and I had each other for company, which gave us confidence. Won would read my statement back to me and say, "Is that wight? Is that wight?" I couldn't resist it, so I would change things and say it was not quite right, and he would have to rewrite it. Before doing so, he would turn to Carter and say, "Is that wight?"

Carter had all the power in the room; anything he uttered was true, and that's all Won Kok cared about. If Carter agreed with it, that was good enough for him. This went on and on. The more it went on, the more I changed my statement, so this scene played out over and over again until, one day, Won didn't turn up for work. He had been rushed into hospital with a suspected heart attack, God bless him! We never saw him again. Carter said it was my fault. He blamed me for giving Won Kok a heart attack. I denied any responsibility.

Luckily, the statements were complete. We were pleading guilty, so the cops put us in a holding cell to await our trial. The cell was much bigger, with about a dozen pre-trial prisoners all waiting to be sentenced. There was a mishmash of Chinese and Indians, all Singaporean nationals, and then there was me and Carter.

I took the opportunity to sleep for a couple of days. My system tends to crash in these high-stress situations: the interrogation, the implications, the feelings of guilt about dragging Carter on a fool's errand, and the sheer stupidity of it all. I crashed and went to sleep. After a couple of days, I began to stir like a bear coming out of hibernation. I started to emerge from my self-imposed cocoon and interact with the others. Carter had got to know everyone by now, and he filled me in with the details. Mostly, they were Triads (Chinese gangsters); the one guy who stood out was this

Singapore Justice!

middle-aged, clean-looking, well-spoken fellow. He was a banker, and he had got caught with his fingers in the cookie jar. They were a good bunch, honest as thieves!

Carter explained the situation with the bullet. When the cops took us back to the hotel room, they were so busy looking for credit cards that when they searched Carter's bag, and this big lump of oil and grass appeared, they dismissed it. Carter said it was sitting right on top of his bag for the entire world to see. As luck would have it, right at that point, I inadvertently moved the peanut tray to reveal the hidden cards, and the cops got so excited with that, and with all their attention on me, Carter casually bent down, picked it up and swallowed it.

I said, "Did you swallow the whole thing?"

"Yeah, the whole bullet. I was off my fucking tits."

I asked, "How did you get on with the interrogation?" He said that Won Kok's face was so distorted at one point that he had no idea where he was or who he was; we laughed at the craziness of it all.

As we were laughing, the banker came over and said, "Why are you so happy? You are in a lot of trouble. You may go to prison." This made us laugh even more. The banker found the whole experience very difficult. His life was in tatters, having gone from being a respectable finance guy to a convicted fraudster; it was hard for him.

Carter didn't blame me for the situation. Carter was a man who made his own decisions; if it went wrong, it was his own lack of judgement as no one had made him do it. He had a strong character, and he was a law unto himself. It just wasn't in him to blame other people for his own failings.

The Rocky Road

* * *

We soon settled into our new environment. Our new cell mates were no different from us, ducking and diving, just like Carter and me, and getting caught, just like Carter and me! In their wisdom as repeat offenders, they thought we would get off, but they said we needed to plead to the judge for leniency. The consensus was that because we were foreigners, the judge would let us go. So we set about working on an alibi, or an excuse, anything the judge would find amenable and let us go free.

We decided to write a mitigating letter to him. The story began with us being down on our luck in Bangkok, with no money, and how we had turned to the Thai criminal underworld for help. They had abused us; taking advantage of us, confiscating our passports and making us work the credit card scam. Basically, we kept the theme of being captives of the Thai gangs, which correlated with the story that we had given to the police. We were thankful that it had all gone wrong and that we had been caught and arrested; the police had helped us escape their clutches. And that was the gist of it. The Triads thought it was a great story, and the judge would see reason and let us go. We were confident that we were going home on a dream boat!

The day of the court case arrived. Carter and I felt confident that this was a done deal; the judge would see the error, and we were obviously not guilty of the crime, just guilty of being victims ourselves.

I had been in court a number of times, as had Carter, so we

Singapore Justice!

knew the drill: stand in the dock, give some lame excuse and hope the judge goes along with it. The cops took us straight to court number one from a holding tank below. The court was really busy. It was a strange scene. In the dock sat at least twenty people, all men. The court official had squeezed us all in at one end; there wasn't room to breathe, let alone seat twenty-two felons. One by one, these poor fellows stood up, a few words were spoken, and then down went the gavel, and they were gone, unceremoniously dragged out of the dock to disappear down the steps. As one went down, another was filtered into the dock. It was a conveyor belt, with just the minimum of exchanges between the judge and the solicitor, then guilty and gone. Everyone seemed to be guilty!

It was noisy, and very difficult to get a handle on it all. Then, through the noise, we heard someone call out East and Matheson, and we stood up. There was a hush in the court for the two foreigners. The judge and the solicitor exchanged a few words that we couldn't hear. We took this opportunity to hand our mitigating evidence to a court usher to hand to the judge; hopefully, this would secure us our release.

The judge gave the sheet of paper a casual glance and said something. We still couldn't quite hear what was being said. Did he say let them go? Much to our dismay, he had said, "Nine months custodial sentence. Let them go back to the cells." What the fuck!

I was back in the clink for another nine months. Carter was as surprised as I was. So began another sentence, prisoner 1903, a new number, a new prison.

Chapter 7

Queenstown or Changi

They forcibly removed us from the dock. Somewhat dazed, Carter and I looked at each other. "What did he say?" said Carter.

"I think he said nine months," I replied. I felt a terrible sense of responsibility and guilt at this point. Carter had been out in Asia for a short stay. OK, he was on a drug-smuggling mission, but he didn't deserve this. I had seriously compromised him. The guilt stayed with me for some time until I realised he was a pragmatist and took responsibility for his own actions. He took to prison life quickly. Once he learnt the ropes and knew where the boundaries were, he could push those boundaries to the limit and beyond. This was very entertaining to watch. He knew how to catch the screws off guard, and they weren't sure what to do with him.

We were now prisoners, the lowest of the low, the dog's doings on the bottom of one's foot. Singapore did not look kindly on the criminally minded. We went straight to

Queenstown or Changi

Queenstown, which was a remand prison as well as a functioning prison for convicts.

It was like I was back in the UK; this was Wandsworth on steroids. It smacked of a Victorian prison, with the same layout and atmosphere as Wandsworth, Pentonville or Brixton. Five or six storeys high, with no landings as such, just a cavalcade of stairways and walkways, like Slade Prison from *Porridge*. In the vast open space between the walkways, the view went all the way from the ground floor to the ceiling, with reinforced netting stretched across from one walkway to the other. The netting was there to catch the suicides, and the undesirables who got thrown over the side of the balconies. Each cell door was reinforced with an eyehole in the middle, so the prison officers (Inchets) could look in without opening the door. The cell was eight foot by ten foot with a toilet in the corner; there was nothing else in there. It was a brick and concrete box, a home-from-home. Welcome home, Dicky.

They processed us, took our clothes and other belongings and gave us a pair of shorts, a vest and a pair of raggedy old flip-flops; that was it, nothing more, nothing less. Then they took us through this empty, soulless expanse of a prison to our cell.

In the cell, there was a man named Deedee, an overweight German who was arrogant and rude, with some personal hygiene problems. An Englishman named Tony was skinny and depressed, and his mental health problems were exaggerated by the circumstances he found himself in. There was also a Chinese guy named Ting Tong; that's right, Ting Tong.

Was it possible for five adult prisoners to share such a small space? The cell was, at best, eight foot by ten foot. Each of us was issued with a plastic cup, and a straw mat to sleep on. The temperature was in the hundreds, and we had a tiny, barred window and no air. The water to the toilet was switched on and off intermittently; it was a crude form of torture. The toilet doubled up as a water fountain, the only source of fresh water. When the water was turned on, you were able to fill your mugs from the lip of the toilet as it was flushed—good, clean water straight from the toilet! We learnt very quickly that this was not a toilet for number twos. It was strictly for number ones.

This prison was a 23-hour bang-up, a hellhole with one hour of exercise a day. The first day was uneventful, as we all got to know each other. We all talked at the same time; they were as excited to see us as we were to see them. We settled ourselves in. The two foreigners were also in for fraud, and they said the prison was a nightmare, banged up all day, the temperature could rise to 140; it was hot, hot and hotter, and they were going stir-crazy.

In the morning, our newfound friends and cellmates instructed us on the morning etiquette, a ritual where all prisoners had to sit cross-legged on the floor. An orderly pattern was formed; it was the "order" of the day. We had to create a square pattern on the floor with one person in each corner and one in the centre. Each morning, an Inchet came round bright and early; he would pop open the eye hole, and we had to sing "Good morning, Inchet." Just after this, the senior officer would make his rounds. We would take up our

Queenstown or Changi

positions again and wait; after some time, the door opened, and there stood the S.O. with two of his henchmen. This was our cue. As one and in harmony, we sang, "Good morning, sir," and the door was slammed shut.

Carter and I started laughing. "Do we have to do this every morning?"

"Yes," our fellow inmates said.

"What, sit there like fucking idiots chirping 'Good morning'? What the fuck for?" No one could really answer that, so every morning, we had to get it together to sit in formation and sing, "Good morning, sir," without laughing.

A couple of days in, Carter and I needed a haircut. We had to put in a request for this. The requests didn't go anywhere fast, so in his wisdom, Carter caught the S.O. one morning as he was doing his rounds, and all the little birds were happily singing, "Good morning, sir." When our door opened, Carter got up and said, "Sir, may I request something?"

The senior officer was a softly spoken man, Chinese with perfect English, and he said, "You may. What is your name and number?"

"Matheson 1904, sir. We need a haircut, sir, and we can't get one."

The S.O. looked bemused and turned to one of his officers, who said, "We will get it done straight away, sir."

The S.O. said, "OK, haircut?" Carter nodded, and the door was slammed.

When they came to open us up later in the day, one of the Inchets took Carter and me to the barbers, where they allowed us to cut each other's hair. We gave each other a number three all over, a skinhead cut; it was refreshing and cool, perfect for the heat of the prison.

The days in Queenstown all melted into one; we got up, sat like good little birds and sang good morning to the S.O., had some tea and Kaya (coconut jam) sandwiches, exercised for an hour, back in the cell, had some rice for lunch, then bang-up all afternoon. Carter and I did a training session, followed by rice and veg for tea, then played chess, read for a while until lights out, then went to sleep. Up the next day to the same routine. Life didn't change much. Carter got into the habit of disrupting the senior officer's rounds with his infernal questions. The S.O. began asking Carter in the morning if everything was OK. I think he enjoyed the interaction.

We were soon to learn that this behaviour was not looked upon favourably by the Inchets, and they were not happy. One day, a Chinese con told Carter that we were pissing off all the Inchets with the daily disruption. It turned out the daily round was sacred, and no one in the whole prison would think of interrupting it; we were on a short leash, and the con advised us to pack it in. Carter was the culprit, but he and I were joined at the hip, so anything he did was us, and anything I did was us. Carter and his ability to push the boundaries!

Personally, I didn't like playing the game. Every morning, I sat on the floor in the silly format and never wished the officer good morning. I just sat with my mouth shut. I was like a petulant child. It didn't go unnoticed, but I thought, "What can they do about it?" It was all part of the small, insignificant mind games of prison life.

Queenstown or Changi

At exercise, we all sat around in a concrete yard with the blazing sun roasting us to death. There was nothing else for it, Carter and I would strip off and sunbathe. I would be down to my shorts, but Carter would be stark bollock-naked, lying right in the middle of the yard with just his T-shirt folded up and covering his genitalia. What a picture! He dominated the whole yard, this big heap of white flesh like a beached whale saying, "I'm here; get used to it." He was pissing up the inmates' and the screws' legs at the same time; it was glorious.

The yard also held the latrine, a hole in the ground off to one side, with no walls, no doors, and no privacy. Carter liked to read while taking a crap. As often as not, while he was taking a crap, a Chinese inmate would wander over. It seemed to be a sign: white man pooing, white man wanting to talk. Sometimes, three or four of them would wander over to him. Carter would be naked and on his haunches, trying to look dignified, newspaper in hand, cheeks all flushed, and squeezing out a big one. Then, to his surprise, he was surrounded; "Hi, my name is Wong. Where are you from?" I don't know what he gave off to attract this attention, but these inmates always wanted to talk to him while he was taking a dump. I would be in fits of laughter as Carter was waving his arms about, screaming at them to "fuck off". Carter would wander back over after his intimate moment with the Chinese, his face all flushed with anger, saying, "What the fuck is the matter with these people? Can't they see I'm having a fucking shit, for fuck's sake?" This went on the whole time we were at Queenstown; the man couldn't have a shit in peace!

The Rocky Road

The next day, Carter and I got a visit from the consulate; the Inchet came to our cell, took us to the other side of the prison and put us in a waiting room together. We were called in one at a time. I was first in. The consul was a slightly rotund lady with shocking white hair, too much make-up and a grumpy demeanour. I had the pleasure of dealing with the consulate in Greece when I served my sentence for "tramping". In my experience, these consular types are treading water, waiting for their pensions and generally having a jolly on the back of the British public's taxes. In my opinion, they're not fit for purpose. If you're a Brit and in trouble abroad, don't bother calling them. In Greece, they couldn't even be bothered to come to the prison; they just phoned. The only support I managed to get was *The Times* newspaper sent over every day.

Looking at this lady, I didn't think asking for *The Times* was a goer, so I didn't bother. She was on the Singaporeans' side; she wasn't interested in me or any requests. In fact, she was blunt and, quite frankly, rude. When my time was up, I went back to the waiting room. Carter went straight in after me. A few minutes passed, and I heard a crash bang wallop; it sounded like a fight had broken out. The next minute, Carter was being marched back into the waiting room. "What happened?" I asked.

"Fucking bitch," Carter said. "I told her she needed to make weekly visits; we could be getting tortured as these people are animals." Carter can be rather forthright in his opinion, and he didn't let her get a word in edgeways, so she slammed her fists down on the table and shouted for the guards to take him away. She never visited us again!

Queenstown or Changi

The Germans had a priest who visited them almost daily, sorting out all their needs and wiping their arses.

The situation in Queenstown wasn't ideal: banged up all day, inedible food, water from a toilet, and the extreme heat. It all added up and took a toll; tensions could get high. Carter tried to strangle one of the Germans, so they moved him out of our cell and into the cell next door. That cell housed more Westerners, one of whom was a man named Matt, a Brit with attitude, rude and arrogant. He was much older than us, articulate with a viscous tongue. He hated everyone: Inchets, cons, Chinese, Indians, Germans, and especially the English. No one was safe from his tongue; he and the Germans got on like a house on fire, they deserved each other. They all struggled with being incarcerated and were at each other's throats for the rest of their prison time together.

Carter and I soon got into a daily routine. We trained together in the cell and played cards and silly word games. It became the norm for us. I would say something mundane, and Carter would pick me up on some insignificant word like "abnormal". Then he would accuse me of using it out of context or using the wrong word completely, and we would have a full-on argument (banter) about the whys and wherefores of the word. No one particularly won, but it was entertaining. We did this every day, much to the dismay of our fellow inmates.

After some weeks, the Germans got right into the priest and badgered him to get them out of this hellhole. It worked, and they moved all the foreigners, including us English, to Changi Prison. A word of warning: Be careful what you wish for.

The Rocky Road

This prison was built in 1936 as a prisoner-of-war camp. The Japs used it to house POWs from all over Asia. The Japs in the Second World War were brutal, and many inmates died there, so it was just the sort of place you wanted to be moved to. It still had a reputation for being brutal. If you listened really hard, you could still hear the screams from the past as the Japs tortured the prisoners.

It was a high-security complex, with prisoners doing life and inmates on death row. They still hung people in Singapore! This was also where they dished out judicial corporal punishment, in layman's terms, "the cane".

Singapore had a reputation for low crime, the reason being that they locked everyone up. For even the most menial crimes, a perpetrator got the five-five treatment, as the Triads liked to call it. Ask a Singaporean inmate what sentence he was serving, and he would raise his hand out in front of him with the palm facing up and his fingers touching each other like he was holding a strawberry with his fingertips. He would separate his fingers like flower petals opening up to the morning sun and perform this motion five times—open close, open close—symbolising the five years and five strokes of the cane, the most common sentence in Singapore. Spit in the street, five-five; steal a can of coke, five-five. They were serious; it was five-five for everything. How we didn't get the cane, I shall never know. I suppose caning Westerners would bring too much attention to this barbaric behaviour, so they saved it for the locals.

For instance, committing suicide was deemed a terrible crime. The police would identify the deceased and leave

Queenstown or Changi

the body where it was, on the train lines, at the base of a car park. It didn't matter where; they would leave the dead body in situ. They would then gather all the close relatives at the corpse and proceed to beat the dead body. Carter and I would have long discussions with the Chinese inmates about this, but we got nowhere. To them, it was perfectly normal, and we were crazy questioning such behaviour.

* * *

Changi Prison had a different setup to Queenstown, and much to our amazement, they took us to the modern part of the prison. The cells here looked like car lock-ups, three in a row, but they didn't have the up-and-over garage doors; these had big bars on the front. Each cell was separated by a wall, but the front was completely open with these bars and a big, barred gate in the middle. It was like something from an American cowboy movie.

Our new Inchet welcomed us "with open arms"; he was a big man of Sikh origin, around six-foot-four. He didn't smile, and it was obvious that he was a brute. We found out very quickly that we were in the punishment block. They didn't know what to do with us, so they sent us to the worst place in the whole prison. The routine here was the same, except we got a much longer exercise period, depending on the whim of the Inchet, of course. So, it was welcome to Inchet Narden's world.

We had to go on a steep learning curve here. The language was neither English nor Chinese; it was Narden's form of sign language: head sign language, if you like. The slightest movement of his head would dictate up, down, this way, that way, yes, no, greetings, clean the floor, cut the grass, sit on your haunches. It had a basic structure, but it meant the Inchet didn't waste his precious time—or, more importantly, his precious words—on criminals. It was, above all else, lazy. We learnt quickly though. Narden had a huge superiority complex and revelled in ordering the foreigners about. He was big and intimidating. This was his domain, his world, and he considered himself the law.

Carter and I got into the rhythm of the day. At exercise, we played table tennis; we could also play chess and, of course, sunbathe. Carter would talk to the Inchet; he needed to know the boundaries to push them to the limit, which he did. I didn't care much for Narden. Quite frankly, I didn't like the man. He grew fond of Carter, though, and the fonder he grew of Carter, the more he despised me.

We still had to do the morning ritual, sitting in a pattern on the floor and all chorusing like good little songbirds. But now it happened twice a day; we had to perform for Narden at noon and at five in the afternoon. He came to the cells, making a deliberate noise so we knew he was coming, and he would stroll past the cells while we all chirped this merry song for him. I had a bee in my bonnet and wouldn't comply with this nonsense. I would just look at him as he walked by and tilt my head ever so slightly in a show of defiance, not the most intelligent thing to do in the present circumstances. So, he hated me, and I hated him.

Carter was a real ducker and diver. He was able to get us Arnnoon, the prison tobacco. He made acquaintances

Queenstown or Changi

quickly and became a close friend with the hard man of the prison, "Babboo". Babboo could get anything and wandered around the prison like he owned the place. It was shocking to see how much freedom he had and to realise we were in the block while this guy almost did as he pleased.

Carter's next achievement was to get us on the garden party. He badgered the Inchet for a couple of weeks, and they put us on garden duty. It was nice to be out wandering around the prison grounds in the open air, even if it did smell of aviation fuel. However, the sun was scorching, and being right next to Changi Airport added an extra 20 degrees to the thermometer. It was 130 degrees in the shade while wearing shorts, a vest and flip-flops, without a hat or any shade. We were given shears to cut the grass. Every day, we would be down on our haunches, clipping away at vast areas of lawn. We volunteered for this! We looked like prisoners of war doing slave labour; all of us in a row crouched down low clipping the grass, a pretty picture. The senior officer came by to see if we were happy now that we were baking in the midday sun. He called Carter up, who assured him we were as happy as pigs in baking hot shit. More often than not, Carter would get into a conversation with the Inchet who was guarding us, and while they talked, the Inchet allowed us a break and a sneaky smoke.

The English guy, Matt, with the bad attitude, got put in our cell; the inmates in his previous cell had forced him out. Carter hated him and wanted to bash him, but he moved in anyway. I don't think I have ever met anyone more hateful in my entire life; he was rude beyond belief, with this blunt, cold, scathing tongue.

The Rocky Road

Carter and I still played word games with each other. It was personal, a man's thing if you like, the same as the banter on a building site. Matt decided, in his wisdom, to join in on our little word game. However, this banter was very personal to Carter and me, and outside interference was not accepted or tolerated. Matt made some remarks concerning Carter's pronunciation of a word, and Carter lost his shit, threatening to give him a kicking. I mediated and calmed the situation down. Later in the day, on exercise, I convinced Carter that it was fine, that all's fair in love and war and that we could surely tolerate this guy. Much to Carter's annoyance, he went along with my suggestion of letting him stay in the cell with us, but Carter wanted him out. I would live to regret that decision.

The days crept on, and the heat was unbearable. We were a mere 80 miles off the equator and overlooking the airport. Inchet Narden would have us all out scrubbing the floors and washing the walls, revelling in his control and authority. One of the Indians had misbehaved, and Narden set about him in full view of the other inmates. It had something to do with smoking, which was not allowed as we were in the punishment block, after all. He beat the inmate with his fists, smashing into his face and head. It was brutal and uncalled for. I watched with bemusement at this display of Narden stamping his authority on the block; any messing with him and his rules, you would be punished. It was just a dick-wagging exercise, plain and simple. He was telling the foreigners, I can do this, and no one can stop me; push me, and I'll beat you.

Queenstown or Changi

Whenever we went as a group from one part of the prison to another, we had to follow the same protocol. The Inchet would lead the way, and we would follow like obedient little dogs. When we stopped for a door, we would all immediately line up along the wall and go down on our haunches. The Inchet would look round and give a little nod of his head, the sign of approval, then open the door. He would then ever so slightly look up and move his eyebrows. These micro movements of the face and head, these signs, were so subtle that the average person would be unable to spot them. It was time for us to get up and move, so we would stand up and shuffle along in our flip-flops through the door and back up against the wall on the other side of the next open door and down on our haunches again. This was an everyday occurrence; we were like little Chinese coolies. Again, Narden revelled in his power, not over the Chinese or Indians but the Europeans. He was a psycho.

Matt (1583) had developed an eye infection. In his wisdom, when he entered the prison, he had never told them he had contacts in, as he feared not being able to keep them, which would have left him half-blind and vulnerable.

There was always some tension in the cell because Matt was just an unpleasant person, which caused an atmosphere. On this particular morning, Narden opened us up to trot us off to the exercise yard. We got in a line, and off we skipped down the corridor. When we got to the junction at the end of the corridor, in front of us was a door to an unknown part of the prison, and to the right was the door to the exercise yard. We stood in line with Narden facing us with his arms crossed, signalling us to go down on our haunches, which we all dutifully did, with our backs to the wall. Narden liked to stand there for a few seconds, basking in the power he wielded over us. Right at this moment, Matt decided to speak up. "Can I see the doctor, please, Inchet? I've got something in my eye."

We were all lined up on the floor, and Narden looked at us and then at 1583. He gave Matt the ever-so-slight look up in the air. 1583 stood up and approached him. Narden took a look at his eye and then said the immortal words, "Who has been fighting with 1583?"

Jesus, now we were in trouble. Where did he get that idea from? Narden looked straight at me, so I stared back at him, giving him a look he didn't particularly like. It was a look of "I don't give a shit, I'm bored, and can we get on with this". Not one of my better moves. With Matt standing next to him, he got us, one at a time, to stand up, walk over to him, and strip naked. As we stood, one at a time, stark bollock naked, he looked over our bodies for injuries, and when he found none, he tilted his head, signalling to go through the door and into the exercise yard. When it got to my turn, I had a look of disdain written all over my face. He got me to strip, and then turn around. Narden looked over my naked body and then signalled to the "door to nowhere". He opened this door and beckoned me through it, telling me to wait in the corridor on the other side. He disappeared back through the open door and shut it behind him. I was left in a long, empty void with not a soul to be seen anywhere. I was fucking naked and standing there like a lemon.

Queenstown or Changi

He sent the rest of the inmates into the yard and then came back through the door, closing it behind him. We stood together in this corridor, just me and him. Narden positioned himself, towering right over me, his face inches from mine and said, "Why were you fighting 1583?"

"I wasn't."

He didn't intimidate me; I considered him a coward. We stood staring at each other for what seemed like a lifetime, eye to eye. He gestured for me to turn so he could look for any injuries on my body. This was a dangerous game he was playing. He was obviously going to give me a whack in the spine and god knows what else. I was naked and alone, and I was truly vulnerable; this guy meant business. I turned my body but not my head, always maintaining eye contact with this bully. I wasn't afraid of him; my heart didn't miss a beat: no adrenaline rush, no nerves. I was ready for this man and fully prepared that the only person who was going to get hurt here was him. The slightest move and I would beat this man, good and proper. I was willing him to make a move. We stood there for a long time, and then, just like that, it was over. He gave me the tilt of the head, indicating I go back to the yard.

I was not a happy man back in the yard. I told this Matt character he had to leave our cell. I didn't want to hear any of his smart Alec remarks or arrogant put-downs; just out you go, son. He left immediately, went straight to Narden and requested a move. Narden looked at me, and I looked at him. But he moved him.

My relationship with Narden now changed; there was a hint of respect from him. He treated me with a slight reverence—not kindness—but he stopped the intimidating looks.

Life then got back to normal. Carter got a job in the kitchen and started producing better food, and he also smuggled Arnnoon back into the cell.

One afternoon, Narden called me in from the yard. He wanted me to go somewhere with him. It was an unusual request, and my hackles were up. We walked with no communication apart from the head and eyebrows sign language until we arrived at another yard. He didn't have a leash on me, but he might as well have had. We made our way to the office overlooking the exercise yard, and Narden gave me the signal to go into the yard with the other prisoners. As I walked into the outside space, a few of the Chinese gave me the nod, nothing threatening, just a casual greeting. So I sat in the shade and watched two guys playing table tennis. When they finished their game, one of the Chinese guys came over and asked if I wanted to play. I looked over to Narden, who was watching me with his fellow officer. I gave him the appropriate head gesture, "Can I play?" He returned the gesture in the affirmative, and I gave the guy a game and thrashed him, and the next guy and the next. I stopped after the third game and gave the bat and ball back. I didn't gloat or look pleased with myself. I just walked back to Narden, who was looking proper proud of himself. Was this the reason he had taken me there? To play table tennis?

After this, Narden and I would spend many trips going from yard to yard, playing other cons at table tennis. On all of our little outings, I never lost a game. Becoming Narden's

Queenstown or Changi

little poodle had value, it seemed. He never played up again, and we never exchanged more than two words for the rest of my sentence, only communicating through this "Narden" sign language system.

Time moved on, and Carter and I got shifted to another cell with some Indians. They were good cellmates as they understood cleanliness. The small space we shared had to be kept clean, or it would encourage ants. Earlier in our sentence, we shared a cell with an English guy, Steve; he was a bit older, maybe in his 40s, scruffy and unkempt, a bit of a tramp. He seemed like someone who might live on the streets back home. A manic depressive, he wished AIDS upon himself because he couldn't cope. If he had AIDS, the Singaporeans would send him home. His sentence was only twelve months—he would rather have the death sentence than do twelve months! He had no hygiene awareness and would leave crumbs everywhere. One night, under cover of darkness, with the full moon giving off its distinctive glow, the ants came a-knocking. Carter woke us with his screams.

We couldn't work it out at first. He said he was being attacked by something. Then, as our eyes adjusted to the moonlight, we could see this perfect line of ants running over Carter's body, heading to the corner where Steve was lying. They were picking up his mess, the crumbs and bits of food he had dropped on the floor. We had an ant superhighway running the length of the cell around Carter's sleeping body and through the bars to freedom with their booty. The ants had outriders, huge motherfucker soldier ants with massive pincers, who were there to protect the food chain, and Carter had just happened to move in his sleep and roll onto the superhighway, so the big motherfuckers ate him alive. It was an easy fix: we cleaned up the area around Steve. Like a fumigation team, we brushed him down, swept the crumbs and debris up and brushed it out of the cell.

Carter obviously wasn't happy and told Steve if he caused any more mess in the cell, he wouldn't be responsible for his actions. Needless to say, there was no more mess from Steve.

The Indian lads were cool, and Carter and I got another insight into Singaporean culture. These guys were at the bottom of the heap in the caste system of Singapore. The hierarchy is white European, Chinese, Malay, anyone else, and then the Indians. These guys were put upon in Singaporean culture, I suppose, like the Pakistanis in Dubai, as slave labour. They liked to talk, with an endless stream of questions about England and English girls!

Carter had borrowed this songbook from Babboo, the prison henchman. In the evenings, Carter and I would sing a duet for the Indians, which could be heard throughout the cell block. Every evening, by request, we would sing, like a couple of old, demented dogs howling at the moon. Everyone loved it. They would all get really excited, shouting out requests. It made me giggle and laugh out loud, more out of embarrassment than anything else; how we blagged that one, I shall never know. To calm things down after our singing in the evening, Carter and I would tell bedtime stories. These stories were listened to by all. I enjoyed this process immensely, but to get himself out of the story-telling, Carter would egg me on with words of encouragement, so every evening, I would make up new adventures.

***

Our time at Changi was coming to an end. Carter and I were due out in two days, and I had more concerns now. They were potentially going to arrest me at the gate for crimes I had committed before. This played on my mind constantly over the two days leading up to our release. I didn't fancy another six months of this, so I was stressed to the max, with my mind working overtime, thinking they were definitely going to arrest me and bang me up again.

The last evening soon arrived, and the Indians wanted a story. I wasn't in the mood. There was no way I could find a story in my brain with all the stuff that was going on in there. They badgered me and badgered me until Carter said, "Come on, Dicky, tell us a story." This took me by surprise… Carter wanted one of my made-up stories. I could hardly believe it. In the end, I decided to tell them a story. To put this into context, the Indian belief system holds the cow in reverence. It is considered the mother, the giver of life, with its sacred milk. I began my story with Jack at home with his mother; they were poor, and Jack's mum sent him off to the market to sell the cow. On his way, he met a man who bought the cow for some old beans. At this point, the cell was in uproar. A cow for some old beans?! The Indians were not having it, and amid all the objections, noise and chatter, I said, "The end," and I went to sleep.

The Rocky Road

In the morning, Inchet Narden came to the cell to take us to reception. Time had changed our relationship; there wasn't the friction anymore. In his office, he shook my hand and gave me a warm smile, a big gesture from the brute, reminding me of when I left prison in England with the guy I had had a fight with. Narden took us to the reception, where we were given our belongings, bundled into the back of a car and taken straight to the airport. I had another little déjà vu moment with the armed police, their weapons clearly visible, escorting us through the airport like a couple of VIP gangsters. An embarrassing moment, but comical at the same time. Just like Greece!

Carter must have put on a couple of stone while we were in prison, where we trained every day. He was unrecognisable. He had broad shoulders and muscular arms. He looked the picture of health as if he had been training all his life. By contrast, I had probably lost two stone. I was slim and fit with a defined muscular physique. I was also buzzing from the fact I hadn't been arrested at the gate, and I was getting out of there. It was like a double whammy, double-gate fever, I was really free.

We made our way to the departures, and our armed security unit bid us farewell. We got on our Singapore Airlines flight and breathed a sigh of relief. Carter and I were literally flying in the air and in our minds. The only place to come down off this cloud was Bangkok, and we were two hours and twenty minutes away. Au revoir, Singapore, hello Thailand.

Chapter 8

Did I Learn a Lesson?

We landed at Don Mueang Airport, the familiar feeling of a bumpy runway and the thrusters forcing us into our seats as we bumped along the uneven surface, giving me a sense of freedom. We were actually out of the grasp of Narden and the block at Changi prison. The roughness of the landing had somehow brought that home to me—gone was the clanging of keys and the sitting in formation on the concrete floor, singing like little birds for their tea.

I was so excited to be back in Thailand. I was feeling fit and healthy; I wanted to dance on the rooftops. I wanted to party. We booked into the Miami Hotel, where nothing had changed: the foyer was still poorly lit, and the carpet was just about good enough not to be renewed. It smelled slightly musty, like a home-from-home.

As we checked in, Cody appeared, stepping out from the lift. He had a big grin on his face as he said, "Oi, oi, fucking hell, when did you get out?" The joy of seeing an old friend, a close friend, a friend from back home!

The Rocky Road

As we embraced, I said, "We got out today, we just flew in. What's happening, what have you been up to?" We had a little catch-up, where he gave me the lowdown on all the lads. It was pretty much business as usual, moving the bullet around Asia and some domestic dealings.

I went off to shower and get changed. Cody was only in town for one night; he was off to Tokyo the next day on some wild goose chase, so we were going to hit the town together.

When we had all showered and changed, we met up in the hotel bar before heading off into the nightlife only Bangkok could provide. Ultimately, Patpong was our destination—party central! Cody said Sebastian was around somewhere, so we were sure to bump into him.

We got into a tuk-tuk, Cody, me and Carter; it reminded me of my first night in Bangkok, and here I was again with two friends racing through the streets with the music blaring and the driver going far too fast for our safety. With the smell of the evening and the warm air on my face, there was no city quite like Bangkok, sin city!

Patpong was rammed with people, touts, street-food vendors and half-naked girls. It was somewhat overwhelming, the noise, the smell of the food, the girls all shouting, "Sexy man, hey you, sexy man, you handsome man." We had gone from the most unstimulating environment with bland food and no girls to this mad world of prostitution and drugs.

We found Sebastian. He was coming out of the King's Lounge, the notorious ladyboy bar. I was with old friends and new, and I remember very little of the evening. I woke up the next day, not knowing where I was, disorientated, in bed

Did I Learn a Lesson?

with a girl who I didn't know or recognise, in a strange room, with a banging headache. It took me some time to get my shit together. I had a shower, saw the young lady off, and went looking for my friends. I found Cody having breakfast in the Ambassador Hotel. We sat and talked for a good couple of hours, including a long discussion about Singapore. I told him how we had been captured, and Cody said, "I told you so!" Which he had.

I asked him what he was up to. He said he was off to Japan as he was loading up a friend of his with some grass; he had it packed in some fancy-arsed way, which he said was undetectable. He wasn't carrying anything himself; he was just safeguarding it. He was safe, or so he thought. My turn to give him some advice: "Be careful, man, it's dangerous up there, the Japs are brutal."

He said, "I know, man. I'm not putting myself at risk, I'll be fine." I waved goodbye to my old friend and then Carter wandered into the Ambassador, looking like the cat that had got the cream. We looked at each other and laughed out loud at the sheer relief of being free.

After a nice long breakfast, we decided to go to Ko Samet, an unspoilt island off the southern coast of Thailand. We took the train to Surat Thani and then jumped on the local bus to the pier, from where an old fishing boat took us over to the island, which had just one circular road. When we docked, an old pickup truck took us to Chaweng Beach, where there was one bar-cum-restaurant with fifteen little bamboo shacks attached. They were right on the beach. We shared the communal toilet and showers with the other guests; the electricity was intermittent, and there was no air con. It was beautiful. It was paradise.

Before we left, we had picked up plenty of candles and mosquito coils and, of course, a healthy supply of the bullet, the mind-bending concoction from Sebastian. We took it easy for two weeks, just washing the scent of the prison out of our skin. We fished in the day, and in the evening, the restaurant cooked our catch. We sat on the beach each day, watching the world go by, and got pleasantly stoned.

Carter had decided that, after the beach trip, he was going straight back home. While we were in prison, his father had passed away, and he had a whole lot of mess to sort out.

I was deep in my own thoughts, and my own concerns. Even though I felt for Carter and his loss, I was contending with my own insecurities and my lack of judgement in getting caught and spending more time in prison. I wasn't impressed with myself. With the time spent on the beach doing very little, I had time, once again, to assess my life and where I was in the great scheme of things. I had never considered myself a failure, and I still didn't; the blips on my path were just that, blips. Whenever I was released from prison, I always felt a sense of alienation. I would feel like a fish swimming through this thing called life, unattached to anyone or anything. Life took on a slow motion, like I was living outside of life itself. Within this state of mind, where the world looked all fuzzy, I came to the conclusion that, as in times gone by, I wanted a risk-free life, so no more crime and no more prison! I decided that Chang Mai up in the north sounded like a good bet; I could go and live there, teach and have a regular existence. I

Did I Learn a Lesson?

had a dream of teaching English and being normal like everyone else. I would become a law-abiding citizen. Good luck with that one, Dicky!

Our two weeks came to an end, and we booked the train back to Bangkok. As we boarded, Carter picked up an abandoned newspaper, the *Bangkok Post*, the Thai-English newspaper. He took a sharp intake of breath and handed it over to me. The headline in big, bold text was: "Two Englishmen caught smuggling drugs into Japan." Cody and his mate, Bob, had their names splashed across the front page. So, my advisor on risky ventures had been caught himself. I didn't see Cody for a while.

When we got back to Bangkok, Carter left for the UK on the first available flight, and I went to Sebastian's house, where the news of Cody's downfall had already landed. Sebastian was ultra-paranoid now and had cleared the house of all signs of drugs or illegal paraphernalia. Sebastian was trying even harder to look like a "legitimate businessman." Everyone liked Cody, so we were all saddened by the news, but we had no idea about the finer details of the situation. He hadn't been sentenced yet, but it didn't look good; four kilos of grass would bring a hefty sentence.

My mind was set on travelling up to Chang Mai and becoming this fantasy teacher that I had dreamed about. Sebastian thought I was crazy, saying there was plenty of money to be made right here in Bangkok. But I was certain that a life of crime was not for me. I wanted out, and I could make a living up north teaching. I did not want to spend any more time banged up in prison. So I said goodbye to

The Rocky Road

Sebastian and headed up north. I would live my days out as a poorly paid teacher and enjoy the rest of my life as a free man! What did Lao Tzu say? "Knowing others is intelligence; knowing yourself is true wisdom. Mastering others is strength; mastering yourself is true power." What did I know?

I knew Chang Mai well. I had been up and down to this part of Thailand many times. I struck up a deal with a local hotelier to stay in one of her rooms for a month while I got a job and sorted out my life. I bought myself a classic pushbike, like something from the 19th century, it looked like one of those old baker's boy bikes, jet black with a basket on the front. I rode it around town like I was the local baker, only I didn't have any bread for sale. I went around scouting for a job and paid a visit to the local university. In reality, I spent most of my time just doodling about, wasting my days. It was sunny and warm, and the air in Chang Mai was clean and free of pollution; it was a joy to ride around town without a care in the world.

As the weeks passed by, I hadn't found a job yet, and then Keith turned up with Sebastian. They had Don with them, one of Carter's donkeys from back home. He was on his way to live in Australia, and he had decided to stay in Thailand for a month or two before heading off to his final destination. He had tagged along with Keith and Sebastian, who were going off into the mountains on a trekking expedition. In reality, they wanted to go into the mountains and smoke opium. They asked me along, so I packed a small backpack and joined them on their little "expedition".

Did I Learn a Lesson?

Before we left for the mountains, Sebastian pulled me to one side and told me he had decided to leave Thailand and head for Hong Kong. He was willing to give me his business, for a price. I could take his house and the bullet business, and I could buy his bike from him. He didn't tell me, but it was obvious, the heat was on. People were getting nicked all around him, and the noose was getting tighter. So he thought he would throw that noose around my neck and then fuck off to Hong Kong and let me hang myself.

Moreover, he would get me to pay for the pleasure. Good friends, eh! I gave his offer a wide berth.

By contrast, Keith took me to one side, determined to shake me out of my fantasy world of being a teacher in the middle of nowhere. He had been busy while I had been banged up, and he had devised a foolproof way of smuggling Ice (methamphetamine) into Australia. He offered to pay me a huge amount of money, much more than the job was worth, to take the drug to Australia. He was convinced I had lost my mind, and this would restore my sanity, get me back on my feet, as it were. Back in the business, more like!

The devil was trying to entice me back into this seedy world! I had two options, but actually, no options. Sebastian's offer was suicide. I would probably end up in a Thai prison for the rest of my life, and I had had enough of risk-free ventures. I told them both that I would think their offers over.

Keith was desperate to go off to the mountains and smoke opium, so he busied himself around town and found a guide to take us up into the jungle. Bright and early the next morning, we headed off with his guide, "Holmes", as Keith had named him. He was a local guide whom Keith had commandeered via a friend.

When we set off early on our first day of trekking, it was cool at first, but by nine o'clock, the temperature had risen, and walking became much more difficult. We made plenty of stops on this first day, but it was still gruelling. We ate up the miles, and by the time we reached our destination, we were all exhausted, welcoming our ready-made beds in the village. We fell into them and slept like babies.

We woke early to the sound of loud insects and a cockerel blasting its early morning call. The sun was beginning to peep over the horizon, and we headed off again. We soon found ourselves at an elephant station in the middle of the jungle. What an incredible experience! We were all allotted an elephant, and we rode off on the backs of these huge beasts. Sebastian was in his element, with safari pants, a white shirt and a panama hat, like the Viceroy of India—all he needed was a monocle and a big moustache. After a few hours, we got to another station, where we dismounted. Keith immediately challenged Holmes, as he wanted opium. Holmes remained calm and said not to worry as we were nearly there. This sort of settled Keith, but not quite, as he had become very anxious. He wanted to smoke some of the local oil, and this trekking was taking its toll on his mental well-being.

We left the elephants and trekked a little further until we reached a tiny little village. Don was also starting to have puppies; he wanted to get on the opium and had become as anxious as Keith.

Did I Learn a Lesson?

Holmes arranged the accommodation in the village. We left our gear in our little huts, and all went for a long shower. Now that we felt refreshed, Holmes took us to meet the chief.

The chief was an old, thin dude who looked like he had smoked far too much of the black stuff. His skin was grey; his eyes were black and sat deep in their sockets. He greeted us with a nod and a toothless grin, beckoning us to sit under a bamboo shelter with cushions scattered around the floor. Our Chief of Ceremonies sat in the centre with a long pipe, an array of paraphernalia and a pot of pure black opium.

We spent the day smoking opium and relaxing. Opium is the dreamers' drug; the worries and the stresses of the day drift away on the manufactured clouds of your mind, and those clouds don't return until the following day when your mind is once again straight. So the day passed in one long dream; everyone was chilled, and we did very little for the whole time. We drank some tea and ate a little fruit; the opium takes the hunger pangs away, so that was all the sustenance we needed.

We drifted along without a care in the world until Sebastian said something that upset Keith. Keith was a volatile character, and, at six-foot-six, it was not pleasant when he kicked off. He began waving his arms about, screaming obscenities. He wanted to kill Sebastian, who by now had become quite docile and was apologising profusely. Keith was having none of it, and I had to step in, somehow coercing him off for a stroll into the jungle. He ranted and raved some more, but once I had him out of the situation, he began to calm down. Once chilled, he would always start to rationalise the situation, so as soon as it had begun, it was over, and he was normal again.

These moments with Keith were always tense as he was unpredictable and prone to violence. The reason he lived in Taiwan was because, in the beginning, when the lads had first arrived, it became apparent quite quickly that he was going to be a liability, so all the lads, as one, had encouraged him to live in Taiwan. It wasn't that he was contained in Taiwan; he just wasn't causing everyone a headache in Hong Kong. He was out of their hair, living miles away, giving someone else grief. Keith was great in small doses, but being around him for long periods could become exhausting. There was a touch of genius and madness about him. However, for all his faults, his friends, including me, loved him dearly.

The next day, we were up early and left the village. After walking for most of the day, we finally came across some hot water springs, where we stripped and bathed our sore and aching bodies in the steaming hot water. Keith and Sebastian had settled their disagreement, and we all relaxed in our jungle Jacuzzi. The trip had been a long one, and we were deep in the jungle. It would take at least another two or three days to get ourselves back to civilisation.

As we were relaxing and chatting about our experience, a white, middle-aged dude came out of the brush and casually walked past us. He looked like he had just come off the tennis courts. He had shiny white Reebok trainers on, white shorts, a white top and one of those daft-looking sun visor hats on top of his head with his hair sticking out of the top. "Hey," we shouted in our astonishment, "where have you just come from?"

Did I Learn a Lesson?

He turned and stared at us, and with this deep American drawl, he said, "We've just pulled over to have a look at the hot springs." We were only a matter of feet away from the road! Our world came crashing down around our ears as we realised we hadn't travelled anywhere; we were right next to the main road leading into town.

We had abruptly come to the end of our journey. Holmes had his vehicle parked in the layby just yards from where we were bathing, fuelled up and ready to go. We had expected another two or three days of hiking just to get out of the jungle, but now we found ourselves climbing into the back of a comfy vehicle and heading back into town. It was like a damp squib.

Back at the hotel, Keith and I talked some more about his proposal. He assured me he wouldn't be sending me off on a fool's errand, there was nothing "dangerous" about it, he would never compromise me, and the gig was one hundred per cent safe. I did trust him, or maybe it was some more misplaced loyalty. Finally, I agreed to the deal and said I would meet him in Taiwan in two weeks' time. I also told Sebastian I wasn't interested in taking on his sinking ship.

Chapter 9

Back in the Game

One conversation and I was back in the game, and within two weeks, I was in Taiwan. How does the saying go? "If you don't change direction, you may end up where you're going"? Exactly, I was heading exactly where I was going.

My mission was to drop off the ice in Perth, Australia, and pick up some cash. I decided to take a pilot's case with a false bottom with me. A pilot's case looks like an oversized briefcase. Pilots used them to move their ill-gotten gains from one country to another by hiding their contraband in the secret compartment in the bottom. I was taking one with me to do exactly the same thing.

Keith booked me a business-class plane ticket to Perth via Hong Kong. Business class on Cathay Pacific! I had travelled business class on Cathay before, but only on short-haul flights. This was long-haul, and I would be flying on the upper deck. For some reason, Cathay had given this quite exclusive area over to the business class traveller. It smacked of everything first class; it had limited seats, catering for maybe twenty passengers; it was very intimate, and the cabin crew were very attentive. For a drug smuggler, it was the only way to travel.

I looked smart. I decided to go with the Singapore look: an Armani suit with a shirt and tie and expensive soft leather brogues. In the scheme of things, it was perfect. A Hawaiian shirt and loud shorts coming out of business class would have drawn far too much attention from the customs boys. As it was, I looked stylish and professional; I went straight through customs without a second glance.

It's nerve-wracking stuff coming through customs with contraband, but the euphoria is as addictive as any drug. The adrenaline was surging through my veins. I wanted to dance like Gene Kelly in *Singin' in the Rain*. But instead, I casually went about my business like the businessman I was.

I was now outside the airport waiting for a taxi. I had well over a kilo of ice in my possession and no sign of trouble. I was back on The Rocky Road. I wasn't falling over just yet, but I was definitely on the way there. The falling-over part was never far behind me.

Time to get on with this little caper. I made my way to the motel that Keith had suggested and called his man, Doug: another country, another copper. He turned up an hour later to retrieve his booty and drop off the cash. It always amazed me how many coppers were involved in the drugs business.

I was expecting to pick up five or ten grand, or even twenty grand; I had my case with the hidden compartment ready to go. Keith's man, on the other hand, had other ideas. He entered my room with what looked like his weekly shopping:

two supermarket carrier bags stuffed with groceries, which was odd. I wasn't sure if he had been shopping or was dropping me off some food. I handed him the drugs, whereby he placed the grocery bags on the bed, turned them upside down and emptied A$ 200,000 of used notes all over the bed with half of it tumbling onto the floor! I said, "What am I supposed to do with that lot?"

He chuckled, saying, "It's a dilemma. Good day, mate," then abruptly left.

I sat there looking at this great big pile of money and, in the end, I put the whole lot in my suitcase and went to find a hire car. I had the contact details of the girl from Croxley whose heart I had quite callously broken. She lived way out of town on the outskirts of Perth. I put my luggage, with the cash, into the back of the car and made my way to her address. She lived on a new development: no high rises. It was an array of smart-looking bungalows with garages and large plots of land wrapped around them. I admired the Aussies' innovative spirit; the development was pleasing to the eye and didn't jar you, something the Brits lacked back home. I wandered up to the door and knocked.

When she answered the door, she looked just how I remembered her, still with the same enthusiasm for life, a bubbly personality and a great big smile. We embraced, and she invited me in. We talked and talked, and there was definitely still a spark there. I think she would have left her husband and run off with me if I had asked her to, which would have been unfair to everyone. I gave her the same old spiel as everyone else: I was teaching English, doing work on films, working in bars, and all the same old phoney baloney. I covered it well. She invited me to stay, and I accepted the kind offer. I stashed the cash in the wardrobe and spent the next week with her and her husband. I must admit that most of the time was with her, alone, which was somewhat difficult as she now made it quite clear how she felt and was still very much in love with me.

I can't say I didn't fancy her, but I'm not so sure she would have been so keen if she knew that I was not being completely honest with her. The last time we had been together, I had been fresh out of prison for drug smuggling, and here I was now on her doorstep, supposedly a new man, with illegal cash stashed in her cupboard, and I had just smuggled over a kilo of ice into her new homeland. How times have changed!

However, time passed very quickly. I had enjoyed her company immensely and was truly sorry when it came time to leave her with her new man. I said goodbye. There were a few tears, and we hugged and wished each other well. Her life was destined to be much, much better without a scallywag villain disrupting it!

The airport in Perth was quite relaxed, but I was still nervous. I had an awful lot of money on me, and it would be difficult to explain it away. A cursory background check with the UK government would have fucked me up completely, and I would have been looking at some hefty bird.

The money was packed inside my check-in luggage, which I took to the Cathay Pacific girl at the counter. She was very polite, and it seemed nothing was any trouble. She made sure I was happy with everything, checked the weight of my bag on the scales, then pressed the button, and the bag was gone, money and all. She handed me my passport. I was checked in and ready to leave. Next, I went through passport control, where they were polite and courteous. I made my way to the VIP departures lounge feeling confident and happy. Then I boarded the plane and waved goodbye to Australia.

The flight was comfortable and relaxed. I flew into Hong Kong with the sun shining through the window, feeling a great sense of relief. I went through passport control and waited with bated breath for my bag stuffed with money to come up from the lower floors and onto the conveyor belt. Just as I was worrying the bag wouldn't turn up, it rose up in all its glory from the lower floor and slowly but surely made its way to my waiting grasp. The bag was heavy as I launched it onto a trolley and headed to customs. I had no concerns with the customs in Hong Kong; if they searched the bag and found the money, they would just stick it back in the bag and wave me through. As it was, I wasn't stopped by any customs officers, and I was out into the arrivals lounge where Mack was waiting to greet me. We both had grins from ear to ear.

Mack asked me about the money and how I got it out of the country. I said, "For fuck's sake, Mack, no one said there would be that much money. I didn't know what to do with it all, so in the end, I threw out half my clothes and stuffed the notes in my check-in luggage." He laughed and said he had had the same problem when he went to Australia. Doug had turned up, emptied all the money out on the bed, said good luck and left him with it. We both laughed.

Back in the Game

Mack hailed a taxi, and we went to his place. He now had this swish pad on a tiny island. He had also bought himself a nice motorbike. Mack was enjoying life. Keith and his new enterprise were changing all of our lives.

At the apartment, I tipped the money out onto the table, and Mack counted it all up and bagged it. I took a shower, and we went into town. Keith and his partner-in-crime were staying at the Peninsular Hotel, one of the best hotels in Hong Kong. They were eagerly awaiting our arrival.

The Peninsular was the oldest and grandest hotel in Hong Kong. It was a colonial masterpiece, even though it had been built by two Iranian Jews in the early twentieth century. It was truly a grand affair with great vaulted ceilings, velvet and gold leaf seating with marble tables. Huge paintings from a bygone age filled the spaces on the walls, hung between these great Roman columns that gave the impression of strength and power. It smacked of old money. The Queen had been on the guest list, as had many of the Hollywood A-listers. Out in front was the fleet of Rolls-Royces, all in the trademark Peninsular Brewster Green, the standard transport for the rich and famous.

Mack and I wandered into the hotel with the confidence of guests and went straight up to the boys' room. We knocked on the door, and Ivan, another woebegone smuggler, answered. The expensive room was very stylish, with chic and vulgar elements all thrown into the pot. Keith, Matt and half a dozen others were all partying. "Help yourselves to the fridge, guys. It's on the house." Mack and I had a few drinks and left them to it. The boys were making big money now.

The Rocky Road

I spent some time at Mack's place, where we discussed Cody and his Japanese prison sentence. Cody and his partner-in-crime had received four years apiece. I broached the subject of Sebastian and his offer with Mack. Mack said Sebastian was definitely moving to Hong Kong, and he suspected that he was smuggling heroin to Australia. Nobody was one hundred per cent sure, but the rumours were rife. None of the lads got involved with heroin; they despised the drug and also the people around it. They wouldn't have it anywhere near them. The idea that Sebastian could do such a thing irked them all. Who could know what was just around the corner?

When I returned to Bangkok, I was a much wealthier person and stayed in the comfortable, upmarket Mandarin Orient Hotel with panoramic views across the Chao Phraya River. I contacted Sebastian. He came over, and we had breakfast together. We discussed his imminent departure from Bangkok to Hong Kong. He again offered me the lease on the house, his bike and connections to get the bullet made. I had already been introduced to his people, so there were no new introductions to be made, we all knew each other quite well. This time round, the deal didn't look so bad, so I took the offer.

Sebastian moved to Hong Kong, and I moved into the house. Eric, the Frenchman, came in with me, and we shared the house together.

Eric had contracted malaria and every so often had to be hospitalised. He had taken a trip many months before to the hills of Chiang Mai and slept on an open-top riverboat with

Back in the Game

no mosquito net. He had been eaten alive and contracted malaria. I witnessed one of his attacks; it was an unpleasant experience. He looked like he was dying. The hospitals across South East Asia were well equipped to deal with this sort of illness, and Eric survived each time. Moral of the story: "Always put a net over you when staying on a mosquito-infested river."

Eric was studying gems and trying to break into the precious stone market. To fund this, he had to take other people's drugs around the world.

Before Cody got caught, he had introduced me to this character, Johnny, from London. A short fellow with this shocking blonde curly hair, a real man about town, he had this swagger and confidence, like a Del Boy on steroids, who knew how to bullshit. Bullshit was common among the woebegone of Bangkok; we all had a bit of it in us.

I spent many an evening with Johnny talking scams and money-making schemes. It turned out that he had a connection in Holland for good-quality coke. The lads in Taiwan were flush with cash, so I enquired about the possibility of bringing coke into Taiwan. A few days later, I got the nod. Now I was going to get into the coke business!

Johnny would fly to Holland, pick up the coke, bring it back to Hong Kong, and then I would take it to Taiwan. On the first trip, I picked up the coke in Hong Kong and flew to Taiwan. Matt picked me up at the airport and took me back to his place. We discussed the situation. He would be the middleman and take me later to meet the buyer, a senior police inspector! I took a sharp intake of breath, but

Matt assured me it was kosher. So that evening, at eleven o'clock at night, we went at break-neck speed through town; no one drove slowly in Taipei. We parked up outside a school. It was the middle of the night! The hairs on the back of my arms were standing to attention, and I felt a ghost walk over my grave. This felt dangerous! Matt had the keys to the school and let us in. He knew exactly where he was going, and we ended up in the school hall, which was pitch black, with just the light from the moon shining through the huge floor-to-ceiling windows. The police officer had a harsh, stony-faced look about him. He also had a strong American accent, which always caught me off guard. He wasn't in uniform, but he was well dressed, with a smart jacket and trousers. There was no messing around, and he got straight to business. He had a test kit; he checked the quality and paid the money. The deal was done, and then, like a spook, he disappeared into the dark corridors of the school.

It was an experience selling coke to a senior police officer in the middle of the night in a bloody school; you couldn't make this shit up. Matt and I went back to his place, where he had a small quantity of China white—heroin—and he asked me if I had ever "speedballed". I had no idea what he was talking about. Speedballing turned out to be coke and smack mixed and snorted up the nose. This was my first experience of it. There was an immediate rush, but then, for me, it was an instant crash. It was unlike anything I had tried before, and I must admit, I liked it. The evening was a blast. The next day, I left for Bangkok.

Back in the Game

The trip was successful, with no hiccups and no great risk, so we began supplying the cops in Taiwan with coke. Johnny and I also started sending grass to Japan. An endless stream of people popped into the house from all over the world, collecting their bullet and disappearing.

I now had an operation going on with traveller's cheques—buying and selling stolen traveller's cheques was big business in Asia. But I was taking unnecessary risks again; it hadn't taken me long, and I was back at the coalface, in the mix, and totally forgetting the promises I had made to myself.

I had fallen over many times, and each time, I had got up and carried on. My lessons in life were harsh, and the short life that I had lived should have taught me something other than getting up, dusting myself off and doing it all over again. I was destined to get a good kick up the arse. I mean, a proper kick up the arse. But for now, it was full steam ahead.

Around about this time, I became ill. The first episode of my illness happened at home in Bangkok. It started with a feeling of queasiness, which led me to need the toilet. It then developed very quickly into severe vertigo. The room would spin out of control, and I had to lie down, but the lying down didn't stop the spinning, and I would soon start to retch. The retching would continue and continue until it was ripping the bile from the lining of my stomach. This constant spinning inside my head went on for hours as I thrashed about on the bed, the sheets saturated, and if I didn't make it to the toilet in time, I would defecate everywhere. The feeling of the cold, wet, clammy sheets on my skin only made the experience worse. One minute, I was boiling hot; the next, I was freezing cold, and all the time, my head would be swimming in a constant whirlpool, never quite settling. Any slight movement or noise would send the vertigo into an uncontrollable spin, and I would be retching again, ripping even more bile from the lining of my stomach. Each time this happened, it felt like I was dying. After many hours of this, I would pass out, only to come round in a heap on my bed, freezing cold with the still wet, clammy sheets stuck to my body. After the episode had passed, I would take myself off to the shower to wash the scent of death from my skin. The illness would plague me for a long time. At one point, I wondered whether it would finally take me, but for now, I was still alive.

Back to risk-taking. I was introduced to Uon, a Chinese fraudster who dealt in traveller's cheque and credit card fraud. Uon was a great big Chinaman, with a colossal stomach—a wealthy belly as it's called in Asia. When he laughed, he looked like he was going to burst. He was full of joy and had a permanent smile on his face. For, as corrupt a man as you could ever wish to meet, he was a lot of fun. We hatched a plan to go to Bali and hit the money changers with stolen traveller's cheques. Bali, here we come.

Bali is a small island in Indonesia. In the 1980s, it was unspoilt, with very few hotels and long, glorious, empty beaches. The Australians used it like the Brits used Benidorm; it was five hours away from Australia, and the flights were cheap.

As we made our descent into Ngurah Rai International Airport, I peered out of the window, and all I could see was clear blue water and beaches. As we came in to land, the thud of the wheels hit the tarmac, and there was that familiar rush from the thrusters, forcing the air from my lungs. For a moment, I was crushed into my seat, and then it was all over. As the doors opened, the distinct whooshing sound reminded me of my old man's dustcart. When I was young, he would take us to work with him on his bin round. The dustcart would start and stop, start and stop, and each time it stopped, the air brakes would go on, making the same whooshing sound as the aeroplane doors. Here I was in Bali, and all I could think about was being in a dustcart!

We disembarked onto the hot, sticky tarmac; the terminal was two or three hundred yards away. Crossing the runway to the terminal, I could see the heat haze rising from the tarmac. It was really hot; the midday sun was at its zenith, cooking the back of my neck and the top of my head. The sun felt good on my skin. I was in a good space, and I had no fear. I don't know why; I suppose if I felt fear all the time, I wouldn't be there doing what I was doing.

We booked into the Kuta Palace Hotel, and Uon wasted no time at all; a quick shower and we were out on the street, casing the joint and working out the best approach to the scam.

The money-change kiosks were little glass or plastic boxes with lone personnel in them. There were no checks; produce a passport, and that was that, you were good to go. So Uon and I hit them all plus the big hotels, which were a little more risky, but only slightly. We were only in town for a long weekend.

It was New Year, and the place was heaving with good-looking Australians, all tanned with blonde hair, and here for the surfing. We hired motorbikes and went round the kiosks changing up traveller's cheques on a monumental scale; it was gruelling work, but someone had to do it!

On the last day, I shot up a dirt track and somehow lost Uon. I couldn't see him anywhere. While I was looking around for him, I saw this policeman on a motorbike coming straight at me. "Shit, here we go again!" The policeman rode right up to me, nearly knocking me off my bike. I pulled over and sat there. The policeman got off his bike and came over to me, demanding my passport and driving licence, which I happened to have with me. When I handed them over to him, he took them, then said I was under arrest, and he was taking me to the police station. I had no idea why I was being arrested. I decided to front the situation. I wasn't going to let him take me to the station; I had ten grand on me, two Australian, one Kiwi, and an American passport, all with my photo on, and I had another ten grand of traveller's cheques. I had to take control of the situation, and fast. I demanded to know what he thought he was doing, nearly knocking me off my bike and asked what the hell he was arresting me for. I told him in no uncertain terms that I wasn't going to the police station with him. I was a tourist on holiday, and he was out of order. It turned out I had been going the wrong way up the one-way street.

"All the same," I said, "you tried to kill me." I told him I didn't have time to come right now, but I would meet him at the station in one hour. To my surprise, he agreed. He took my real passport and my driving licence and rode off with them. It was a close shave, and with my heart in my mouth,

Back in the Game

I watched him race off with my documents. With the dirt from the road flying up in the air and the tail end of his bike disappearing into the distance, I thought to myself, "That was fucking close."

I went to the station an hour later, minus the money, cheques and passports. I picked up my licence and paid a small fine. It could have been much worse. Sometimes, the gods look out for you.

That evening, we had dinner and then wandered down to the beach, which was a mass of people, all there to observe the sunset. The sunset on Kuta Beach was like no other, it was a fitting end to a slightly risky weekend.

When we got back to Bangkok, we sorted out all the money. Uon had bills to pay for passports, licences and some of the cheques. He was an honest crook, and we both walked away a lot richer than when we started out on our little Bali venture.

The risk I had just taken was unnecessary. I was making plenty of money in Bangkok, but I was still a victim of my own personality. I took risks for risk's sake, but for much of the time, they were unnecessary. Talking of risks, another one soon plonked itself on my doorstep.

I received a message that Keith needed a quantity of opium. Not only did he want the opium, but he wanted it delivered to Taiwan. I let Keith know that I could deliver that for him. I got the green light, and I took the plane to Chiang Mai.

I booked into my friend's hotel. It was quiet and calm, no hordes of people coming and going through the front door. It

The Rocky Road

was a relief from my hectic life back in Bangkok.

The last time I had been in Chiang Mai, I was fresh out of Changi Prison. I had come here to get away from all the drug smuggling and fraud. The pipe dream of being an honest teacher was now long forgotten. I was up to my neck in it. I was moving copious amounts of drugs, smuggling them all over the world, committing fraud wherever I could. All I needed now was another crash landing and another lesson, but I couldn't see that happening any time soon. The voice in my head that said, "Don't do it, Dicky, don't do it!" was lost in the noise of corruption, fraud and drug smuggling.

I hired a motorbike and zoomed off to the mountains; the scenery around Chiang Mai was stunning, lush green with vistas as far as the eye could see. Riding high up into the mountains was spectacular, with the waterfalls, rickety old bridges crossing deep ravines, and great views of the mountaintops. In the moment, with the hum of the bike's engine and the gentle sensation of the tyres rolling over the tarmac, my mind drifted off to the potential scenarios that could go wrong. I decided my mind was playing games with me, and I shook myself out of it. I pulled over and took in my surroundings. I turned the bike's engine off, and the chorus of crickets, cicadas, frogs, and God only knew what else was so loud it was deafening. The heat of the midday sun with the cacophony of noise quietened my thoughts, and I jumped back on the bike and rode to the Bhubing Palace, where the royal family spent their time from January to March. It was also open to tourists, but at this time of year, it was out of season, and the palace was shut.

Back in the Game

I pulled up in front, and two security guards casually waved me away. One guard strode forward and spoke to me in broken English. He told me that the palace was closed to the public, but if I carried on down the road, there was a community of Karen, the local tribal people who were worth going to see. I thanked him, and as I was about to leave, he asked me if I would give him a lift on the back of my bike as he was heading down there himself. I obliged, and he got on the back of the bike. He was a nervous passenger and constantly whispered in my ear, "You safe rider, you go slowly, you go slowly." It was a funny ride with the constant twitter of his voice in my ear. I rode the bike at a pace that he liked, and when we arrived, he was very pleased and looked quite relieved that he had made it alive. He congratulated me over and over again.

The Karens are a colourful tribe, in bright clothing, with the tradition of the females wearing many rings on their necks, supposedly for protection from tigers, but today it's considered a mark of beauty. There were stalls set up all along a dirt track, and my passenger seemed to know everyone. He wandered over to each of the stalls, exchanging the odd word and a handshake, then moving on to the next stall owner. When we reached the end of the line of stalls, he turned to me and said, "You like to smoke opium? Very good opium, best opium in Thailand."

"Yeah," I said, "I would like that." So we went off to find the chief, who he informed me was his very good friend.

We trundled along the dirt path through the village until we came to the chief's forlorn-looking shack, a round wooden building with a part-thatched and part-corrugated roof.

The Rocky Road

The chief was home, and I was introduced as a friend—a friend who wanted to smoke some opium. The chief was an elderly man. Like the last chief, he had black teeth and a dreamy look about him. He was happy to oblige, and we went into his shack, which was one big open space. It was similar to the chief's house that Keith, Sebastian, Don and I had visited the last time I was here. The cushions were scattered about on the floor, and the pipe was laid out in the middle.

We soon got down to business. The chief and I took it in turns, lying on the floor and puffing on this four-foot-long pipe, resting between the puffs while we waited for the effects of the opium to take over. As we rested, the security guard from the palace asked if I was happy and if I wanted to stay for more. Although the chief and I were in an opium-filled dreamland, I still had my wits about me, so I said to the security guard that I was a little concerned. Maybe the police would come by, and I would be arrested. My newfound friend assured me that the police wouldn't do that. In fact, he took out his ID and handed it to me and said there was nothing to worry about as he was the "CHIEF" of police! Well, blow me! We both laughed, and then everyone started to laugh. I smoked a couple more pipes with the dreamy old man, and then it was time for me and the police officer to leave. The police chief asked if I was OK to ride back, and I assured him I was fine, and we made our way back through the stalls to the bike. The chief again went to each stall, but this time, I realised what the game was. On the way in, he had told the stall holders that he wanted his protection money and that he would pick it up on the way back through. He had ponced a lift off me to the village so he could pick up his money. What a cheeky bastard!

Once he had collected his ill-gotten gains, we jumped on the bike and made our way back to the palace, again with him chattering in my ear with the words, "Slow, slow, very good, *farang*." After I dropped him off, I waved him goodbye and rode back to my hotel. With the afternoon sun warming my soul and a head full of opium, I sought out Holmes, Keith's guide from the last trip. When I found him, I asked if he could take me to score some opium. He said, "No problem, Mr Dicky," he would pick me up later in the day from my hotel.

It was late afternoon by the time he picked me up, and we jumped in his jeep and headed off into the mountains. The night closed in fast, and we ended up deep in the jungle, where it was pitch black. The track was narrow, and as we made our way along, it dwindled down to nothing, and we finally came to a standstill. When Holmes shut off the engine and turned off the lights, the jungle immediately closed in on us. It was so dark that I couldn't see more than three or four feet outside of the vehicle. It was somewhat spooky and other-worldly. Here we sat in the middle of the jungle in the middle of the night; it felt dangerous. Holmes opened the door and said he would be back in a minute, and the door slammed shut behind him as I watched him vanish into the night. What the fuck! In the blink of an eye, the dark ebony jungle consumed him. I was looking all around me. All I could see were weird eyes staring back at me. For some reason, I started thinking of ravens, big black fucking ravens,

The Rocky Road

like I was in a scene from *The Omen* or something. I had spooked myself, and I couldn't get out of this sense of panic. I just sat there like a fucking lemon; the cunt had fucked off and left me in the middle of the jungle, and I couldn't see shit. I sat there for ten minutes, then twenty minutes, with nothing happening. I had not seen this coming. I was sure I had been set up.

The area of Northern Thailand reaching right up to the border of Burma was the territory of the heroin warlord, Kuhn Sa, known as the "Opium King". Rumours were rife that he had shot two American DEA officers in this exact area. I was fit, strong-looking, with a military-style haircut—I looked like an American GI!

The look was deliberate. When I passed through airports, customs officers would often treat me with deference and inquired about which army unit I was with, so I would breeze through easily. Now, it wasn't such a great look. It didn't benefit me in the slightest, and now it put a target on my back. With that in mind and the darkness playing tricks on my eyes, I started to see people moving about. The jungle was moving, and my eyes couldn't adjust to the sheer inkblack void. I felt a knock on the jeep door; as I turned, a face was staring straight at me through the window. Then there were more faces; the vehicle was surrounded by men with machetes. I really thought I was fucked.

The faces stared at me, and then one of them tried the door. I could hear the driver's door being tampered with; the fuckers were trying to get in. The eyes were all around me now, staring at me like a caged animal. The driver's door burst open. I grabbed my bag, and I was about to throw it at the person coming through the open door when I realised it was Holmes, with a big fucking smirk on his face. With his Thai accent, he said, "Hey, Mr Dicky, sorry man, too long, too long, me have much problem," He looked around and saw all the faces peering into the jeep. He waved them away, and they moved back. He fired up the jeep, spun the wheels in reverse, and sent dirt and debris flying into the air, spraying it all over the men with the machetes. As we flew backwards, I said, "For fuck's sake, man, where have you been, and who were all those fucking men?"

"No problem, Mr Dicky, they just local, no problem here," and he handed me a package all wrapped and sealed.

We drove out of the jungle and out onto the open road. I must have looked relieved because Holmes started laughing and said, "No problem, no problem, Mr Dicky. These people, good people." Fucking halfwit. The whole episode scared the life out of me, and he was sitting there laughing his bollocks off.

Soon after that, I flew back down to Bangkok from Chiang Mai and Monty, my old school friend and Keith's so-called partner-in-crime, met me at the airport. We grabbed a taxi and discussed the opium. Keith had asked Monty to come and collect it and take it back to Taiwan. Monty didn't have the bollocks for it, so I told him not to worry, I'd get it over to him in a couple of days. Monty liked the new plan and left for Taiwan.

I got back to the house with the opium and searched around for a pair of Reebok trainers that Sebastian had left behind. I remember him saying he had this pair of Reebok trainers "specially made" for smuggling drugs; they had secret compartments in the bottom. However, when I found them, they looked like someone had torn out the bottom section. They were useless. I found out many moons later that Monty had used them to transport grass from Thailand to Taiwan. Unfortunately, they had sprung a leak, leaving a trail of fresh grass behind him at both the Thai airport and the Taiwanese airport, like a snail's slimy footprint, all the way from Thailand to Taiwan. No wonder he wasn't keen on using them a second time.

Again, I had no reason to volunteer myself for such a hare-brained operation; the consequences could be dire if I were caught. Nonetheless, I stuffed the opium into the Reeboks and went off to the airport.

Going through Don Mueang airport was never an issue. If the drugs left Thailand, who cared? At least they were not coming in. I was still self-conscious walking through the airport though. Smuggling drugs concealed in your body, whether swallowed or up your backside, gave the smuggler a boost of confidence. Inside, you knew the chances of being caught were next to zero. So the sheer act of smuggling the drugs, with zero chance of being caught, was exhilarating. Carrying them on the outside was very different. I couldn't say I had ever smuggled drugs in a pair of shoes before; it was quite terrifying.

I was doing a good impression of Herman Munster as I slapped these oversized trainers down onto the hard floor; the sound was deafening, echoing through the vast openness of the main hall. My adrenal glands were working overtime, and my hearing was so acute I could hear a pin drop. In reality, the trainers were making no more noise than other people's footwear in the airport. But I still thought I must be standing out like a sore thumb. Self-conscious, but somehow looking quite relaxed, I made my way through the airport.

Once through passport control and customs, I felt much more at ease. Sitting quietly in the corner, mulling over my situation, I had one leg crossed over the other. I looked down at the Reebok trainer perched on the end of my foot. It was basic and quite crude looking, not very professional, to say the least. I had a little shake of the head to myself and wondered why I was sitting in an airport with these stupid-looking things on the ends of my feet stuffed with opium. How had I talked myself into this one? I wasn't even getting paid for it, for Christ's sake!

Lost in thought, wondering about my lovely-looking footwear, I heard a voice say, "Dicky?" As I looked up, I saw Jin standing in front of me. Jin? He was one half of the ballet couple from my lunch date in Taiwan, the one where the two gay guys were trying to hit on me. I stood, greeted him and asked after Hok, his partner. Jin pointed over to where she was sitting. They were just returning to Taiwan from their honeymoon in Thailand. Hok was having a photo taken by a professional-looking guy with all manner of cameras thrown over his shoulders. As Jin and I wandered over to his wife, I asked him about the photographer. He said the *South China Post* was doing a piece on them, following their wedding and the honeymoon—the Asian version of *Hello!* As it turned out, these two were the premier ballet dancers of Taiwan and were, to my surprise, seriously famous. We chatted while we waited to be called onto the plane. They were keen to hear what I had been up to since we last saw each other; obviously, I had been teaching English all over Asia!

I stayed with them as we boarded our plane, chatting like old friends. Our seats were close to each other, and they gravitated towards me, telling me all about their wedding and their upcoming tour.

The flight passed quickly. With my mind on my shoes, I carried on with the conversation with the two celebs. Before I knew it, we were landing in Taiwan. I had quite forgotten I was on a mission until I stood up, and Herman Munster appeared again. I was surprised that they didn't mention how tall I had become.

In the airport in Taipei, we walked along together, laughing and chatting about nothing in particular, but I stuck to them like glue. Passport control didn't give me a second glance as they stamped my passport, and then together, we went to collect our luggage.

We grabbed our bags and put them on trolleys. As we made our way to customs, as they were famous, they received a lot of attention. It was assumed that we were together, which no one questioned. I was given the VIP treatment with my friends and ushered through without delay. With my shoes stuffed with opium, I wandered through the airport with the Beckhams of Taiwan. Once outside, I arranged to have dinner with them, which was the least I could do after they had helped me smuggle opium into the country. I wished the Beckhams farewell and jumped into a taxi.

Back in the Game

I booked myself into a hotel and gave Keith a call. He said he would go pick up Monty and come straight down to the town. By the time he reached the hotel, he was beside himself with anger. He hadn't known that I was coming to Taiwan, and he had only just found out on the way down the mountain that I had brought the opium with me. Keith found it difficult to forgive Monty. We were friends, and as far Keith was concerned, Monty had compromised me by asking me to smuggle the opium to Taiwan. It never crossed my mind, but in retrospect, Keith was right.

As I was in town, I went to see Matt and did some speedballing with him. This had become a ritual for me. Whenever I was in town, I'd take some coke over to Matt's, and we would speedball. Speedballing is not addictive, as far as I know; it's a heady concoction, and quite frankly, I didn't know any other person who took such a mix of highly addictive drugs and who had convinced themselves it wasn't addictive.

I flew back to Bangkok and returned home. Eric was in, and he was flouncing around the house like only a Frenchman can. I was convinced he was gay, but it may just have been his Frenchness. He was always hanging around with the ladyboys in town, with some pretence of fancying a girl named Mim, who never left the company of the ladyboys.

I had been back for a couple of days when I had one of my many attacks of ill health: extreme vertigo, headache, hot and cold sweats, involuntarily emptying of my bladder, diarrhoea, and retching for hours and hours until the bile was ripped off my stomach lining. I felt like a cursed man.

On the lighter side, life was moving along quite nicely, and there was plenty of money about. Keith had become wealthy. Mack was ticking along nicely, teaching a little English in Hong Kong and doing other side-lines, which he didn't elaborate on. Sebastian hadn't been seen for a while, so the chances were that he was nursing a habit somewhere. Monty was Monty doing what Monty did, which was very little. The only downside was Cody doing bird in Japan.

The sickness hung over me like a dark cloud. I had some irons in the fire, and the coke and bullet were both running themselves. A little people-smuggling and traveller's cheques held it all together like glue. I just couldn't shake off this feeling of doom and gloom though; I thought it may just have been the after-effects of the illness. I could not have been more wrong!

I hung around Bangkok for three months, doing very little. I liked to get stoned, pleasantly stoned, not monged out, but stoned enough to slow the planet down.

Friends would pop in, and we would smoke, listen to music and put the world to rights. Eric was always good company, and the house was never empty, with either his friends or mine wandering through. The calibre of these travelling nomads was always high. Jonathan, an Australian, was never far away, and he would often stay with us. He had a broken leg from a motorbike accident, and the Thai doctors had wanted to amputate it, so he went back to Australia, where they saved it for him. When he came back, he had stainless steel scaffolding built around the break. It was an incredible piece of engineering, and the surgery was first-class. The scaffolding had to be in place for four months, so he had decided to convalesce in Thailand. He was on crutches but mobile and spent most of the day sitting around the house getting smashed and telling funny stories. He was a linguist who spoke many languages, telling the maids jokes in their native tongue. As he got to the punchline, the laughter and joy from the girls would fill the house. He had spent many years in Africa, smuggling fuel from Somalia. He spoke Somali, Swahili, and Makhuwa, which is spoken in Mozambique. He would take tanker loads of fuel all the way down the east coast of the African continent. Smuggling fuel was big business, and he had been risking life and limb. It was a typical scene: big characters and even bigger stories.

Late at night, I would often go to Patpong, the red-light district, which would be heaving with people there for the sex tourism industry. Patpong was two streets running parallel to each other with an adjoining road in the shape of the letter H. I would sit outside a bar where the two roads met. I liked to sit for hours drinking coffee and watching the world go by.

Man's primal instinct is to procreate, but here, in the middle of this flesh market, there was no baby-making, just the cardinal sin and the lust for flesh. Bangkok catered for everyone's taste; any wild sexual fantasies were indulged. One evening, I watched a ladyboy wander off up the road with an old white guy. Half an hour later, the ladyboy was back, on his own, and back in the bar. No sooner had he entered the bar than he was back walking up the road with another old white guy, then a young guy, and another young guy. Did these men know they were going off to have sex with a bloke? Who could know?

The Rocky Road

At one point, the ladyboy caught me looking and came over. I received the stock phrase, "You sexy man, you want?" and he made the gesture with one hand closed like a fist, positioned it to the side of his mouth while he pretended to suck a lollipop; very ladylike! I rejected the offer but invited him to have a coffee with me. He wanted a beer, but I insisted on coffee. The bars were a rip-off when purchasing beer, but the coffee was reasonable, so it was coffee or nothing. He wasn't going to win, so he sat down with me, and we drank coffee together. It was an enlightening moment; the men had no clue that she was a he. He took them off, gave them a blow job, took their cash, and went off to find the next punter. The ladyboys were complex creatures, generally above average intelligence, and, it must be said, good company.

* * *

Time was ticking along, and my visa was running out, so I got the train down to Penang, Malaysia, to renew it. The run down to Penang was a well-trodden path for the traveller who wanted to extend his stay in Thailand. Once there, it was a simple process of dropping off your passport at the Thai consulate and picking it up the next day. The train ride always fascinated me. The Thais are predominantly Buddhist, and they have a wonderful nature about them. It is the land of smiles, as they say. Malaysia, on the other hand, is predominantly Muslim. There is nothing wrong with the Islamic religion per se, but it doesn't leave much room for laughter and joy. As the train made its way to the border, the faces became sterner, with no smiles. The people looked exactly the same, but now, if you smiled at them, instead of smiling back, they would scowl at you.

On the way back to Bangkok, I stopped off at Pattaya, a seaside town. Pattaya was basically one big whorehouse town on the southern coast. The town had grown out of the heady years of the 60s when the American naval ships from the Vietnam War would dock, and the men would rock into town to party. Pattaya would become a Wild West Show, drawing in the whores from Patpong and further afield. The place would literally go wild; it was a 24/7 madhouse. My friend Brad lived nearby with his wife, Nin.

The surrounding area around Pattaya was quite beautiful, and they lived a stone's throw away from the action, just far enough so that when the naval ships came into town, it didn't affect their tranquil lifestyle. Their house was on the sea, built on stilts and tucked away in a sheltered bay. From the mainland, a long, rickety jetty took you to their timber-framed home. It was a basic structure, painted light blue, a single-storey with a pitched roof. Inside the house, it was open plan, with a simple kitchen in one corner and two bedrooms and a bathroom taking up the other corners. Its appearance was deceptive; from the outside, it looked small, but once inside, it was somehow cavernous, like a Tardis.

The house was built to make the best use of the beautiful views and utilise the cool breeze that came off of the sea. Once the back door, the front door, and all the widows were open, the sea breeze gently cooled the house. The views from each side were quite dramatic, like beautiful paintings. It was as if he had a Van Gogh painting on each wall, with vibrant colours, the aqua blue of the sea, and the lush green of the shore. I spent a great deal of time with these two, who were great friends. Nin was from Thailand, and Brad was from a small village in Cumbria. He was a fighter, a thick-set guy with a huge heart, and an honest man, one of the few genuine people I had met in Asia.

Brad had his flaws, as we all do. He would dip in and out of a smack habit, but he had the strength of character to beat it every time. I enjoyed his company as he enjoyed mine.

He had made numerous connections while in Thailand. He knew a lot of people in the heroin business. He introduced me to some big players. I had already been bitten playing in this game; heroin always came with consequences. The money was big, and so was the punishment, on a karmic and on a personal level. It also attracted the more unsavoury type of character; the people he introduced me to were ruthless and very dark.

In among these harbingers of misery, he introduced me to his friend, Adam. Adam was English, short with a thick mop of gingery blonde hair, large eyes and an oversized smile. He was well-spoken, obviously well-educated, articulate, and very confident. He had that certain arrogance and entitlement you often find with the public school boys. He had a habit when I first met him, but he was what they call a functioning addict. He could still operate as a normal human being but needed to jack up every once in a while. He also happened to be a good friend of Matt from Singapore, the cause of my near incident with Inchet Narden. A friend of Matt and a junky! Not a good combo.

Back in the Game

Putting the negatives aside, I liked Adam; it may have been his over-confidence that appealed to me. I often found people with this self-assured attitude quite fascinating, and I would often find myself being drawn towards them, which may well have been due to my own lack of confidence. Underneath this veneer of self-assurance lay a poorly equipped human, contending with a world he didn't really understand. My fascination would more often than not be short-lived, though, as I soon recognised my own traits within them. I realised they were as flawed as I was, and behind their over-confident persona lay an insecure small child. We are, by our nature, a fine balance between weakness and strength.

Adam lived in the most hedonistic place on earth, Pattaya, where he was wandering around trying to find himself while having every temptation known to man thrust upon him. He was looking for the meaning of life while sex and drugs dominated him.

I spent a great deal of time with Adam, often talking with him into the long hours of the night. We would be stoned and drifting into the esoteric world of Madame Blavatsky and the Theosophical Society or the world of magic with Aleister Crowley. We never came to any meaningful conclusions, but those types of conversations rarely do. One evening, after a long discussion about Christ, he gave me a book to read, *The Spear of Destiny* by Trevor Ravenscroft. It was about a spear that had supposedly been thrust into the side of Christ while he was on the Cross. As the story goes, every person who held the spear held the destiny of mankind at their fingertips. Hitler, Genghis Khan, and Napoleon had all supposedly possessed this talisman of power at some point. Once they lost possession of the spear, it was all over; they were defeated, the spear passed on to the next tyrannical leader, and another chapter would begin for the destiny of mankind. Every time I bumped into Adam, we would discuss this book, with the discussions becoming very other-worldly. We got stoned, dismantled the human race and put it back together, over and over again; it was heady stuff. As any stoner will tell you, getting stoned in the right company can get rather deep and meaningful.

After my time with Brad, Nin, and Adam, I felt refreshed and at ease with myself and life in general. Over the coming months, Brad and I spent a great deal of time in each other's company. Brad would often be in Bangkok running this makeshift hotel called Windy's. It was owned by a German fellow named Hans. He owned the top two floors of a block of flats and turned it into a hotel—only in Thailand can one pull this sort of stuff off! Most of the guests were German backpackers. It was bohemian and rustic; it wasn't really a hotel, but a *sort* of hotel! It had a "reception", it had basic rooms, and it was cheap. I hung out at Windy's with Brad, and quite often, Hans would pop by. He was young for a guy who owned a hotel! He was a good-looking guy, tall with blonde hair and very charming, which was odd for a German.

I got talking to Brad and Hans about ice (methamphetamine); they had never tried it and were keen to give it a go. I hadn't actually tried it myself, but I was just off to Taiwan with some coke, so I said I would bring some back with me.

Back in the Game

The next day, I flew into Taiwan, dropped off the coke, did some speed-balling with Matt, and then picked up the ice. It came with a stern warning from the lads; they advised me to be very careful. It was a powerful drug which had the ability to send you bonkers. I got the drift. The reason it had the street name of ice was that it actually looked like little ice cubes.

I returned to Windy's to a fanfare; not only were Brad and Hans there but also their partners and Jerry from the Singapore days. All were desperate to try ice. The protocol was the same as chasing the dragon: you cut a small piece from the main block, placed it on a section of tinfoil, lit a flame underneath the foil and chased this ever-decreasing lump of ice as it gave off a trail of toxic smoke, chasing it until it disappeared into nothing.

Hans and Brad had both been addicts in their time, so they knew the score and chased this substance like old hands. It was the exact same process as chasing heroin. I had a go and got an immediate rush to the head; the boys were correct, this was powerful stuff. As with all amphetamines, like speed, your brain goes into overdrive, so we all started speaking at the same time, babbling nonsense at each other. We took a little bit more, and a little bit more, and we carried on until we overdid it. At that point, it was too late. We had consumed far too much, and we were all smashed. In among the noise of our chatter, we decided to go back to our homes, shower and go out on the town.

Sometime later, we all managed to get it together and meet up in Patpong. We went straight to the King's Corner Lounge and headed up the stairs to be met with this exceptionally loud and bright disco. I peeled off from the group and stood on my own for a moment. I wasn't particularly enjoying the experience; the drug had exaggerated the sound and colours in the room; it was overbearing and making me feel claustrophobic. As I looked around, I caught the eye of a European couple sitting at a table below; they were staring right at me, so I stared back at them. They quickly diverted their attention, turned their heads towards each other and started nodding, which made me paranoid. They looked up once again, and they didn't hide the fact that they were talking about me; they might as well have pointed a finger at me and said to everyone, "Look at that guy." I shrugged my shoulders and looked over at the bar to where Brad and the gang were standing.

I couldn't believe what I was seeing. Each of them stood out like a sore thumb, eyes as big as saucers. In a group, they looked like space aliens from a sci-fi movie out on a jolly to Planet Earth. The optics in the disco had exaggerated the whites of their eyes, and they looked crazy mad.

Every person in the disco was focused in on them, as their eyes stood out like great beacons, warning the ships not to come too close. I turned to the mirror next to me. I hardly recognised myself, as my eyes were huge, and I had the look of a madman too. I glanced down at the couple at the table again. They were staring even more intently, and they now had a look of concern about them. My paranoia was getting the better of me. When I reached the gang, I said, "We need to go, like now, come on, let's get out of here. Have you guys seen yourselves, you look fucking mental."

Back in the Game

Each of them turned to a mirror and, with horror on their faces, said in unison, "Let's go." We left the disco and left Patpong. We neither laughed nor cried; we just walked up the road in an abject state of misery. As the evening progressed, the misery became worse. Ice isn't a laughing drug; it's a drug of misery, and we were in a perpetual state of sad paranoia. We talked and talked into the night, but it wasn't stimulating in any shape or form, and in the early hours of the morning, we went our separate ways.

I didn't sleep. The drug was full on, and the thoughts in my head were racing, going from one lobe to the other. I made myself go to bed in the end, even though I wasn't in the least bit tired. I made the decision to just lie there and watch my thoughts. I surprised myself by using this time to be constructive. I planned new scams and discussed with myself where and what I was going to do over the next year. I let my mind go free, and my thoughts went to home, to childhood, to family and friends, and to my insecurities. And so it went on, bouncing round and round my brain. In the late morning, I got up, had breakfast and showered. I felt refreshed, as if I had actually been asleep. I headed over to Windy's to see the boys. They were still up from the previous night. They looked like shit, and they were starting to regret having taken the drug as they had had no sleep and were feeling slightly depressed.

The next evening was exactly the same: no sleep, but now the depression had truly got hold. I put myself through the same process as the night before. I went to bed and watched my thoughts through the night. The depression was still there the next morning, but it wasn't as intense. I rode over to Windy's, where the gang were still together. They still hadn't slept and were now suicidal. Hans said, "Dicky, when does this stop?"

"I don't know," I said. "How do you feel?"

"Like shit."

"I'm sad, unbelievably sad; it's relentless. I have no energy, and I feel like I want to cry forever."

"I'm sure it will be fine by tonight," I said, not believing a word of it.

That evening, I went through the same process again: I went to bed and watched my thoughts. I did this all the way through the night until I got up in the morning. I was gloomy; all signs of happiness had truly been vanquished, and in a state of unhappiness, I rode over to Windy's to see everyone. They were all climbing the walls by now with the depression that came with the toxic drug and the lack of sleep. The men were crying, and so were the girls, pleading with me to make it stop. The day was long and truly sad: three days, coming up to the fourth night. We all thought it couldn't possibly go on for longer than that.

That afternoon, we all crashed out in the reception area of the hotel and woke the next day after a long sleep. No one fancied taking ice again!

Shortly after this unpleasant experience, Brad and Nin were offered jobs as extras on the movie *Air America*, which they were shooting in Chiang Mai. The 80s and early 90s were a boom time for Thailand and Hollywood; many films were being shot in Thailand, as it was cheap. Movies such as *Good Morning, Vietnam* and the like were shot there on location. Brad had been in every film that came to town, and so had Nin. They disappeared up to Chiang Mai and encouraged me to follow them.

With Johnny looking after things in Bangkok, I made my way up to meet them in Chiang Mai. The town had been taken over by the Hollywood production teams. After some searching around, I found Brad, who said he would meet me after the shoot and introduce me to the man who did all the hiring and firing.

I wandered around the set, taking in the madness that is the film industry. I bumped into Mel Gibson at the catering truck and had a chat; he was the most unassuming and pleasant man. I found Brad, and he dragged me off to find the boss, who was in this makeshift office. He welcomed us in and sat us down with an ice-cold coke. Brad was one of those people that you immediately liked, and his charm had obviously worked on the Hollywood man. He was proper familiar with the guy, as though they were old friends.

Brad and I both had the same look: young, healthy and super fit—that deliberate ex-military look. I gave the appearance of someone much younger than my years. When Brad introduced me as a potential extra in the film, the chap said a resounding "no". They couldn't have anyone on set who looked younger than Robert Downey Junior. We were the same age, but I looked much younger, so eat your heart, Robert. This chap then asked me where I was from as we were both English. I said I was from Watford. Usually, when asked this question, I would say London, as it was lot easier than explaining where Watford was and talking about Elton John.

The Rocky Road

This guy was English, so I assumed he would know Watford. He repeated it back to me, "Woutford?" It wasn't looking good if he couldn't pronounce Watford.

I said really slowly, "WWWaattfooord."

To my surprise, he said, "What? Watford near Ricky?"

"Yeah, Watford near Ricky." (Rickmansworth)

"I went to Clement Danes School in Chorleywood."

Chorleywood is a stone's throw away from where I live. I couldn't believe my luck. I said, "I'm actually from Croxley Green." This led to a long discussion about all things local to where we were both brought up. After our long catch-up, I asked him again, "How's about giving me a job, then?"

He still said, "I can't do it, I'm afraid. We really cannot have anyone on set looking younger than Robert."

What a blow; there I was, halfway around the world, in the middle of the bloody mountains, with a guy from my hometown, and he wouldn't even give me a job. So we left him and went for a drink.

To get me involved around the set, Brad came up with an idea: why didn't we offer him our services as security guards for the film set? We both looked like ex-military guys, young and tanned with these flat-top haircuts and not an ounce of fat between us. Plus, we could speak Thai, so we were over-qualified. Brad was convinced he could talk the guy into hiring us, so the next day, we went back to see him. Brad was a talker; he gave him some spiel about red berets, tours of duty, and unarmed combat, then said the crowd were out of control and he needed our help. Just like that, we were in. The guy was so impressed we were hired on the spot as heads of security! We just wandered around the set, "acting" like security; how ironic!

When the gig was over, I left for Bangkok. No sooner was I back in my comfort zone than I was sick again; the vertigo hit me like a steam train. One minute I was fine, then the next, I was incapacitated and lying in my own shit and vomit. The fever came and went just as Keith turned up at the house; he was making a fortune but wanted to make more. Now he wanted to get into the heroin business.

There was no need to veer into this business; he had no stress, his operation was stone-clad, no one was getting caught, and the money was beyond his wildest dreams. His life was ticking along just fine. We spent the day discussing his proposition. It sounded preposterous; it was a high-stakes poker game, and if you got dealt the losing hand, it could be curtains.

I gave Keith my honest opinion on the idea; it was a bad product, it came with its own unique karma, and it would come round and bite us all on the arse. He was having none of it. "Karma, fucking Karma Bastarma," he said. "It's all bollocks. There's no such thing as karma. Life is life. Get on with it, Dicky."

The statement caught me off guard. Keith was a deep thinker. He was prone to outlandish expressions of violence, verbally and physically, but deep down, he was very sensitive and a profound philosopher of life. He had an uncanny, intuitive mind. This didn't sound like the guy I knew though. He had always steered the boys away from this particular drug and had suspected Sebastian of dealing in it and despised him for it, but now here he was, trying to convince me it wasn't so bad after all.

We spent the best part of a week chewing it over, with me trying to convince him how bad it was and him telling me how good it was. Truthfully, Keith was well aware that karma was a real thing—what goes around comes around—and this was definitely not a good idea. I had already had my fair share of this drug and its "unique karma"; the consequences could be dire. But he badgered me and badgered me until I relented to his hare-brained scheme. I gave him my word that I would have a kilo of China white in Hong Kong by the end of the week.

The Rocky Road had just become a lot more dangerous. The words "Dicky, don't do it, don't do it" did not do it justice. I was about to fuck it up—again!

I contacted Adam. He said he could have a kilo delivered to Bangkok the next day.

I silenced the voices in my head and somehow convinced myself all would be fine.

As I waited in the Mandarin Hotel for my man to turn up with the kilo of smack, the room felt lonely and cold. I could feel the dark clouds above me, emptying their contents onto my head; the rain was filled with bad karma, soaking me with the stench of foreboding. A knock on the door shook me out of my lonely thoughts. It was Adam, dropping it off personally. He came into the room and handed me the drugs, and then we shook hands. His hand was clammy. Nothing felt right about this. He had the look of someone on edge; I couldn't grasp the significance of the shifty look and his urgency to leave. Was

I being set up? It must have been the junky in him because nothing happened. I concealed the drugs in the bottom of the pilot's case and dropped it off to a chap called Bob, the man who Johnny and I used for our coke runs from Holland. I saw him off in the taxi and crossed my fingers.

I went up to Windy's to see Brad for a beer. Brad had a phone line at the hotel, so when the time was right, I phoned the boys in Hong Kong to see if Bob had made it. They said he hadn't arrived yet and put the phone down. Those were tense moments; it was way past the deadline. I was praying that he had made it undetected. I made another call. He still hadn't come through customs, and the conclusion was that he must have got caught at the airport. I was devastated. How could I have been so stupid as to get involved with this business again? I now had to live with the thought of sending a man to prison. Moments later, the phone rang. It was Keith; he said it had been a false alarm, as Bob had turned up safe and well with the drugs in hand. What a relief.

The next day, I bought a ticket and flew to Hong Kong. I met up with Bob, who gave me the whole story. The customs officers had put the bag through an X-ray machine and could see an anomaly. There was something wrong with the bag, but for some unknown reason, they couldn't find the drugs. It had been a close call for Bob, who was shaken by the whole experience. I gave him some extra cash and sent him on his way.

After this episode, the plot thickened. Keith had organised for a friend, Tommy, to take the white to Australia. But he neglected to tell Tommy it was smack, saying it was coke. It was a deceitful move.

The Rocky Road

So Tommy had a kilo of what he thought was coke in his possession. His girlfriend was partial to a line of coke, so they decided to open the package, and Tommy's girlfriend stuck her big hooter in it and took a big snort. She woke up in intensive care having overdosed on smack. She survived the ordeal, but Tommy felt he had been betrayed, which he had, so he ran off with the drugs. No one ever saw the drugs or Tommy again. This really wasn't going well... but in for a penny, in for a pound!

Plan B. I was involved now; I couldn't help myself. I was the forever chancer. I arranged for another kilo to be delivered to Australia this time. I had put together a ham-fisted operation with all caution thrown to the wind. Tony, one of Brad's mates from back home, was in town, so I arranged for him to go pick it up in Australia. I put Tony on a flight and sent him on his way. We arranged a coded message and place where we could meet up. It was all a bit of an off-the-cuff thing, with no planning. In fact, it was a straightforward kamikaze run, very risky and very stupid, but I thought it might just work. The details aren't important, but the stupidity was astounding.

Four days later, I flew into Perth, Australia. I wasn't at all concerned as I wasn't carrying anything illegal. So, without a care in the world, I passed through passport control, picked up my bags from the carousel and headed off to customs. I had nothing to declare, which should have made life easy for me. However, I was stopped by some random customs officer who wanted my passport. As he flicked through the pages, he visibly changed; the expression on his face became stern, and his stance took on the composure of

Back in the Game

authority. He ordered me over to one of the customs desks and thrust my passport in my face. He was very aggressive. He stood there pointing like a football referee giving a player a red card. I took my passport and wandered over to the customs desks.

I looked along the five desks and each one was busy. I assessed the options in front of me and decided to go for what looked like a pleasant-looking customs officer. I hoped he would be mild-mannered and just wave me through. How misguided was I!

"Passport, please, sir," he said.

I duly gave it over to him, and he looked at it and said, "I see you've been here before, Mr East?"

"Yes," I said.

"So what's the purpose of your visit, sir?" he said.

I had a bad feeling that this was not going to go so well. I wasn't carrying anything illegal, but if he checked me out, I would almost certainly get taken away, thoroughly searched and grilled, and, at the very least, deported, if not arrested on suspicion of something. I'm sure they would be able to make something up and make it stick. Having a criminal record can be a pain in the arse sometimes.

I said I was visiting friends and asked if there was a problem. He ignored my question and emptied my bag all over the counter, taking out my tube of toothpaste and squeezing all the toothpaste out. He began ripping everything apart, feeling the linings of my clothes, checking them thoroughly, and then throwing them down onto the countertop with contempt.

I said, "Are you OK? What are you looking for?"

The Rocky Road

He asked if I knew it was illegal to bring drugs into Australia.

I couldn't believe this guy, he was brutal, and again, there was this over-aggressive behaviour. He then picked up my passport, held it aloft and began shouting at the top of his voice, "Passport, passport, passport control, is there anyone in passport control?"

What the fuck was he doing? There were a lot of people around, even though it was five in the morning, and this was seriously embarrassing. I wanted to tell him to keep the noise down, but I kept my mouth shut and acted like the confused tourist. Then he stopped shouting. He looked at me with contempt, then peered over the counter and looked down at my shoes. I said, "You're kidding me, right? You actually want to look in my shoes?"

"Yes," he said. "Take them off and put them up here." This guy was acting like a psycho. I was a guest in his country, and he was almost stripping me naked in public. I took off my shoes and handed them to him one at a time. He looked in them and found nothing. He picked up my passport again and started shouting for passport control. For all of my feelings of being embarrassed by the whole situation, deep down, I knew the clock was ticking. If someone from passport control took my passport away, I would be dragged off screaming and shouting my innocence. I would get the finger up the butt routine, be questioned for 48 hours, and then be booted out of the country.

After wandering off shouting at the top of his voice, with no reply, he came back, handed me my passport and said,

Back in the Game

"Oh well, it seems there is no one on duty at the moment, so you're free to go, sir."

As I started packing all my stuff back in my bag, I told him that I loved coming to Australia and that I was coming back in a month: "Will I receive the same sort of treatment?" He said it would be worse, and, as a passing comment, said, "Have a good day, sir, goodbye."

I left the airport with a sense of euphoria, as if I had gotten away with something. I hadn't at all; all I had done was get over a hurdle. I found a motel and left my bags there, and then I went to find a pay phone to ring Tony. Tony's phone rang and rang. No answer. I left it until the next day, and I rang again. No answer. I was getting concerned. I rang the next day and the next. Finally, on the fourth day, someone answered the phone. The man on the other end was suspicious; he wanted to know who I was, what I wanted, why I was phoning, and who had given me this number. I assumed it was the cops. Tony had obviously been nabbed, and now I was compromised. I slammed down the phone. Now I really was in the shit. Tony had been arrested and he would almost certainly spill the beans. He had no loyalty to me and cooperating with the cops would bring his sentence down. He knew too much about me, so he was the weak link in the chain. I should have used someone far more removed from my close group of friends. As it was, he had the info the cops wanted. By now, they would be looking for me; they would know exactly who I was and what I looked like and have all my personal details at hand. I was stuck in Australia, and as soon I made a move to leave, I would be arrested. I was looking at some serious bird. I had royally fucked up this time. What had I said to Keith? "This stuff has bad karma." And here I was with it biting me on the arse.

I was stuck, with no way out. I didn't know where to turn. I spent a good deal of time stewing in my room, looking at my options. I was driving myself mad with the whirring noise in my head.

I had friends in Perth, so I hired a car and went to visit them. I stayed with my friends, pretending that life was great, and my teaching career was booming, but underneath the veneer was a panic-stricken fugitive on the run.

Don, who had been on the opium-smoking trip to Chiang Mai with Keith, myself and Sebastian, was in hospital in Sydney; he had been involved in a terrible motorbike accident and was in hospital in a coma. So, with nothing much else to do, I decided I would head over to Sydney to see him. I guessed they would only be looking for me on the international flights, not the domestic ones. I flew to Sidney with no issues.

Once in Sydney, I found myself a hotel, with my mind racing. I had to find a way out of Australia; luckily, I was still free, so while I still had my freedom, I got on a bus and made my way over to the hospital where Don was being looked after. On the bus, I analysed the predicament I found myself in, and the stupidity of it; getting involved with this drug was always going to end badly for me. I had compromised myself on a level, and there was no going back, I had become involved, and now I was going to pay the price.

As I watched the world go by through the bus window, my thoughts went back to the first time I had been transported in a sweat box from the police station in Watford to Brixton prison. I had been looking out from the small window of the prison van, wishing with all my heart for the freedom that everyone enjoyed as I watched them go about their daily business. Right there, in downtown Sydney, Australia, I wished the same! Even though I was still free, I wasn't really; I was treading water until the cuffs went on. In my mind, I was already a prisoner.

When I arrived at the hospital, there was quite a crowd. Don's dad had flown in from England, and there was a contingency from St Albans, friends of Carter's. I introduced myself to the St Albans crowd, and they said, "Oh my god! Dicky? Bangkok Dicky?" Yeah, Bangkok Dicky. No more introduction necessary.

Don had many friends around him from back home, which was a comfort to his family, who had to make flying visits, staying for only short periods of time. The St Albans gang invited me to stay with them at their apartment.

They lived in a ramshackle place, which was a complete mess. Among the chaos were a couple of big, old sofas, deep burgundy in colour, pitted with the tell-tale signs of the hash smoker. Tiny burn marks—little potholes—were quite visible, all caused by the hot embers that escaped the joints as they were endlessly passed around. It seemed that no one cleaned or did the washing up; it was a real home-from-home.

No sooner were we through the door than one of the guys was skinning up. With the social norm of the smoker, the joint made its way towards me. I declined the offer. In the circumstances, I couldn't smoke; my paranoia was at an all-time high, and it would have tipped me over the edge. One smoke and I think my brain would have turned to mush. I also needed to stay straight, to keep my wits about me; if danger was coming, I wanted to see it coming.

I hung out there while I decided what to do; it crossed my mind to go down to the harbour, jump on a ship and become a castaway. These were just flights of fancy though; I had no idea what to do. In the meantime, I visited Don every day; he was still unconscious but looked peaceful in his hospital bed.

Through the haze of the endless smoking, I got to know this ramshackle lot from St Albans. They were all chancers, not drug smugglers or lawbreakers, just a bunch of girls and boys pushing the boundaries, taking on any old jobs to fuel this hedonistic life of smoking and partying. I mentioned *The Spear of Destiny* in a conversation, saying it was a very esoteric read. One of the guys suggested I might like to meet his girlfriend's mum, a Māori, an elder, the keeper of ancient knowledge, as he described her. She sounded interesting, so I arranged to meet her the next day.

She came to the apartment and introduced herself. She immediately put her arms around me and embarrassed me, saying she had been dying to meet me! I wasn't sure what that meant and why she would want to meet me.

Her name was Francis. She was a typical Māori lady, with olive skin, jet-black hair, a somewhat round face with high cheekbones, and deep dark eyes. She had a warmth about her; she felt familiar to me. The mind can play tricks on you, but I definitely felt we had met before, maybe in another life! She embraced me, and as she did so, I could feel all my anxiety

Back in the Game

floating away. It was an odd feeling, like a dark cloud had been physically lifted from me. We talked for hours, though she was doing most of the talking while I was asking the questions. The meaning of life, reincarnation, spiritual entities, Jesus, Buddha, Muhammad, God... she had views on it all. It was fascinating stuff. She also had the ability to heal the sick, and she had clairvoyance: a soothsayer, or a witch of the past.

Francis had caught me at a vulnerable time, there was no question about it; I was open to anything. The noose around my neck was getting tighter and tighter. I was looking for hope, and she looked like she had some. Who knew the truth? Maybe she had the answers, maybe she didn't, but she definitely had my attention.

She spoke of the connection between us, saying it went back many lifetimes, and Francis was here in this lifetime, to help me, or save me from myself! I was intrigued by the outrageousness of the statement; if she wanted to help me, she could start by getting me off this island. I told her I would soon be leaving, and I waited for a word of warning from her. Surely, if she was someone who could see the future, she would warn me against taking a flight. No such warning came, and as unlikely as it may seem, I booked my flight on the back of her lack of concern.

Three days later, I was at the airport to catch my flight back to Asia and freedom. Francis came to the airport to see me off, and I found her having coffee at one of the many bars. She was cheery, but she said she felt the loss of me leaving; she had much to tell me, but alas, there was no time. We had an hour or two to burn, so as a parting gift, she told me her story: the introduction to the mystery schools and her knowledge of life after death, the gift of seeing energy all around, her connection to God, light beings, and the work of the Masters of Earth. It was heady stuff. She finished her story and said she wanted to give me some advice.

When I returned to Asia, I was to talk to my five friends and advise them all to go home. She said their time had run out, as had mine. She warned me of an impending catastrophe that would befall us all if we didn't heed her words and go home and stop doing whatever it was that we were doing.

I was shocked by her advice and knowledge of my close friends and that we were all up to no good. I had always kept this veneer of respectability as the language teacher. I had never spoken of the lads and our close relationship; I certainly hadn't mentioned any skulduggery.

We spoke some more, then it was time for me to go to departures. We hugged each other, and I thanked her for her advice. She repeated her warning: "Be very careful," she said. "It will not end well for you or your friends."

When I left Francis at the gate, I was unusually emotional; I felt like crying. It was a very odd feeling. At this point, I knew I wasn't going to be stopped or arrested. It seemed impossible—surely this woman, the woman I had spent the last three days of my life with, would have known and told me it was dangerous and not to leave. My sense was correct; no one took a second glance at me. I just strolled through passport control and customs and onto the plane.

On the aircraft, I had a long, cool glass of beer; it was hard to believe. For the last three weeks, I had been convinced I was being hunted by the Australian authorities, yet here I sat, a free man. The relief was tangible; my body felt relaxed, and my mind was clear. I had escaped the clutches of the Australian authorities; I was on my way to Hong Kong, mentally exhausted.

The whole experience had shocked me to the core. I had berated myself over and over again, cursing myself for being so naive and stupid. I hadn't listened to my own judgement; I hadn't taken into consideration my own experience with this substance. Keith had convinced me of something I knew I shouldn't do. The price for playing with heroin was always very heavy, and I considered myself to be extremely lucky not to have been doing a long prison sentence. I had fallen over for the last time; I made the decision to return home, thinking that was enough of that.

Francis had made an outlandish prediction about me and my friends, and for some reason that I couldn't quite fathom, I took her words seriously. Some might say I had gone slightly crazy (and they did), but I took on board what she told me: things would not go well if I carried on with this path, and the same applied to my close friends. What was waiting for us, God only knew. There's no telling why I should have believed such an utterance from someone I had just met. I had only spent three days with her, so I hardly knew the woman. However, I did take her seriously—I was going to leave Asia and head home.

Chapter 10

The Crazy Man Returns

Living in a place like Bangkok can easily spin you out of control, swallow you up, and then just spit you out without a care in the world. Bangkok has no feelings; it's a city, so if it grabs you and sucks you in, you can lose your way, and yourself, becoming one of its many victims. I had seen it so many times; guys would get involved in the drugs and start dating the prostitutes. The girls may have been in this situation before, and they would know the ropes. The punter would become a lifeline, a source of income; she would have her fish firmly on the hook, and she needed to keep him on there. In the process of trying to keep him, she would slowly boil him alive, turning him crazy. The girls of Patpong were victims of an insane world—the sex industry—turning tricks and trying to look like they enjoyed it. No love: it was enough to send any girl mad. In the end, deeply damaged, the "fish" would have to be sent home, generally never recovering fully.

When I finally got back to Bangkok, I spent the following weeks clearing the decks and tying off loose ends. The first person I talked to was Cocaine Johnny. I told him that I had met someone extraordinary who had given me a warning, and I was off back to the UK. He tried to talk me round, saying I had nearly been caught by the cops and that I wasn't thinking straight. I was adamant. Sure, I was in a vulnerable state—I had nearly been caught—but Francis had freaked me out.

Then I flew to Hong Kong to see Mack and Sebastian. I explained what I had just experienced, and I gave them the warning. They thought I had lost my mind, but I wasn't bothered; it had spooked me enough. Then I flew to Taiwan and told Keith and Monty. I gave them the warning of doom, and they also thought I was crazy, a victim of Bangkok. They asked why I didn't move to Taipei. The truth was that all I could do was tell them what had happened to me and leave it at that, it was up to them. I was burnt and I was going home.

Chapter 11

The Journey Home

I flew back to Hong Kong and bid my friends farewell for the last time. I was off to China to catch the Trans-Mongolian Express from Beijing to Moscow. It was a seven-day train journey! I had to get a visa for both China and Russia; once I had those, I passed from Hong Kong to the Chinese mainland through Shenzhen and on to Guangzhou. There, I got on a train and made my way across China, all the way to Beijing, where I was going to catch my train home.

Beijing was an enormous city with a population of ten million. The city was in two very distinct halves—one half with the new modern high-rise buildings, all ugly, made of concrete with no life, and the old quarter, with narrow lanes and two-storey houses with courtyards and plenty of life. The push was on to demolish the old part of the city and rebuild with these ugly high-rise monstrosities.

I stayed in the old part of the city and soon became friends with a local professor from Beijing University. He spoke perfect English and was my guide for the entire trip. He gave me

The Journey Home

the lowdown on the one-baby policy, Chinese Communism, the Tiananmen Square fiasco, and families hiding their children under their houses so the Chinese authorities couldn't take them away. At the time, China was buzzing; the boom was on, and everyone was making money.

I visited the Forbidden City, which was a disappointment. Chiang Kai-shek, who had been the chairman of the national party back in the 1930s and 40s, had jumped ship when his party lost to the Communists, fled to Taiwan and took all the treasures with him. They are now in a museum in Taipei. Consequently, there was nothing to see when I went to the Forbidden City; it was bare.

I rented a push bike with its own number plate. The main form of transport was a bicycle, thousands upon thousands of bicycles, with, I might add, bicycle police! At road junctions, the bike police would monitor "bike law". I couldn't resist a little law-breaking and shot through a red light; I was duly pulled over and reprimanded. This drew an enormous crowd, maybe up to 200 people. Nothing happened; he didn't fine me. He just took my number plate down and let me go. I pushed my way through my audience and waved goodbye to them, which got a round of applause. I wonder if it made the main news; it was a real spectacle. I saw a road rage incident, or "bike rage": two guys slugging it out, which also drew a massive crowd. I was asked to move along by some guy who was watching. "Not for your eyes," he said in perfect English, but I ignored him completely; it was a fantastic punch-up.

I had to go and reserve my bunk on the train, so the professor and I went to the station. He had said it would be

The Rocky Road

chaos, and I would need his help and guidance. He wasn't wrong. There must have been 1,000 people or more crowded around the ticket desk, so he told me to follow him, and we barged our way to the front, knocking people out of the way. He was right; I don't think I would have assessed the situation in quite the same way. A queue is a queue, right? You wait your turn. Well, not in Beijing! If you want service, get yourself to the front by any means necessary.

We got my ticket and reservation sorted and wandered off. I was leaving in a day or two, so my friend and guide took me for dinner at a famous snake restaurant. We ate snake-and-cat soup: delicious! As we ate our meal, two well-dressed businessmen walked into the restaurant. The staff cleared an area right in the middle, the tables cleared or moved, and this tiny little table and chairs were hurriedly placed right there in the centre of the restaurant. It caused quite a commotion; all the diners stopped eating and watched the pantomime unfold before them. I asked my friend what was happening. He said the two gentlemen were from Taiwan and they were extremely rich. The restaurant was the most famous snake restaurant in the whole of China, and these two gentlemen were about to be served fresh snake blood. The scene was captivating, with a hush and anticipation from the entire room. The chef appeared, holding two live snakes. He deftly slit them precisely at the point of the liver, and then with expertise and a deft squeeze, the blood filled the shot glasses. The two diners clinked glasses and downed the bright red liquid. It received a casual round of applause, and then everyone turned around and got on with their meals. I asked what

The Journey Home

this was about. My host said this was a sign of their status and wealth; it was also supposed to be an aphrodisiac. I had to chuckle to myself. This outrageous display of bravado, and they were telling everyone in the restaurant that they weren't virile and couldn't get it up. It didn't seem very masculine to me, even though I think that was the idea.

The next day, I went to the Great Wall of China, which I must agree is one of the wonders of the world and one of man's greatest building projects. It is the longest garden wall of all time!

* * *

It soon came time for me to leave. I said goodbye to my professor, and I boarded the train. This was the Orient Express on steroids; the train was ancient, with sleeping compartments with pull-down beds and a quaint buffet carriage with dodgy candelabras. It was musty inside the compartments, like the smell of your nan's place when you were young. The seats were covered in moquette, which comes from the French word for carpet, which says it all. They were hard and prone to giving you carpet burns, and the colours were deep burgundy. Maybe not so much Nan's place but more like a musty old whorehouse. When we pulled away from the station, the fumes from the diesel engines filled the compartment with black smoke, which was forever in the air, no matter where you went on the train. This was my home for the next seven days.

My first experience in the buffet carriage would stay with me forever. I was served by the Arthur Daley of Russia. I

The Rocky Road

was to meet these characters everywhere I went on my trip through Russia, but this one was Arthur Daley "the waiter". I picked up the menu and asked him about the trout; I got an abrupt Russian. "NO."

"How about the steak?"

"NO."

"The chicken?"

"NO."

"Mm, what have you got, my friend?"

He pointed to the soup and bread. The menu was extensive and very cheap, but everything on it was off.

"OK," I said, "you must have more than soup."

"You have American dollar?"

"Yeah, sure."

"What do you want, then?" he asked me. Everything on the menu was available, but it was valued in hard currency, US dollars, and much more expensive than the printed menu prices. I had to go through this process every mealtime.

As we made our first few stops in China, the travellers would jump off and exercise their legs. The platform was awash with local food vendors selling steaming dumplings, bao buns and rice dishes. The stops became the daily entertainment. We would jump off, hoping to find delicious food; we generally got wonton soup with dumplings and a good old bao bun!

We travelled through the Gobi Desert, which stretched on for miles, just sand all the way to the horizon, with the odd herd of camels and nothing else. The view from the open window out into this vast landscape was breathtaking. It was warm, with the desert sands swirling into the air, stinging my face, so I had to keep the windows closed.

When we reached the border with Russia, the wheel frames had to be removed and replaced with wider sets. The gauge on the Russian side differed from the Chinese side, so the wheels came off, and new ones went on. This odd situation resulted from the conflict between Russia and China in the 1960s when the border was closed, only to re-open in the 1980s. In their wisdom, the Russians and the Chinese decided to use a different gauge track from each other. At the border, I jumped off the train to watch. It was an incredible scene. A huge crane lifted the carriage off the railway lines while workmen quickly unbolted the undercarriage mechanism. The crane then lifted the carriage onto the new frameset, and the workman busily bolted this back onto the carriage. It was then lifted back onto the Russian lines.

There were no safety barriers as such. They relied on the passengers to have common sense and not get in the way. Amidst this mayhem, I jumped back onto my carriage, only to be lifted in the air while they changed the wheels. These were the great days when health and safety didn't rule, and the natural sensibility of man prevailed. It ran like clockwork!

Without any interference, the men got the job done, super-fast, and we were on our way in no time at all. We were now in Russia, heading to Moscow. We reached Lake Baikal, the deepest freshwater lake in the world, which is 600 km long, and we stayed with it for a good part of the day.

On the train, I made friends with Bernard, a 75-year-old English folk dancer whose claim to fame was guesting on *The*

Generation Game with Bruce Forsyth. Bernard travelled the world while his wife chose to stay at home. They had been together for over fifty years, with him periodically disappearing off into the wilderness. He said he was fulfilling a lifelong dream, riding the Trans-Mongolian railway across China and Russia. His main mission was to visit the Bolshoi, the home of ballet, when we reached Moscow.

When we arrived in Moscow, Bernard and I checked in at the local university: tourists could either stay at designated hotels or bunk in the universities.

We wandered the streets of Moscow together, and when we found the Bolshoi, it was closed for refurbishment, so Bernard and I decided the next best thing was to eat at the brand new McDonald's, the first in Russia, which had just opened that year, 1990. When we arrived at McDonald's Pushkin Square, we were met by at least 10,000 people queuing. I was told that, on some days, this figure could triple. The Russians were dressed in their finery: smart suits for the men and flowery dresses and hats for the women. What a sight!

The queue was immense, to say the least, but it moved quickly. They allowed forty people in at a time, and ten tills were manned constantly. When the forty people in front of us were served, and the tills were free, another forty got the chance to buy the latest food craze! The restaurant was all gleaming and bright, with these eight-foot-tall statues of iconic landmarks from around the world, like the Eiffel Tower, the Empire State Building, and Big Ben—very chic, very cosmopolitan! The Russians sat at their tables with mountains and mountains of this rubber food. I think the Russian people thought they had finally arrived.

Moscow was a city caught in time; the architecture was incredible, from the Kremlin, Red Square, and St Basil's to the stark, colourless communist housing. The grey, lifeless-looking buildings had an other-worldly sense about them, preserved in a time warp, pristine and magnificent, albeit with the smell of oppression.

Bernard left for the UK, and I hung about in Moscow, travelling around on the railway network. The stations were opulent, with grand chandeliers hanging from great, vaulted ceilings. One station, Taganskaya, paid homage to the soldiers of war from a bygone age. The artwork in the station was breathtaking.

I walked through Gorky Park, where a wall of death had been erected. It didn't draw much attention, so I watched the riders do their thing with no other spectators. They went round and round this giant wooden barrel. It made me dizzy; heaven knows what it was like for them. I walked aimlessly until I came across the tourist hotel, the Intourist, on Tverskaya Street. The hotel was the best Moscow had to offer; this place also had the old-world feel of the past. Outside the hotel, I was approached by another Russian Arthur Daley. "Hey, tourist," he shouted with a thick Russian accent.

"Yeah?" I said.

He came towards me in his long grey coat and trilby hat. "You want caviar, you want champagne? Best prices!" Then, like a cartoon flasher, he proceeded to open his great big grey coat, from top to bottom, revealing an array of deep pockets, all stuffed with caviar and small bottles of champagne. It was all laid out within his coat in symmetrical rows, with the caviar on one side and rows of champagne on the other. I felt as if I were in a comedy sketch. I had a wry chuckle to myself and bought one of each.

Back at the university, I made friends with some of the students, and they gave me the grand tour of Moscow. We visited all the places I had seen already: Red Square, the Kremlin, St Basil's, the Bolshoi, and the GUM shopping centre. We also made our way through the tenements and the poorer areas, which looked grey and bleak, and the lack of food in the shops was evident. In the evening, we went to Aragvi, a top-end restaurant where the KGB and the cultural elites would dine. The price to get in? US dollars, which I had, so in we went. The place was grand, with high ceilings and great arches, beautiful ornate tables and chairs, and the white of the linen tablecloths stretched out like a huge hospital ward. It was unbelievably noisy; one of the students informed me that the Georgians were in town, and they were rich. They had taken over the restaurant lock, stock and barrel. The music was theirs, as was the dance floor, at least the area that the Georgians had turned into a dance floor. It was acceptable behaviour in Moscow; if you had the money, you could basically buy and do whatever you wanted. The extraordinary amount of food being served was disturbing, as most Russian people had only the bare minimum to live on. It was a thought-provoking evening, watching the rich get fat while the poor get thin.

The Journey Home

My time in Moscow was short. I got back on a train for a 24-hour journey to Warsaw. From there, I jumped on another train to Budapest, where I booked myself into the Citadella on top of Gellert Hill. It overlooks the city with spectacular views. It was basic as far as rooms went; however, it was situated in the best possible vantage point.

From there, I took a boat on the Danube all the way to Vienna, where I booked into a hotel. I was going to stay for a couple of days. I wanted to visit the Hofburg Palace, where The Spear of Destiny was kept.

The next day, I visited the museum that housed this ancient spiritual relic, the spear that was thrust into the side of Christ as he was nailed to the cross. To be honest, it was just a spear in a glass box, nothing much to report; it didn't inspire anything in me.

Vienna was beautiful, clean and tidy; pristine would be a better description, with fabulous buildings. St Stephens Cathedral was an architectural masterpiece, along with the Hofburg and Belvedere Palaces. The list went on. I felt at ease with myself in Vienna. Asia was far behind me now, and I was nearly home. I had no idea what I was going to do when I got home, but I would worry about that when I got there. My youngest sister was always good to me, so I planned to head to hers and see if I could stay for a while, just long enough to find my feet. I wasn't carrying any baggage; the drug scene felt like a distant memory, so I wouldn't be compromising her hospitality. So, the next day, I picked up a bus, and 22 hours later, I arrived in London.

Chapter 12

Life in a Loop

I made my way to my sister's. I hadn't forewarned her, so she was somewhat surprised to see me. To my relief, she was glad to see me and offered me a bed before I had a chance to ask. It was an extraordinary gesture. Life at her flat was pretty crazy, with five boys and all. It was hectic, and there was a lot of crying, laughter and love. It was like The Waltons on steroids. I did love it there, and it reminded me of home somehow.

I was only back a week when I was struck down with my infernal illness again. I told my sister that I was going to be ill for six or seven hours, and there was nothing to worry about. I told her I had caught some type of infection or parasite while I had been away and that now she was going to witness me vomiting, pissing and shitting myself, and I would look as if I was dying. I assured her I wasn't going to die and that it would pass. I apologised and locked myself in a bedroom for the duration of this horrendous experience. The room spun out of control, and I was contorted on the floor, writhing around

Life in a Loop

uncontrollably, begging for the pain to stop. The six hours of misery came to an end, and then, clammy and exhausted, I took a shower and had that familiar feeling of being cleansed.

Carter was in the UK, living in St Albans with his girlfriend, so I called him up and arranged to pop round to see him. We had a close relationship, having spent six months together banged up in a foreign prison. Prison is one thing; being locked up in a foreign prison is another; the need for an ally, a friend, someone you can trust in a situation like that is paramount. Luckily, we had each other. It created a great bond between us.

Carter was still at it, selling grass and a few pills. He liked to keep himself under the radar, so he didn't get involved in Class As. Good karma, as they say. We saw each other most days over the coming weeks, which meant that I was still around the drug business, still pushing the boundaries, even if I wasn't involved, but if he got caught, I would have been banged up purely by association, so it was not very bright!

I hadn't been in England long before Keith contacted me. He had a problem and wanted me to sort it out for him. Mark, with whom we had done the credit card scam, had ripped him off. He asked me to go round and do the necessary and collect what was owed.

I didn't want to get involved, but again, out of some sense of loyalty, I agreed to get it done. I phoned Mark and said I was coming over to pick up what he owed. He was defiant on the phone, telling me he would stick an axe in my head and some other nonsense. I said I would be round in the morning, so he should get his axe ready.

The Rocky Road

The words of warning from Francis were still ringing in my ears. I needed to change my direction, she had said. It would not end well, she had said. Francis had obviously made an impact on me, so much so that I had left Asia. Now, here I was, back in the UK and back in the game, picking up drug money, with menaces. Some people never learn!

Bright and early the next morning, I got up, showered, and left my sister's flat. I was going over to Mark's to pick up the money owed to Keith. I had the use of my brother-in-law's car, and as I walked over to it and opened the door, I could feel eyes upon me. Over time, being around drugs and generally misbehaving, I had developed a sixth sense; my observation skills were acute for anything out of the ordinary, the unfamiliar face, the face that you would see more than once, or undercover cops, who generally stood out like a sore thumb. They didn't dress right, they didn't walk right, and they were bad actors.

On top of that, I had that uncanny ability to feel something in the ether; it was an unmeasurable thing, but it was real all the same. I could feel something was not right. I noticed the guys straight away. I was being observed. There were three cars, each with two passengers, parked in different spots. They were obvious, too obvious. The only assumption I could come to was that Mark had grassed me up; out of self-preservation, he had tipped them off. Mark was an untrustworthy character, friendly with many police officers, solicitors and judges, and he was spooked. Clearly, he had gone into fight or flight mode and had decided to go for the "flight" option. He had set me up, hoping I would be arrested and go to prison and out of his hair.

Life in a Loop

I got into the car and drove off like there was nothing wrong. Each of the three cars started their engines and pulled in behind me. It was glaringly obvious. I knew I had a problem, a serious problem; my record spoke for itself. If I got caught still messing around in the drugs business, the judge would not look favourably on me.

As I drove along, I could see all three cars. I couldn't believe how predictable they were being. The roads were busy, so I nipped in and out of the traffic, pushing my way through. I pissed off a few drivers with my aggressive manoeuvres, but I wanted to make sure I wasn't mistaken and that these guys really were on my tail.

At one point, I lost them; then, out of nowhere, they were back on my tail. I drove around the middle of town. The traffic was heavy, allowing me plenty of time to confirm my worst nightmare: it was definitely the Old Bill, and they were stuck in my rear-view mirror. I wasn't sure which squad they belonged to, but they were the authorities, and now I had to get rid of them. I decided to drive back to my sister's flat.

I was uncertain what to do with this situation, but I pulled up outside my sister's flat, got out of the car and headed into the flat, calm as you like. I didn't want to spook them and give the game away. The Keystone Cops parked up in their original positions and watched me casually walk into the flat.

I told my sister that I was being followed and asked her husband if he could give me a lift to the railway station. He said, "Won't they just arrest you if you go back outside?" He was right; the chances were that I was going to be arrested.

The Rocky Road

I had an idea: I would put on a disguise, and then we could see if it worked.

Many moons earlier, back in Hong Kong, I had gone to a make-up artist and had a beard made for me. At the time, I had some wild idea of a scam for which some dressing up was necessary, so, on the spur of the moment, I had a beard made. The process was great fun. I went to the film studios and was shown to an on-site cabin; inside, it was decked out like a scene from an old Hollywood set. A big, old barber-style chair was sitting in front of a huge mirror with lightbulbs all around the edges. It was bright and hot. Three or four girls were busy with dummy heads, clipping away at the hair pieces plonked on top of them. It was buzzing with energy; the girls were up and down and all over the place. There was all this Chinese chitchat, shouting and laughing going on. I think I may have been the butt of most of it.

One of the girls sat me down and asked me what I was looking for, so I explained how I wanted the beard to look. They began by taking samples of my hair and put this mock-up version on my face, using some type of glue to stick a meshy material to my chin and cheeks. Then they trimmed it up so that it fitted the contours of my face and then unpeeled it from my cheeks. They asked me to return the following week for the final fitting.

I went back a week later, and the girls went through the same routine, laughing at my expense as they sat me down for the fitting. One of them disappeared for a moment and returned with this dummy head with an enormous beard. She unpeeled it from the dummy, stuck it onto my face, and

Life in a Loop

then trimmed it. Finally, when I was happy with the look, the girl offered to take it off, wrap it in a soft linen cloth and box it up for me. No, I said, I'll keep it on thanks. I was meeting Mack for lunch in Ned Kelly's, and I thought it would be funny to turn up with a full-on Grizzly Adams beard. The girls were laughing as I left the cabin to make my way across town. As I headed to the MTR to travel all the way to Nathan Road to Ned's, I felt like an undercover agent on a secret mission.

I entered the bar and saw Mack sitting in one of the cubicle-style seating areas. As I approached, he clocked me and started laughing. I struggled to laugh as the beard was restricting my facial muscles; it felt as if I had a sheet of wet paper stuck to my face. I sat down, and Mack had a good pull on it. He said he was impressed; it looked real and felt real. The waitress came over to serve us, and Mack asked her to give us a minute, so she turned her back on us and served the table opposite. As she turned, I said to Mack that I didn't think I could eat with the beard stuck to my face, so Mack suggested I take it off. Just at the point when I was removing it, the waitress turned back around and said, "Are you gentlemen ready?" She didn't blink an eye; one minute, I looked like Grizzly Adams, and the next, a clean-shaven young man, but there was no reaction. Mack and I roared with laughter as she walked away with our order.

So I had my beard, and I also had this big Russian trench coat and a dodgy-looking hat. I glued the beard to my face and put the hat on. The trench coat was massive, more like an army officer's coat than a trench coat. I put it on and pulled up the collar. I tied the bootlaces on my walking boots, which gave me a few extra inches of height. I stood back from the mirror and had a good look. I didn't even recognise myself, so it looked good enough. When I came out of the bedroom, my sister began to laugh, which made everyone laugh. I asked her for something resembling a walking stick, so we fashioned a broom handle, and I limped out of the flat with my brother-in-law. I played the part of the Old Russian trooper well; they didn't even look at me as I gingerly climbed into my brother-in-law's van. As we moved off, I casually glanced at the six-man team. Who were they? Customs? The drug squad, or maybe the local Old Bill? Whoever they were, they had just lost their target.

I got my brother-in-law to drop me off at the station. I said I was sorry for all the aggravation I had caused, and that when the heat had died down, I would pop by for a visit.

I used the public phone and called Carter, giving him a brief outline of what had happened, and he said he would pick me up from the station. Sometime later, he pulled up next to me and said, "What the fuck do you look like?"

I said, "I can't believe you recognised me." We laughed, and I jumped into the motor and told him the whole story about how Mark had grassed me up. Carter wasn't surprised; he had never trusted him.

Carter said I could stay at his place. He was still busy moving dope around. He had become much busier than I had realised and was moving large quantities of hash all over north London. He dragged me along on his daily delivery route, like some latter-day milkman delivering daily goodness to the public. He introduced me to some rather unsavoury characters: honest, law-breaking bank robbers and hard men from back in the day, big and strong. The types that would open a door for a woman, give up a chair for the fairer sex, never swear in the company of females, and treat them with reverence. But in the same breath, they had no problem sticking a shotgun in her face if she was a cashier. The contradiction always amused me.

Carter's customers were all ex-bank robbers. This band of merry men had soon worked out that selling dope was far more profitable than bank robbing, and the bird was far less. I don't mind admitting these dudes were scary.

I received a call from Keith; he had yet another problem that needed sorting out. He was sending ice over to a friend in Camden, and the guy had been arrested. He wanted me to go and see the guy's girlfriend and get the lowdown. Carter and I decided to go and case out the flat where she lived to see if she was under observation. We sat around for the day, but nothing looked out of place. Late in the afternoon, the girlfriend appeared and made her way up Camden High Street. I got out of the car and followed her. No one was watching her, so Carter pulled over, and we basically snatched her off the street. She was screaming a bit, but I quietened her down as we sped off up the road.

"For fuck's sake," I said. "Shut the fuck up. Nothing is going to happen to you. We just needed to be sure you weren't being followed." She was still screaming and trying to open the door. I said, "You're not going anywhere. We need to ask you some questions, so be quiet." She finally stopped making a fuss, and we found somewhere out of the way to pull over. After a long conversation, we were finally able to make sense of what had happened.

Mick, the boyfriend, was selling the ice from their flat. One day, he had a knock on his door; it was plainclothes cops. They questioned Mick about his next-door neighbour, who they said was a drug dealer, someone they had under observation. Mick told them he didn't know the guy, and the police left. It wasn't behaviour I had ever come across before. Cops knocking on the drug dealer's neighbour's door to ask questions about his neighbour? Nonetheless, Mick had carried on, even though he knew the cops had the flat next door under observation. I wasn't sure where Keith had dug this guy up from, but his behaviour wasn't normal.

Within the week, the cops kicked his front door in and arrested him. It must have been a case of mistaken identity. The cops had obviously been given a tip-off and had gone to the wrong flat. It was Mick's flat that they should have been watching. I suppose the game was up when the cops saw everyone going next door rather than to the flat they were actually watching.

The girlfriend was calm now. She realised we were friends of Keith's, who she had dated in the past, and that we were only trying to find out what had happened.

I got the girlfriend to send me a visitor's order to visit Mick in prison, and I went to HMP Wormwood Scrubs to see him. I was taking a massive risk visiting this guy. I had no idea what he had told the drug squad or if they were watching his visitors.

Life in a Loop

I was back in a London prison, only visiting, but that was enough. The Scrubs, as it is fondly known, is another of London's surviving Victorian prisons. I went through the rigmarole of emptying my pockets and receiving a casual pat down. All the visitors were shown through to the visitors' area, a room with semi-private cubicles lined up against the wall. We all got our allotted numbers and sat at the cubicles, and then the prisoners came out one at a time and found their "guests".

Mick sauntered up to the table in the cubicle, wearing his light blue stripy shirt and ill-fitting jeans, the rank-and-file uniform of UK prisons. He sat opposite me; there was no screen, but we had to keep our distance. I was surprised when he sat down, as I realised I had met him before. Keith hadn't told me exactly who I was going to be dealing with, probably because I would have refused to have anything to do with him. I had first met this guy in Bangkok; his character was best described as Rodney Trotter, or maybe closer to Trigger.

He had come out to Bangkok to pick up some bullet. I hadn't spent a great deal of time with him, but on one occasion, we had to go and meet someone together at the Shangri-La Hotel.

Before we left, I showed him a little trick we all used in Asia. I removed a couple of tailor-made cigarettes from a packet. Gently, one at a time, I rolled the cigarettes between my thumb and index finger, coercing the tobacco out. Once all the tobacco was drawn, I replaced it with grass, twisting off the end so the mix couldn't fall out. The two elegantly-made joints were then placed back in the cigarette packet. These were the smash-and-grab emergency joints.

We met our man in the foyer. As we were talking, Mick decided to spark up a cigarette, so he pulled out one of the joints from his packet and began puffing away like a steam train. Quite casually, I leaned over and whispered that he might want to take the joint outside before we all got nicked. He then started looking from left to right in this exaggerated Trigger-esque fashion. It was comical, but I was aware of the danger he had put us in, smoking a joint in the foyer of a top hotel. We had also met at a rave once, where he was the DJ. I turned up on an invited VIP list and freaked out all the ravers because my friend and I looked like coppers.

These were the only two times that I had met Mick, and now I sat opposite him in the visiting room of the Scrubs. He had been nicked with Keith's ice. What a predicament! He didn't particularly like me; my attitude towards him had never been polite or courteous. He sat there like a lemon, and I said, "Keith wants to know what you've told the Old Bill." He began explaining what his girlfriend had already told me, so I bluntly told him that I had heard the whole story, I just needed him to tell me what *he* had said. I wanted to say, "You buffoon," but that would have complicated matters, so I kept my thought to myself.

He said the cops had no idea what the powder was and were getting it analysed. He hadn't admitted to anything, and he was refusing to cooperate with them. It sounded plausible. I didn't want to pass the time of day with the guy, so I got up and said goodbye. I gave Keith the message that, in my humble opinion, everything was cool and there was nothing to worry about. I didn't visit Mick again.

At this stage in my life, I could quite easily have fallen back into my old habits. With things as they were, my mind wasn't settled; the cops were on my tail again, for whatever reason, and so, in my utmost wisdom, I decided to up sticks and go to South America.

Chapter 13

South America

I booked a flight to Caracas, Venezuela, via Portugal; it was a cheap flight with just one stopover. No one stopped me at Heathrow; the age of technology hadn't caught up yet! The flight was delayed in Lisbon, and they put us up in a hotel for two nights. I got friendly with three guys: a Kiwi, a Frenchman and a Brit. They were all on a gap year and were going travelling in South America. We all got on well and agreed to stick together in Caracas.

Caracas, the capital of Venezuela, was a sprawling metropolis of two million people; it was hot and humid. When we arrived, we all got our backpacks and headed for a hotel. Each of us had the Lonely Planet guide to South America, the go-to guide back then, full of interesting facts, transport information, places to eat and places to stay. We found a hotel, and I ended up sharing a room with Bruno, the Frenchman. He was a wispy little fellow with jet black hair; his character was very much like Eric, my old housemate back in Bangkok, all *va va voom*, French accent and

South America

flaying arms. He had a good grasp of Spanish, much better than mine, which made me lazy, as I let him get on with it. By the time we got settled in, it was early evening, and we went for a walk to find a restaurant. It was a humid evening, and we wandered aimlessly around Caracas.

An hour later, sweating like pigs, we stopped opposite a row of about fifteen shops, with one open-fronted takeaway restaurant in the middle. There were lots of people milling around. I sat down on the curb at the side of the road as the three guys stood around me discussing something. As I sat there, I couldn't help but notice three sets of extra feet milling around. It was busy enough around us, but these three sets of shoes kept appearing. When I looked up, I saw they were attached to three young men who didn't look friendly, so I stood up and beckoned the boys to the restaurant. We all went in, and I sat at the back to get a good view; I wanted to weigh up the situation. We had barely been in the country for four hours and were already in trouble. My travelling companions stood at the counter, looking up at the menu on the wall, unaware of the danger they were in. I found that quite incredible.

My teenage years had been spent in the pub environment, getting drunk and fighting. The weekend fight was something we all took for granted. All the surrounding villages and towns would converge on my village, meeting up at one of the many pubs, and then all hell would break loose. I look back on it with fondness. It was like stag rutting season in the forest; only the strongest survived. It could be brutal in the pubs if you didn't have your wits about you. Clocking who was on your case and the potential danger was the best way to prepare for such situations. So you kept your senses alert for the danger. It had equipped me well for the present situation—these guys were clearly up for it.

I sat at the table and watched The Three Bandidos. There was no mistaking it; we were being weighed up for the kill. Two stood outside, pretending to wait for a bus, while the third was standing in the queue for food. Then, the two at the bus stop came into the restaurant, and the third stood in the bus queue outside. This was not good. Back home, three muggers wouldn't even entertain going for four guys in their mid-twenties; four guys would put up a fight, so it would be a fool's errand. In Caracas, either this rule didn't apply, or it didn't bother them. For sure, we were in a life-threatening situation, so I called my guys over one at a time and explained the situation. I told them not to make it look obvious that they were aware. I warned the Frenchman last of all. My plan was to walk out of the restaurant into the middle of the road, hail a taxi, get in and be gone. For some reason, none of them believed me; they didn't take me seriously at all. They said I was seeing things, then went back to the bar and bought food as if nothing was wrong. I wasn't concerned whether they believed me or not. I knew exactly what I was going to do, and it didn't include getting stabbed or shot.

There were far too many people around for them to try anything. I knew they would wait until we were somewhere much quieter. It was now or never, so I stood up, beckoned my pals, walked straight into the middle of the road, hailed a taxi, and jumped in. I had the back door open and encouraged

South America

them to get in. They all just stood there like lemons. In the background, I could see the bandits of the night getting agitated; their meal was getting away. Sitting there in the back of the cab, I finally got Bruno to tell the taxi driver where our hotel was, then I said, "Jump in, Bruno. There is danger, just get in."

He waved me away like a true Frenchman, with flair and a confident pomposity, and said, "I am here to be with the people of Venezuela. I'm not going around in a taxi." He then muttered something obscene about the Brits and stormed off. There I sat in the back of the taxi, with the Kiwi and the other Brit standing next to the open door. I said, "Get in, lads. We're off to the hotel."

One of them said, "What about Bruno?"

"You can go with him. See yah later," and I went to shut the door. Then, all of a sudden, they had a change of mind and jumped in. On the way back, I gave the guys my thoughts on the situation. I could be wrong, or I could be right; either way, looking at that situation, I wasn't taking the risk. I wasn't going to fight three guys who thought it was OK to take on four young, strong-looking blokes. They were either stupid or heavily armed with knives or even guns. I didn't know which, but if they were heavily armed, we could get severely injured.

Back at the hotel, we waited outside for Bruno. I wasn't overly concerned. I thought he would be fine, because mugging one guy didn't necessitate shooting him. Then, out of the darkness, Bruno came walking with his arms behind his back and his head down, muttering to himself. We went over to him, and he explained that three guys had stopped him for a light and then held him up at gunpoint, so he had given them what he had on him. He looked at me and said, "You knew?"

"Yeah, I told you in the restaurant, but you wouldn't listen." He walked off cursing "the fucking English". It was a baptism of fire; welcome to South America; one day in, one robbery!

It soon became obvious that, as a tourist, you were a cash cow, someone to rob. In Asia, the atmosphere was very different; as a tourist there, you had the status of a welcome guest, revered to a certain extent, and locals were pleased to see you. You were still a cash cow, but they had other ways of getting into your pocket and relieving you of your hard-earned cash. There was no need for violence. Pulling the tourist in with a broad smile was easier for the Thais. Smiling came naturally to them, and the effect on the unsuspecting *farang* was disarming. Once you were in the arms of this trickster, he would rob you blind, steal your credit card, and sell you untold fake goods at a premium, smiling all the while. I enjoyed the battles in Asia; they were non-violent, the big con, and if you lost out, you took your hat off and bowed in honour of the ingenuity and the gall. Here in South America, things were quite different; being a tourist made you vulnerable; you had money, and it was there to be taken, and if need be, taken by force. I had gone from the top of the food chain to the bottom purely by moving from one side of the planet to the other.

Bruno didn't hold it against me for long; we soon left the Kiwi and the Brit behind and travelled together. First,

South America

we headed to Isla Margarita, the holiday island for the Venezuelans. We followed the coast to the port, from where we took a boat across to the island. Isla Margarita is a beautiful island with long, golden beaches, a clear blue sea, and a lovely, welcoming vibe, though some were more welcoming than others. We spent a few days lying about in the sun and bumped into the two guys from Caracas again.

We all hung out on the beach for the day and then arranged to get up early the following morning and visit the other side of the island. Bright and early, we made our way across the island. We noticed the locals would stand by the side of the main road and put out their thumbs. Invariably, vehicles would stop and give them a lift. This was not an unusual form of transport to me, as I had often thumbed a lift when I was younger and also when I was in Israel. On the way out of town, we caught the bus, but on our return journey, we decided to go local and thumbed it. We thumbed a lift from Punta de Piedras all the way to Porlamar. The Avenida Juan Bautista Arismendi was the island's superhighway, stretching from one end to the other.

It was dark by the time we got to the highway. The road was well-lit, but from the verges onward and into the brush, it was totally black; not a single light could be seen. We stood by the highway with our thumbs out, and it wasn't long before a pickup truck pulled over with a couple of young dudes in the front. We stood out as tourists, fresh meat on the market.

"Hey," they shouted, "*donde vas?*" (Where are you going?)

"*Porlamar, mi amigo,*" we shouted. They were cool, laughing and joking, and possibly slightly drunk, and they waved us into the back of the open-back pickup truck. I jumped up first and sat close to the cab window. I watched as the two amigos in the front rummaged around, looking for something. The driver got a blade out of his pocket and placed it on the dashboard. He motioned to the passenger, who began to rummage around some more, desperately searching for something. He found what he was looking for and began displaying it to the driver; it was a short machete, which he slipped into his jacket. I couldn't believe it; whenever I was with these guys, someone would try to rob us. We were almost certainly in trouble… again!

What were the odds of this happening twice in such a short space of time? Honestly, you couldn't make it up. The driver pulled away off the sandy verge and onto the tarmac. I called to the others, "Come here, listen, guys, we are in trouble again. The driver just got a knife out of his pocket and put it on the dashboard, and the other one has a big machete tucked in his jacket. They are going to try and rob us."

As they again started debating whether I was right, the guy in the front climbed out of the side window and into the back. "*No problemo, no problemo, mi amigos,*" he started. He then continued in Spanish. I couldn't make it out, but I knew "*no problemo*" meant we had a problem.

The truck suddenly swerved off the tarmac road and onto the sandy verge and skidded to a halt. The driver got out, shouting in Spanish. I asked Bruno what he was saying. The gist was that they had to make a detour down this sandy road to pick up his brother, who was waiting for them. It was a classic scene; the meat was in the truck, and it had to be delivered to his brother. The problem was we were the meat!

South America

It was dark, but the motorway was light enough. The bandidos wanted to drive through a gap in the brush to meet the brother; it looked like the road to hell, with no lights, just a mass of blackness. I immediately jumped off the back of the truck and made my way to the lights of the motorway. I wanted high visibility. I shouted out, *"Adios, amigos."* Then the driver started shouting, which got his friend all agitated, so he started shouting. I yelled, "Come on, lads, we're out of here," and I walked off. I got myself close to the road and put my thumb out, deliberately putting as much space as possible between me and the two armed men in the pickup. Then my three friends came hurtling up the road after me, running as fast as their legs could carry them. I wasn't far ahead, so they soon caught me up. Out of breath, they all started asking me if I was sure about the situation, saying, "They had seemed like nice blokes."

So I said, "If you think that, go back and get in their truck, then. See you later."

They didn't go back, and we made our way along the road until another vehicle gave us a lift.

That evening, we all ate together, and the discussion was all about whether I had been right or wrong. My argument was that the two guys had knives, and they were leading us down a dark and gloomy road, a road that looked like hell. I knew I wasn't mistaken. I sat and listened to my naive friends and wondered how long they would survive in this hostile environment.

We stayed on the island for a week or two, and then the Kiwi disappeared. Shortly after that, the Brit went, and Bruno and I were back as travelling partners.

The Rocky Road

We didn't hang around in Venezuela for too long. We headed back to Caracas and took a bus to Cartagena, Colombia. It was 800 miles and 22 hours away!

Cartagena was a bustling sea port on the Colombian Caribbean coast. On the seafront is the old walled town, dating back to the sixteenth century. There were cobbled streets and colonial buildings, all dressed up in beautiful pastel colours. We hung out there, looking at the churches and architecture. Down by the port, we were approached by a Colombian who wanted to know if we were tourists. He asked where we were from and then offered us jobs crewing yachts. I took his details down and was excited by the prospect of sailing; we had spoken to sailors on the island of Margarita, and they had been an odd bunch, insular and suspicious. The idea of sailing appealed to me, but Bruno was reluctant to take up the offer. On returning to our room, I retrieved my trusty Lonely Planet travel guide and read up on Cartagena. There, highlighted in bold print, it said, "Beware the offers of crewing yachts; they take you out to sea, rob you of your belongings and throw you overboard!" It was another close shave, but this time Bruno saved *my* arse.

South America was much more challenging than Asia. Just three weeks in, I had escaped two potential robberies, and now I had been offered the chance to be food for the sharks. It was dangerous, but I understood the game.

Bruno had a friend who owned a house in a small fishing village just outside Cartagena, so we made our way there. It took a little while to find the property, but after asking some locals, we finally found ourselves in this tiny little house perched on top of the hill looking over the bay and out to sea. His friend, Phillip, was in France and had given Bruno permission to stay as long as he liked. We were settling ourselves into our new accommodation when a friend of Phillip's turned up, an Afro-Caribbean guy by the name of Carlo. He was tall and jet black with this mop of frizzy hair.

"Welcome," he said, and his face lit up with his huge smile, displaying perfect white teeth. He was very charming and put us at ease straight away; he was full of local info and asked if we wanted some grass. Well, this was a nice welcome. We assured him that, yes, we would like some grass, and off he went to collect it. He came back a short time later with his arms full of marijuana; he must have had at least a kilo, but he only asked us for ten US dollars.

Bruno and I sat on the veranda with this spectacular view overlooking the coast, and we got pleasantly stoned. They were a dreamy few days; the grass was potent, and the days were long and leisurely. We didn't do much of anything apart from watching the lizards and geckos vying for territory in the garden. Carlo popped up every day. He did our shopping and our laundry, and sometimes he cooked for us. We became very lazy and just sat up at the house doing very little apart from getting stoned. One day, Carlo asked if we wanted some *coca*. "*Si. La coca, Carlo,*" was our reaction, so he went off and was back in no time with four or five grams of coke for $15: three dollars a gram.

Given how cheap it was, we spent the next month snorting coke and smoking grass, day after day. Time stood still as we got our daily routine sorted: up late to fresh Colombian coffee and a joint, and by lunchtime, the coke was calling, and we would get on it until we could do no more.

This all ended abruptly a month later when I started to find it boring and monotonous. Coke is coke. If you like it, good luck, but I found it a waste of time. I had played devil's advocate with myself, tempting myself with this highly addictive substance. I had pushed it to the limit, doing line after line, day after day, and in the end, I came to the conclusion that it wasn't all it was cracked up to be, and I stopped. It was really rather boring.

I had tried heroin in the past, but heroin was a completely different animal; any ideas of hammering that for a month, doing line after line, day after day, would have left me in tatters. I would have struggled to stop. Once heroin has you, it has you. In my opinion, coke is a mental addiction, not a physical one. Heroin is far more dangerous; it is not a drug to play games with.

We left Phillip's house and headed for Cartagena to catch the bus to Magangue, then on to Mompos, and finally to Bogotá!

Like any other city, Bogota is a hustle and bustle place, but this one was dangerous. We took a taxi to the hotel, and the driver immediately advised us not to go out after sunset. "*Muy peligroso,*" (Very dangerous) he said. At the hotel, we got the same advice. There was a rumour that a Brit had recently been warned of the dangers and completely ignored the advice; he had last been seen lying in a pool of blood near the financial district. Only the Brits!

South America

The next day, we headed up to Mount Monserrat. A cable car took us all the way to the top. From 10,000 feet, the views were incredible; Bogotá was huge.

The old city was full of beautiful architecture and vibrant colours, but I felt like I was being watched constantly; the men had a habit of standing in doorways looking dodgy like they were up to mischief. It may have been quite innocent, but from the perspective of a guy who watches for danger, it looked like danger. I stood out like a sore thumb; all that was missing was a handkerchief tied in the corners and plonked on top of my head. I felt like I had a big sign on me saying, "Tourist: rob me"! I had good cause to be suspicious after all the previous exploits. I had also been robbed in Santa Marta by a teenager, a tall, gangly youth, who ran past me, ripped the chain from my neck and bounded down the road like a young gazelle. I watched him in the mid-day sun as he effortlessly skipped down the road with my gold chain. I didn't give chase; I just watched him running down the road and thought I couldn't catch you even if I tried. After that and the other episodes in Venezuela, it was best to be alert.

We hung out in Bogotá for some time, then made our way to San Augustine and to Tulcan, just over the border into Ecuador.

In Ecuador, we took a train ride from Ibarra to San Lorenzo. The Trans-Siberian Railway journey is without a doubt the most impressive rail route on earth, but the eight-hour journey on the Ibarra to San Lorenzo line, was the most exhilarating train ride you were ever likely to take.

The Rocky Road

The Ibarra train station looked like any other train station, but this train ride to San Lorenzo was quite unique. The carriages resembled the local buses, except on rails; they were identical to the buses that transported the local people by road, but somehow, they had been transformed into rail carriages by attaching railway wheels to them and putting them onto the railway tracks. There were five carriages, each a separate entity. It all looked ominous and exciting at the same time.

We purchased our tickets and climbed aboard. As the train pulled away, some of the passengers climbed out of the window and onto the roof, so Bruno and I followed suit. We looked back and watched the other carriages leave one at a time. Each carriage propelled itself along individually, as though we were one giant fairground ride. We all moved along as one but separately. The passengers on the other carriages had also climbed up onto their roofs, and we waved to each other and hooted and hollered like big kids, and then we all sat back and watched the jungle go by.

All of a sudden, someone shouted, "TUNNEL," and we all flattened ourselves out, lying with our faces down as the approaching black hole consumed us. It was a dangerous game. Who knew what was in the tunnels or how low the roofs were? The space between the passengers and the tunnel ceiling was minimal, with only inches to spare. There was a constant scream of "TUNNEL" as we all ducked down with our hearts in our mouths. The ride was like no other, as the carriages made their way through the dense, green jungle for a good eight hours. The train finally arrived at San Lorenzo,

South America

and we were all in one piece. We climbed off the makeshift carriage and boarded a bus to Esmeraldas.

Esmeraldas was a sleepy coastal town, very peaceful and quiet, with beach shacks for hire. We found ourselves a place to stay down by the front and went for a walk along the beach. It stretched for miles, with no people, rubbish or pollution: just an endless, glorious stretch of sand that went on and on for as far as the eye could see.

I loved it there. The peace and tranquillity suited me well, as did eating fresh fruit for breakfast, smoking a joint or two during the day, and eating fresh fish in the evening. I would walk on the beach every morning, and the feeling of freedom took my mind back to the prisons, where I had had the misfortune to spend periods of my life. The freedom that nature provides has, since my first incarceration, given me a true sense of freedom.

The affinity that we have with our surroundings is somewhat underplayed in the societies we live in, especially in the West. We all feel calm and relaxed when we are in the arms of Mother Nature, only to leave her behind and go back to our brick houses and travel on our concrete roads, separating us from our undeniable relationship with the trees, the flowers and the earth. I would often have these moments of melancholy and reflection when in a natural environment with no people around; feeling at ease with the world, my mind would wander into flights of fancy and the path that I had trodden.

Over these past few years, I had been given plenty of warnings of incoming danger, but I had generally ignored them. The gut feeling, the whispers in my ear of "Don't do it, Dicky, don't do it": I listened to them, sometimes, and other times, I didn't; sometimes I got caught, and sometimes, I didn't. Francis' words were like a warning shot over my bow, and I had heeded her words well and left a life behind me that almost certainly would have ended in tears. Here, I was free and enjoying the moment, looking forward, not backwards. Could I make the transition from scallywag to upstanding citizen, a pillar of society? Only time would tell!

The longer we stayed, the more I felt at home. Walking the beach every morning was a joy: long, peaceful walks without a care in the world. One morning, while walking, I happened upon a seagull on the beach. It was way off in the distance, just standing there, facing the sea as the waves washed up just short of its bright blue feet. It was unfazed as I approached, so I sat down beside it, and we looked out to the sea. This bird was huge; it measured the same height as me, and we were eye to eye, with me sitting and the seagull standing. I had never seen a seagull like this before. Sometime later, I found out it was a blue-footed booby. It was large and somewhat spooky-looking; up close, it had these piercing blue eyes, which were so intense that I felt the bird was looking right through me and into my soul. I sat with this beautiful-looking bird for quite some time, talking gibberish and asking it about its plans. I was having a one-way conversation with a seagull on the beach!

We sat together, man and bird looking out to sea, wondering what the future held for us. He had to take off and fly, and so did I!

South America

After an hour or so, I got up and stroked it on the head; it neither cared nor was bothered with my intimacy. I left it staring out to sea and wandered back up the beach. As I walked along, I wondered where we would both end up. I was fated to get to wherever my destiny led me, but the question is this: is the path written before we take it, or do we write it as we go along?

Time in this small haven drifted along. Bruno was quite temperamental and would have moments of deep melancholy. Sharing the bungalow (or shack) on the beach, with such beautiful surroundings, with a man with such dark moods, became increasingly wearing. More often than not, I left him to his own devices.

One evening he returned to the shack, quite drunk. I was sitting in the corner reading a book, and as he came in, he nearly fell over himself as he saw this large spider stalking a cockroach. He panicked and began falling about the place in a drunken stupor, screaming French profanities. As he panicked, the spider picked up the Frenchman's vibe and disappeared straight up to the ceiling. Attached by a thread, he made his escape before the mad Frenchman could splatter him. The next morning, we shared breakfast with some fellow travellers, and I mentioned his erratic behaviour the night before. I joked that the spider had been so big that it could have eaten him.

He had no sense of humour and began flaying his arms about again and cursing the English. I do admire the French for the way they aren't inhibited in any way; his gesticulations and his French accent were a thing of beauty. I was laughing at his expense, and he didn't appreciate it, so he stormed off as he had done on so many occasions.

There was a tension between us now that never really resolved. Not long after his tantrum, we headed off to Quito, and at this point, we went our separate ways.

* * *

The capital of Ecuador sits nearly 3,000 metres above sea level, and the oxygen is thin. I was quickly out of breath and became ill within days. I had booked into a cheap hotel with a shared bathroom, and, as the vertigo took hold and the vomiting began, I needed the toilet. I found myself in just my pants, crawling from my room across the corridor to the bathroom. I don't know how long I stayed in there; it could have been hours. Finally, I gathered the courage and the energy to make the journey back to my room. Again, I found myself crawling along the floor. I was much worse than usual: the head-spinning was severe, and I was retching for hours with the cold sweats and the sense of doom. The symptoms eventually left me, and I decided it was time to leave and go back to the UK for treatment. I feared that if I had another episode like this, I would almost certainly die.

I headed back to Colombia and to Medellin, the centre of the world's cocaine trade. I stayed there for a while to gather myself. Like Bogotá, it was a dangerous city, not the sort of place a tourist wandered around at night.

South America still held a couple of surprises for me. While in Medellin, I went looking for a bookshop, and as

South America

I wandered the streets, I came across a Colombian army unit in the middle of an operation. They were split into two groups, one unit on either side of a long, tree-lined avenue with a cathedral at the end. The two units were making their way to the cathedral, moving in unison, getting coverage from the doorways as they made their way to their objective. So, with my roving reporter head on, I retrieved my trusty Canon AE-1 from my bag and followed close behind, like David Bailey! It soon became apparent that it was just an exercise. At the end of the avenue, by the cathedral, they stopped the manoeuvres, made their way to a waiting truck and proceeded to climb into the back.

I put my camera away with some disappointment and continued with my search for a bookshop. I was in an age without Google Maps or the internet; when looking for a shop, a town, or whatever, you just asked someone for directions. On this occasion, I wandered over to the soldiers in the back of the truck. In my best Spanish, I said, *"Donde esta la libreria, por favor?"* (Do you know where the bookshop is, please?) This was not a good idea; every soldier in the back of the truck grabbed a rifle or a handgun and pointed them at me. I was in the shit.

The soldier closest to me demanded, *"Tourista, tourista se passporte."* I could see myself being lifted into the back of the truck and kidnapped. With this thought in mind, I rummaged around in my bag, found my passport and handed it to him.

He repeated what he had said and then added something I couldn't understand: *"Dama de Hierro, Dama de Hierro?"*

"*No comprenda!*" I said.

Then he said in English, "The Iron Lady, Margaret Thatcher."

"*Se, se*, Margaret Thatcher," I said.

"*Muy Bueno*," (Very good) he said. Everyone in the truck laughed, and they all put down their guns. The officer gave me my passport back and pointed me up the road. "*Adios, amigo*," he said, and I left as quickly as I could. It was a scary moment, the feeling of vulnerability with so many weapons pointing at me. I put as much space between myself and these gun-toting, trigger-happy soldiers as I could. I had never experienced having a dozen guns pointed at me, and I have never again asked an army officer or policeman for directions. I eventually found the shop, and they didn't have the book I was looking for anyway!

* * *

The illness was bothering me, the episodes more frequent, and I needed to go back home to get to the bottom of it. I threw caution to the wind, returned to Santa Marta to see Carlo, and grabbed a few ounces of coke to take home with me. With just a small quantity, I could make 15 to 20 grand; smuggling it into the UK would be easy.

I had obviously lost all sense of reason. Life in South America was good. Potential robberies aside, it is a beautiful part of the world, with so much to offer and so much to see. But I couldn't stay because of this infernal sickness, so the best thing was to risk it all again and head home with some coke! I thought I had left that life behind, but I couldn't resist the temptation. Francis had said it would lead to disaster, and I had believed her—but just one more little trip wouldn't do any harm, would it?

I arrived in Santa Marta and met up with Carlos. I told him what I was after, and he said it wasn't a problem. Then he made a few phone calls, and we headed off into town. We made our way to a local bar and waited for his man to arrive. Again, this was one of those spit and sawdust joints where the locals eat. I stood out like the tourist I was, and the bar staff asked me where I was from. They were amazed to find out that I was English, and then we laughed and joked with each other. Suddenly, two cops came into the bar with their guns out, waving their weapons around and shouting something in Spanish. Everyone got up and quite casually walked to one of the walls. We all had to stand facing the wall with our hands behind our heads. The cops had twenty of us all in a line, and they began at the opposite end, patting everyone down and searching their bags. I had a couple of grand in cash in my bag. I couldn't let the cops discover it, or they would take it. I had to think fast, or these guys would rob me. One of them approached me, and I said to him, *"Tourista, senor."*

The cop stopped short of me and shouted, *"Tourista? Passporte?"* I handed him my passport and then I had one of those déjà vu moments, as he said, *"Inglaterra, se?"*

"Se, Inglaterra," I replied.

He then said the immortal words, *"Dama de Hierro, Dama de Hierro?"* The cops burst into laughter; they didn't bother searching me as they ushered me out of the bar with

Carlo. It was a close call; Margaret Thatcher had saved my bacon twice now, what a lady!

Soon after this little interaction with the cops, we found Carlo's man and scored the drugs. I didn't hang around Santa Marta for long; I just said my farewells to Carlo and got on a bus to Caracas to catch a flight home.

I arrived in Caracas and rescheduled my flight for the following week. I spent my last days in South America wrapping coke into small packages. The best way to smuggle it back into the UK was to hide it in my backside. While serving my first prison sentence, I had carried dope up my arse every day through my whole sentence. It may seem crude, but it was a failsafe way of keeping your contraband hidden and undetected.

The day of the flight soon came round, so I secured the coke and boarded the plane. It's not comfortable having a large object in your back passage. Needless to say, it was a long old haul back to Lisbon.

Before I left Caracas, I had decided to fly to Lisbon and grab a bus for the rest of the journey back to England. Flying directly into Heathrow from Caracas would have been dangerous, so I figured getting the bus would camouflage me, and no one would even look at me as I arrived at Southampton port on a bus from Lisbon.

I knew it was dangerous and a fool's errand. How many more times did I need to learn this lesson? Maybe once more!

I went through Lisbon Airport without a hitch and found a hotel, where I spent two days in my room mulling over my situation. I seriously thought about not doing it, thinking it was far too dangerous. Prison is never an enjoyable experience at the best of times, so heading back to the UK with coke would certainly win me a long sentence if I got caught. Yet here I was, sitting in a hotel room, preparing to risk everything. I was setting myself up for a big, old fall. And so began the journey of journeys.

The coke was weighing down on me; it was more uncomfortable than ever as I was carrying a backpack, and the pressure from the coke inside me was unbearable. It was a relief to finally get on the bus and sit my arse down and take the pressure off. The bus moved off, and we were on our way through Portugal, Spain, France and then on to England.

The illness I was suffering from could come out of nowhere; one minute I was well, and the next, I was puking all over the place. Of all the times, right now was definitely not the time to be ill, so when my head started to spin, I knew I was in trouble. I knew the signs. I was heading for a major attack. I stood trying to control the feeling of vertigo that had consumed me; nothing I had ever done in the past had slowed it down, and when it was on me I was doomed. I needed water. I asked a man close by, "*Agua, por favor?*" (Water, please?) It was the last thing I remember as I began having an epileptic fit and passed out.

Chapter 14

Nearly Meeting My Maker

I came round in an intensive care unit. I could hear voices. I was in a semi-paralysed state, and I could feel my limbs but couldn't open my eyes. I had tubes in every orifice, rigged up to a life support system. Somehow, I felt trapped inside my own body. I tried to move my arms, but they were restrained. My legs were restrained too. I was manacled to the bed. I knew I was in trouble. I started to recall my situation. I had collapsed and passed out on the bus with cocaine hidden in my body.

I could hear voices in the room—male voices. I was definitely in trouble. One of the voices spoke in a heavy accent, "Richard, you are OK now. Open your eyes." I was paralysed. I couldn't open them. I began to shake and writhe around on the bed. I felt many hands hold me down—the fear and the claustrophobia! I was in complete darkness with no way out. I thought my eyes didn't work, and I was blind. The same voice said, "Richard, open your eyes. You are OK now." I couldn't open them, which led to more panic. Unknown

Nearly Meeting My Maker

hands were still holding down my limbs. I couldn't move. Then, I felt someone pinch one of my nipples; it hurt like hell. Then there was more nipple-pinching. What the fuck was going on? The pain from the nipple-pinching was unbearable. I motioned with my hand as though I was writing in the air, and someone placed a pen in my hand. I wrote: "Open my eyes."

Finally, I felt the fingertips of someone lifting my eyelids, with the sound of Francis' voice ringing in my head, "It won't end well for you, Dicky." My eyes were open, and I was surrounded by half a dozen suited men. Cops! I was nicked. The inevitable end, just as Francis had predicted!

The End

About the Author

He's still alive!

BV - #0086 - 190325 - C0 - 198/129/25 - CC - 9781068552823 - Gloss Lamination